THE HEALIUM WAY

THE ART OF BEING *EXTRA*ORDINARY AND LIVING WITHOUT REGRETS

PART 1 *of* 2

JIM PEERA

The views expressed herein are those of the author alone and should not be taken as professional advice. The information presented is intended for informational purposes only. The reader is responsible for his or her own actions.

ISBN: 978-1-7375950-0-7

To all of you unconventional movers, shakers, lovers and peacemakers...

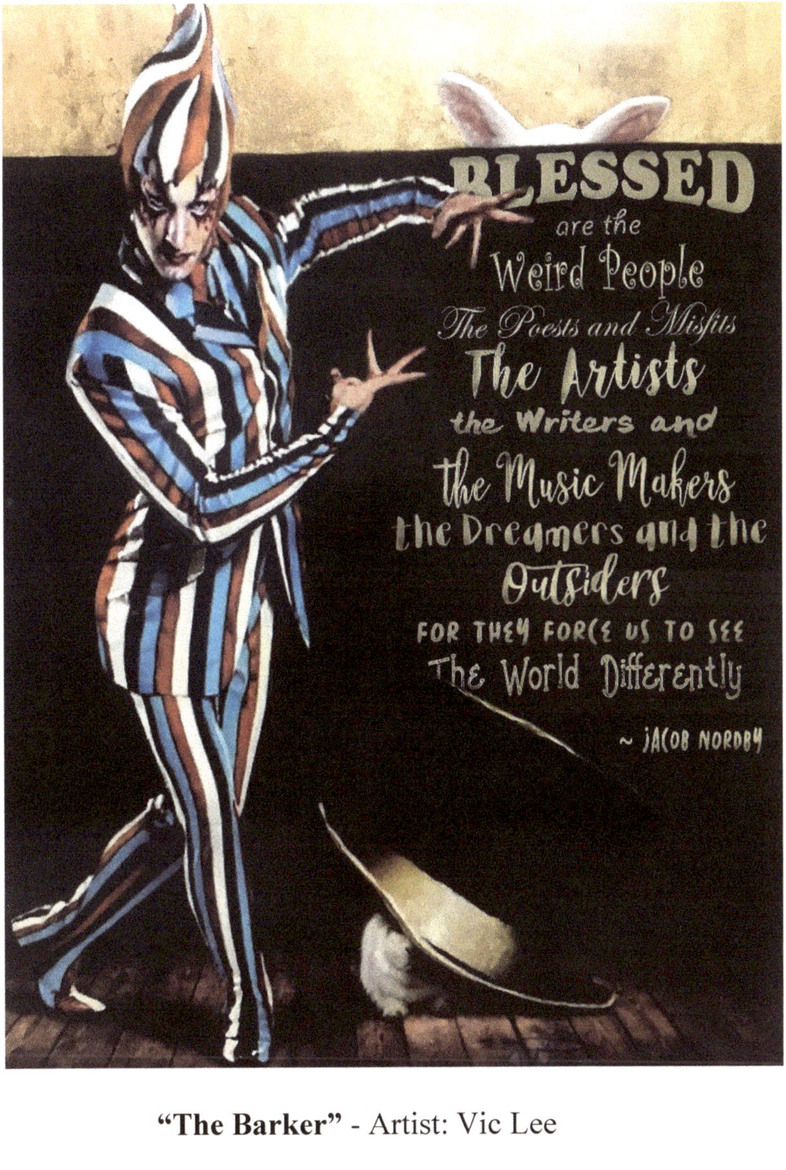

"The Barker" - Artist: Vic Lee

Table of Contents

Prologue

It was a beautiful, hot and humid Sunday afternoon in Dar es Salaam, Tanzania. Our large, two-story white house near the Indian Ocean, sparkled with gemstones and minerals that were part of our multicolored-stone driveway. While sitting on the front-covered porch behind a wrought-iron laced screen, my eyes were drawn to all the broken crystals and semi-precious stones. This batch of minerals came from a mine that our family partly owned with the government. The sun-kissed stones glistened so brightly that even my pet tortoise left his shady wooden shack to go check them out. I was only seven years old, but I knew that our wealth and comfort was untypical in Africa. We had house servants who cooked us three meals a day, did all the housecleaning, landscaped the garden, chauffeured me to school — even wiped my butt at my command. I recall how that particular Sunday started out as being rather peaceful, without the usual weekend distractions. The sweet smell of white gardenias and red roses attracted the bumblebees and finches to our manicured front garden; the atmosphere was unusually serene. There were no uninvited visitors, neighbors or friends popping in, and all the servants had the day off. My older siblings were out of the house, and my grandma was sleeping in her room. Beside me was my baby chimpanzee, Whiskey, a mischievous pet who loved drinking water out of empty alcohol bottles. But this perfect moment was about to be shattered. The sound of angry voices was coming from my parents' bedroom. Suddenly, I heard a loud bang. My mom and dad were arguing, and my mom had slammed the door, causing my little monkey to scream in fear and latch on to me. Mom was yelling at the top of her voice, as she rushed down the stairs in her clanky wooden slippers. I dropped Whiskey by the steps and we both ran into the living room, curious about the loud ruckus. Mom and I met at the bottom of the stairs, and she furiously pointed her finger at my head, yelling, and in our East Indian dialect and mother tongue of Kutchi, *"You're not my son, you're not my son, you are my problem, you're my problem!"* Next, she banged her head against the white plaster wall and spewed even more vile words at me while pulling her hair out. Shocked, I cried profusely and tried to cling to her waist as she aggressively pushed me away. I, too, started knocking my own head onthe asbestos tiled floor in a frenzy, crying out in my mother tongue, *"What did I do, Ma? What did I do?"* Then, like an angel's wings, the comforting arms of my grandmother swooped me up off the floor, she held me lightly. My grandma was a large and strong woman who could carry a grown-up man if she had to. She checked me for injuries but I was OK, and she soothed me by rocking me on her lap.

I'm not sure what happened to my mom that day, but I was later informed that she had to be restrained. Then, she was medicated and treated with shock therapy at a local sanitarium. Mom had broken down multiple times before and no conventional treatments seemed to have worked. I didn't see her for some time, and Grandma Kulsum took over her duties at home. My grandmother was a true family matriarch. She was bold and unconventional, smart and intuitive, and above all, a natural peacemaker. I remember that as I was crying that day she explained that Mom was having a nervous breakdown. That it wasn't my fault. That her vitriolic words were part of her sickness and were not directed at me personally. I don't know what I would've done without her. I'll never forget how my Grandma Kulsum kept on repeating to me on that day and the weeks that followed how I was very much loved. She went on to tell me that I was a blessed child,who had been protected by God.

At the time, I didn't quite grasp what she was saying as she explained how I was born a four-pound preemie,and caused my mom to bleed incessantly during childbirth. That Sunday, while she consoled me and wiped tears off my face with the bottom of her long flowery dress, Grandma recounted how on that tenuous day of my birth, my dad had been forewarned by the doctors to prepare for the worst. They painted a grim picture that one of us — my mom or myself — would die in the morning unless we showed signs of improvement during the night. She told me that she and my dad prayed at our bedside in the intensive care room that frightful night. With Divine intervention, their prayers were heard, and for some higher purpose, both my mom and I made it through. As I recollect this traumatic story of my childhood today, I'm obviously indebted to my maker for sparing my mom's life and mine. The doctor at the scene said it was a miracle that both people lived without any serious life-threatening damage. Looking at it now, I can say that my childbirth undoubtedly caused some collateral damage with my siblings that affects our relationship to this day. Beyond that divine intervention, I am also grateful for my grandmother's love and care for me following the days and weeks of my mom's breakdown. While my mom was getting her psychiatric treatments, my grandma was instrumental in making sure that I was cared for and helped me stay playful and happy. She inspired me to build sand castles on the beach and play cards with her. She allowed me to play freely in the rain and collect tadpoles in jars. She bought me colored pencils to draw, and encouraged me to write poetry and letters to my family members overseas. What my grandma did was quite extraordinary for that time. This wise woman was giving me some basic tools to express myself freely, to release any pent-up emotions within, and allow me to have a normal and fun childhood. This was a game changer for improving my mental wellness, and in due course my mom's violent episode that Sunday afternoon became a faint memory. By the time my mom got better and apologized to me, my emotional wound was pretty well stitched up and we enjoyed a functional mother and child relationship moving forward.

MY LESSONS

I initially wanted to call this book, *Art is a Wound Turned into Light,* from a brilliant quote by the twentieth-century French artist; Georges Braque. Then, I realized that it would only be read by people who acknowledged they were somewhat screwed up and/or considered themselves artists. That of course would eliminate a lot of people. Plus, this book is not so much about art as it is about understanding balance, living life without regrets and working towards being an extraordinary human being. Specifically, it's for those of us adults who have allowed our overworked and unbalanced lives to suck the joy out of us, have lost touch with our true selves and are imprisoned in our man-made containers of thought. Much of this imprisonment is sowed during our childhood, which is reaped and manifested into adulthood. Using my own personal childhood story that I just recounted as an example, I could have easily gone and stayed in a victim box and carried that dead weight narrative of not being loved by my mom into my adult life. But I chose not to. That's because we each hold the key to our liberation, and to experience our limitless possibilities. That traumatic Saturday was my necessary life lesson to learn that I was much stronger, resilient and powerful when I operated from an unconventional and non-imprisoned mindset. From that day forward, I've led my life on my own terms and it's been highly fulfilling. I believe I can help teach you to be in charge of your own destiny by being a better observer of life's many unhealthy trappings instead of being seduced and consumed by them. Therefore, this is a book about self-transformation and self-love that my extraordinary grandmother would be proud of, if she were alive today.

THE INSPIRATION

From the fateful night of my birth to the present, my life's survival mode has never been about befriending fear or surrendering to the status quo. As the youngest of five children, I've had my share of emotional and financial roller coaster rides. From the rich beginnings of a rather spoiled child in Africa, to being poor in France, to attending a Catholic boarding school in England, to pursuing my dreams in America, a country that almost bankrupted and killed me, my adventures are definitely worth closer introspection. Having survived some jaw-dropping and momentous events in my 60 years, the past two-thirds of my life has been about fighting against many injustices and protecting my underdog status in America. My pursuit for success and peace has not come easily however, with a painstaking journey acclimating to the wounded American South and choosing to live in racially charged Atlanta, Georgia. As a nonconformist thinker, the road less traveled has always worked out for me, as the best possible outcomes are always achieved without being attached to any particular dogma or agenda-based philosophy. So I thought sharing some of my novel ideas in an unconventional manner would inspire you to do the same — on your own path. In order to become the best instrument of change and peace, it requires all of us to be open minded and pluralistic in our thinking. This includes being unshackled from any particular religious belief or programming that holds a set bias, judgment or constraint to our self-growth and metamorphosis.

Both my wife and I are self-admitted rebels and detest the practice of preset and rigid philosophies. It must come from being forced to do things that we didn't understand or want to do during our respective childhood. She was indoctrinated at an early age in her neighborhood church, where she sang choir and followed the teachings of Catholicism and the Son of God, while I grew up memorizing Arabic prayers that I did not understand and praying to a religious leader as if he was a living God. Having tasted the conformities and boundaries of a religion I was born into, via Islam, and having witnessed similar experiences of my wife's religious upbringing by way of Christianity, it became apparent to us that we both craved for a better alternative to feed our individual spiritual hunger. Thankfully, we didn't have to look too far. We were already connected to this abundant source of upliftment and empowerment that helped us navigate through life's many challenges. For me it was the creative arts. For my wife it was the healing arts and Shamanism. As you are about to find out, both the creative and healing arts are seeds that are planted and granted to us by our maker at birth, regardless of any artistic or medical training. They're Divinely inspiredand driven. It is why each of us is capable of creating a more healed life for ourselves. When my wife and I combined these two innate gifts into our individual lives, we noticed an immediate difference. We were able to attain more peace, joy and balance within us. We did not miss going to church, the mosque or any worship center that bubble wrapped or strapped us down with fear and guilt in any way. We were creating our own spiritual sanctuary in our home that was way more fun, liberating and rewarding than anything the world had to offer. My son who is thirty-two and my daughter who is twenty-nine as of this writing, learned to be spiritually powerful and creative adults by deploying a similar philosophy of non-tribal and non-dogmatic healing while growing up. Over time, we all deployed these creative and healing tools into every aspect of our daily routine to help our mental state of mind, cope better with life's challenges and get along with all types of people. This is exactly what we needed as a young family — and what America needs more than ever today. That is why I dedicate this book to my fellow Americans. By testing and utilizing the proven Principles in my own life, I have transformed myself from a rather anxious and capitalistic young man into a more spiritual, balanced and grounded person. Some of this is due to the accumulated wisdom of experience, travel and aging, but a lot has come through trial and error and testing these Principles in the laboratory of life. I have changed for the better in all aspects of my life and I believe you can too. I call these life-altering principles, The Healium Way; a universal philosophy for achieving peace, contentment and balance within us all. The title of this book and the accompanying Principles are aptly named and inspired by Healium Center, the interactive wellness-with-the-arts sanctuary I founded in 2014 in Atlanta, Georgia.

All the stories in this book are true and many of the ideas presented here have been validated and proven during a seven-year period.

TWO PARTS

Having lived a full life without regrets and always with the goal of going above the ordinary, this author's story is itching to be told to the world with passion and vigor. My childhood and adulthood traumas, trials and tribulations have been instrumental in providing me with opportunities only my Creator could have planned. What seemed like curses, turned out to be blessings and what seemed like never ending calamities, turned out to be temporary setbacks. All were universal lessons in life that I am grateful for. And I will be sharing some of those personal stories with you. But this creative body of work is not about me as much as it is about getting you to be the most balanced, joyful, enlightened and best human you can be, regardless of where you fit into society. In fact, it is my hope that as we go into our adventure together, that you remove all your societal labels, predispositions and expectations and see yourself as a human first. It is what has helped me stay true to myself. So I write this book in part as a memoir and part as a self-help guide to try to make a difference in your own life. Due to the vast amount of exciting and useful material to share, I've split the work into two books. Part 1 is packed with many deep and personal heart wrenching journeys that encapsulate the inspiration behind The Healium Way. While Part 2 unpacks the tested Principles for you to deploy in your own life. Both are necessary reads to complete the literal adventure and compilation of The Healium Way.

I also write this book as an American immigrant who's spent over four decades in the United States. Sadly, the America of today is nothing like the one I first arrived in. That America that I adopted was a country of joyous, compassionate and united people. These days, Americans walk around with their heads hanging low and their Souls tethered. There's a sense of hopelessness on one end, and darkness on the other. It's quite disturbing and concerning. What has changed for the worse is the society's eroding moral values and misplaced priorities. It is detrimentally affecting people's judgment, mental health and ability to peacefully coexist with their fellow citizens. But why is that, and what can be done about it? I will offer my diagnosis and practical remedies for a peace plan to fix our unhealthy imbalances and provide lessons that will lead to your own growth and transformation.

OUR COMMON CONNECTION

With the entire nation succumbing to and being torn apart by a polarized political climate, America is revealing its fragility and manifesting its unhealed wounds on itself, one person at a time. It's happening to your neighbor, your coworker, your partner, your boss, your local merchant, your family member — to you and to me. Whether we're rich, poor, white, colored, liberal, conservative, gay, straight or any other label we put on ourselves, we're all hurting and manifesting our respective pain in some fashion. That's because we're all interconnected. Some of us hide our true feelings better than others, but all of us know our collective cuts run deep, and the Band-Aids are not sticking too well on our thin-skinned society. Our conventional prescriptions have had sickening side effects, and it's time to find a better doctor with unconventional remedies.

THE DOCTOR IS IN

The good news is that there's this doctor who will nurse our wounds and get us on the path to recovery. This doctor is you. It's me. It's the higher spiritual entity within us that is capable of healing our open wounds and helping us recover from our emotional sickness and imbalances. The unconventional prescription is The Healium Way. The medicine is the creative and healing arts. And the medicine man and the healer is none other than you. Specifically, it is the higher vibrational version of yourself. For The Healium Way to be effective and make a difference — you, the doctor and healer in charge of your wellness has to be all in, to do the work. This means having faith in your abilities and taking action without any excuses or resistances. If you're not prepared to do that, close this book now and return it to me for a full refund. You may not be ready to explore and self-prescribe The Healium Way. And that's perfectly OK.

Otherwise, keep an open mind and be prepared to take a cathartic interactive trip inward. But unlike visiting a therapist, this will actually be a fun experience. In many ways, an intended side effect of applying the Healium Way principles into your life is staying young at heart and having a matching lifestyle attitude. You will still have all the common human imperfections: problems, bad days, disappointments. But with The Healium Way, they will be more manageable and not be allowed to survive in your renewed self. You will understand how each of us possesses the ability to self-care and create balance in our life. You'll learn the value of being true to yourself by detaching from the man-made obstacles to that personal growth. At the very least, you will move closer towards possessing those attributes.

If you stay the course and apply the Principles of The Healium Way to your life, you might just begin to unleash unbounded personal power, find limitless joy and passion and manifest a renewed sense of purpose.

THE INTERACTIVE JOURNEY

When I first began contemplating writing this exciting adventure, I wanted to create a book unlike any other. The result of this desire is an interactive journey that activates your emotional receptors and personal willpower, driving you to take action for your own self growth and transformation. This body of creative work was conceived and written to engage you in the process of self-discovery using real-life stories, creative visuals and exclusive online content. As a person who is not a trained psychotherapist, a doctor, a scientist or even an accredited professor, I am not going to spend a lot of time picking apart our complex behavioral psychology. That's not necessary for The Healium Way of living. In fact, the reason our Center has had such a positive impact on its participants is all about our simplicity. We are not clinical or analytical in our approach. Our mission is to keep it simple, stupid (K.I.S.S.) and demonstrate what solutions work most practically and effectively in a no-nonsense manner.

If you've been a part of the Healium community or participated in any of our activities, this book will be even more exciting and beneficial for you with new insights and revelations never presented before. Writing The Healium Way was not easy for me, as it was created during the Covid-19 pandemic during a time when I had to close The Center.

I also contracted the virus twice, and tragically lost both my mom and my mother-in-law to the disease. These losses of mine and the hundreds of thousands of others were a reminder to me of life's fragility and underscores the importance for each of us to mine that extraordinary version of ourselves and live a life without regrets, while we still can.

So let's get started!

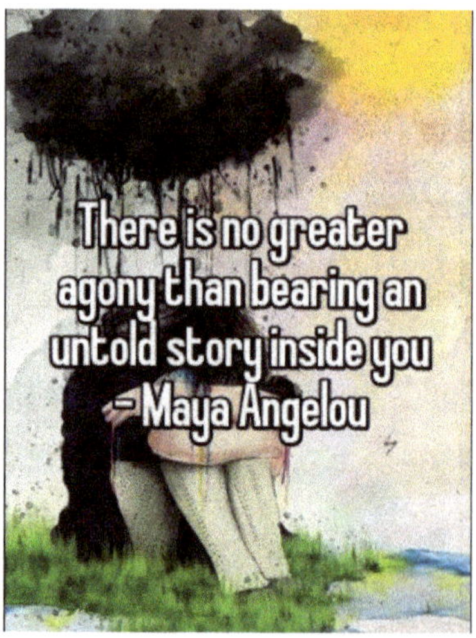

1
A Lofty Idea

"The best way to find yourself is to lose yourself in the service of others"

— Mahatma Gandhi

It was past midnight on a clear southern moonlit Saturday night. I was upstairs in my private hangout putting some finishing touches on a clay sculpture that I had been working on from the previous night. About thirty feet from the ground, this airy loft atop a three-story modern house in the suburbs of Atlanta, was my creative hideaway, where I could escape from the distractions and the grind of the world below. The hooting sounds of resident owls penetrated through the asymmetrical double pane windows around. Often, I'd press my head against the glass and see their glistening eyes pierce through mine. These insightful birds always kept me company atnight, from their oak tree rest. That night, as I glanced around the room crowded with over fifty pieces of my surrealism-styled artwork, I realized how each of them was special and carried a personal story of pain, pleasure and uninhibited freedom in my life's journey. Thiscreative hobby was my medicine. I thought, and I felt blessed that other members of my family also found solace in creative art. Both my teenage kids self-prescribed art and music as medicine for their personal growing pains. My daughter would sit in her room each night and either strum a song on a guitar or draw out her dark emotions on paper, while my son would compose his music and rap his poetic verses until dawn, often screaming out loud in a healthy release. My wife found solitude and benefit in playing crystal bowls, chanting, drumming and freestyle dancing. On some occasions we'd all collaborate on a spontaneous idea and create magic together.

I remember a time when my son was composing a new instrumental song for his mom's birthday gift without her knowledge. He invited me to hear it and as co-producer, I gave him some pointers to improve and edit some parts. Soon he got my daughter to put an electric guitar riff in it, and asked my wife to sing some background vocals. None of us had any professional artistic or musical training but that didn't matter. We found tremendous joy and satisfaction in what we were creating in our own safe space. Unbeknownst to me, what was happening was highly spiritual and we were self-prescribing the medicine of the creative and healing arts. At any given time, one would find the entire house filled with friends and family where everyone was engaged in a creative and spiritual activity of some sort. It was an uplifting and fun-filled environment that provided a lot of needed release, relaxation and recharge. To many visitors, our home was a novel sanctuary that was full of life, inspiration and peace; not dissimilar to a church — but without judgment, hypocrisy and dogma. What many people didn't know however, was that behind the facade of pleasure, hid a lot of underlying individual pain that was being surfaced from within. My kids had their respective first love and school issues, my wife had her past unhealed child scars to heal, while I had a combination of old open wounds and new business-related trials and tribulations. We were an emotional mess, but we all found that art was soaking in and providing release we all needed.

Then the kids left, and as with many empty nesters' harsh reality, my wife and I felt quite lonely. The house was not the same.

It was quieter and we missed the interactive arts nights with the kids and their friends. As a couple, we spent quality time together and went out on more dates but didn't find anything exciting and adventurous to quench our creative thirst. On some Saturday evenings, while my wife cooked a nice meal and enjoyed her creative activities, I would take a glass of wine up to the lost and get lost in my world of sculpting for the entire night listening to the Bee Gees; my favorite songwriters and musical group. So on this particular Saturday night, something very special happened. While sipping a glass of red wine, my eyes turned to that piece I created a couple years earlier called *"Out of the lion's mouth."* I wasn't sure at the time why that particular piece spoke to me and pulled me in like a magnet. But I felt my heart racing. As I was staring at this sculpture, which was of a man getting out from a mouth-shaped red rock (a specimen dug up from a vortex in Sedona, Arizona), I felt tears trickle down my face. Then, all my work on display started to trigger memories from the past decade. Every creation was cathartic and beautiful in its own way and executed freely out of my imagination. Individually, each told a particular story and collectively they seemed to reflect a body of uninhibited art of self-expression. Some works were light and humorous, but most were deep and thought provoking. I took a few minutes to savor the creations as many chapters of my life flashed right before my eyes. I was not inebriated but there was an out of body experience in the making. While there was not a sound in the house and my wife was fast asleep in the bedroom, I found myself hearing the kids in the living room playing music and jamming with their friends. I looked down from the loft into the living room but it was pitch dark and empty. For a split second it appeared I was hallucinating, but it wasn't spooky; rather I felt safe and peaceful. That night in bed, I kept dreaming in and out of that particular incident in my subconscious memory. Although I didn't understand the significance of that loft hallucination when it happened, I pieced it together the following day while sipping my morning rocket fuel cup of macchiato.

MANIFESTING THE SIGNS

The loft incident had some underlying meaning, I realized. But what? Was it a sign from my maker or guardian angel to do something? My mind had been preoccupied with the idea of doing something spiritual for the community. Could this be it, then? I took to understanding it as a two-part message that confirmed a premonition. First, it reaffirmed the power of art as a healer. It was clear how I was going through a cathartic moment and was essentially using my own art to provide some therapy for myself. Even many years after their creation, my sculptures still had the power to affect me and help heal my past wounds, such as my brush with death in Africa and a life-altering ordeal I had just overcome in Alabama; a story I will unfold for you in detail in this book. The second lesson was that of an awakening. Were my Spirit guides directing me to help serve others? Was this my sign to take action and start a new spiritual and artistic project? Was art going to be the vehicle to take me on this spiritual journey? Were the voices, musical instruments and people laughing in the house that night giving me some message? These were all questions running in my mind. It was as if I longed to re-create a fun, judgment-free creative place (like we all had enjoyed as a family) for the benefit of a larger community. It was apparent this was going to be an ambitious task, so I took a yellow pad and a pen and started jotting some questions. I asked myself, is it possible that there could be millions of empty nesters like us who need to re-activate their inner-creative to find joy and fulfillment? Is it possible that many adults have forgotten to play, be creative and have non-competitive fun? What has happened to our inner child who kept us light, adventurous and without judgment or ego? Why aren't we building more creative-based spiritual community spaces to connect, uplift and empower people?

These were some of the voices talking in my head that morning in the days that followed. About a week later I tossed the idea to my wife of testing this concept out as an '*Interactive Healing Arts*

Center for Adults.' She chuckled, rolled her eyes and wasn't too keen on the idea of opening another business. As we were edging close to retirement age, she hoped we were done working hard and would travel abroad more. Dissatisfied with that response, I tried my kids; *"That's crazy, Dad, it's called an Art Center for Old People!"* or *"That just won't work dad"* is what they came up with. Then I floated the notion to my friends (mostly those in real estate), and they thought I had gone insane. *"So, let me get this right Jim, you want to put your hard-earned real estate money into making no money in art?"* and *"Are you nuts?"* were some common rejections.

NO MEANS YES

With all the naysayers discouraging, I did what I've always done in my life when people say "No" I say "Yes" or at least, "Why not?" I quickly began doing some research and discovered that the idea of opening a community arts center, especially one that was unconventional in its approach, was going to be more of an altruistic project, rather than a profitable venture. After all, *"Starving artists are called that for a reason!"* a struggling art gallery owner chuckled when I asked him for advice. He went on to complain to me how our society sees little value in supporting and prioritizing the arts. Soon this nice man became a casualty of his own prophecy and closed his doors soonafter. In America most art galleries fold within three years of opening. With the high rate of failures in the art and music industry and low priority of arts funding in our society, I knew how this project would only be possible using my own savings. And because I wanted it done right, it would be a substantial investment and a high-risk endeavor. I quickly wrote up a small business plan, calculated the burn rate (negative cash flow) and with the best-case scenario estimated being in the black in the second year. That model showed how we would lose money for a considerable time, just to prove if this "Wellness with the Arts" concept worked on a community level. But that was a risk and gamble I was prepared to take. The amount of money needed to launch this idea only worked if we kept the operating expenses at a minimum. We had some money saved up for our world travels but I persuaded my wife to re-allocate some of it to this project. We compromised and agreed to take a family trip abroad before we embarked on this new adventure. But before we took this leap of faith, I asked my Spirit guides to give us another sign. I had a few conditions and requirements. First, we had to be in a good location near public transport. Second, we had to find a good deal (pay below market price) and third; we had to have a large enough space to conduct an array of workshops and events. Within a short time, I found the right building in the right location, but there were over thirty people bidding for it. I did not get anxious or aggressive and self-deflated my ego substantially. I simply prayed and surrendered to the universe to guide me, wherever and however it saw fit. The universe soon spoke and miraculously my offer was accepted. Although it wasn't the highest price, it was the winning bid and dumbfounded the realtor and the other bidders. I thanked my guardian angels for confirming the property and promised that I would make them proud. After I closed on the property, I had two very good offers at a big profit, but I respectfully declined and told them I was set on opening an art center instead. It was no surprise that they both were infuriated with that response, and yes, called me crazy for not taking the money. And I probably was. But I had a laser-focused mission that no amount of money could buy. Soon the concept of a novel and rather unproven healing with the arts center was officially born. It didn't take long to come up with the name *Healium* accompanied by the slogan *Uplifting You with the Arts* and a cute happy logo. I envisioned The Center to be a place unlike any other where participants would call it their creative spiritual home and be authentic and without judgment. I specifically wanted the logo to have an imperfect handwritten and spontaneous feel to convey a place to celebrate people's raw but perfect imperfections.

Moreover, I highlighted the U in red to signify the importance of *doing U, by U and for U.* The concept of a judgment-free, interactive arts space that fused the creative and healing arts into one experience was officially germinated and formed.

Healium Center opened its doors a few months later in early 2014 and as of this writing has served over 6,000 people and produced over 600 interactive events since its inception. It became a 501(c)(3) nonprofit organization in 2019.

At our grand opening, I wrote this 'welcome' poem:

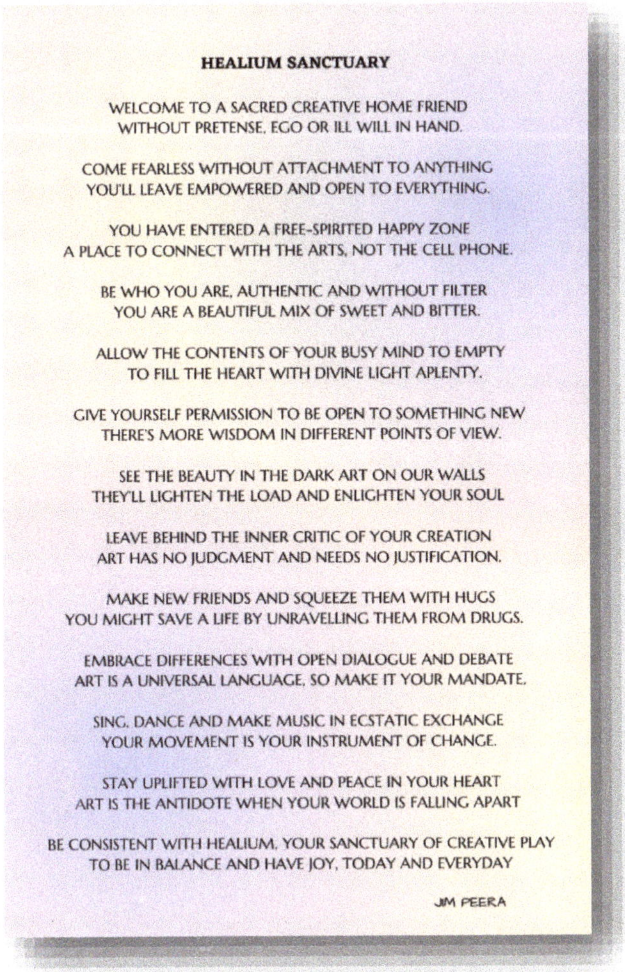

HEALIUM SANCTUARY

WELCOME TO A SACRED CREATIVE HOME FRIEND
WITHOUT PRETENSE, EGO OR ILL WILL IN HAND.

COME FEARLESS WITHOUT ATTACHMENT TO ANYTHING
YOU'LL LEAVE EMPOWERED AND OPEN TO EVERYTHING.

YOU HAVE ENTERED A FREE-SPIRITED HAPPY ZONE
A PLACE TO CONNECT WITH THE ARTS, NOT THE CELL PHONE.

BE WHO YOU ARE, AUTHENTIC AND WITHOUT FILTER
YOU ARE A BEAUTIFUL MIX OF SWEET AND BITTER.

ALLOW THE CONTENTS OF YOUR BUSY MIND TO EMPTY
TO FILL THE HEART WITH DIVINE LIGHT APLENTY.

GIVE YOURSELF PERMISSION TO BE OPEN TO SOMETHING NEW
THERE'S MORE WISDOM IN DIFFERENT POINTS OF VIEW.

SEE THE BEAUTY IN THE DARK ART ON OUR WALLS
THEY'LL LIGHTEN THE LOAD AND ENLIGHTEN YOUR SOUL

LEAVE BEHIND THE INNER CRITIC OF YOUR CREATION
ART HAS NO JUDGMENT AND NEEDS NO JUSTIFICATION.

MAKE NEW FRIENDS AND SQUEEZE THEM WITH HUGS
YOU MIGHT SAVE A LIFE BY UNRAVELLING THEM FROM DRUGS.

EMBRACE DIFFERENCES WITH OPEN DIALOGUE AND DEBATE
ART IS A UNIVERSAL LANGUAGE, SO MAKE IT YOUR MANDATE.

SING, DANCE AND MAKE MUSIC IN ECSTATIC EXCHANGE
YOUR MOVEMENT IS YOUR INSTRUMENT OF CHANGE.

STAY UPLIFTED WITH LOVE AND PEACE IN YOUR HEART
ART IS THE ANTIDOTE WHEN YOUR WORLD IS FALLING APART

BE CONSISTENT WITH HEALIUM, YOUR SANCTUARY OF CREATIVE PLAY
TO BE IN BALANCE AND HAVE JOY, TODAY AND EVERYDAY

JIM PEERA

A SAMPLE OF HEALIUM EVENTS

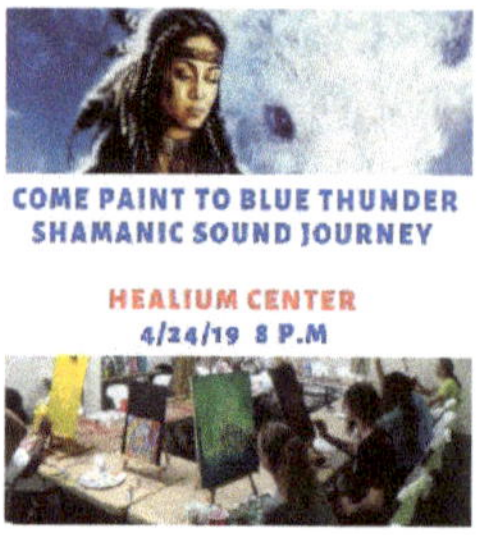

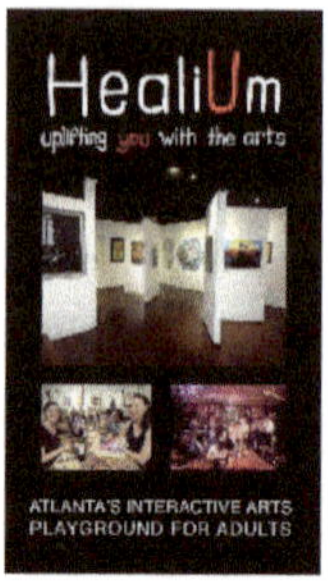

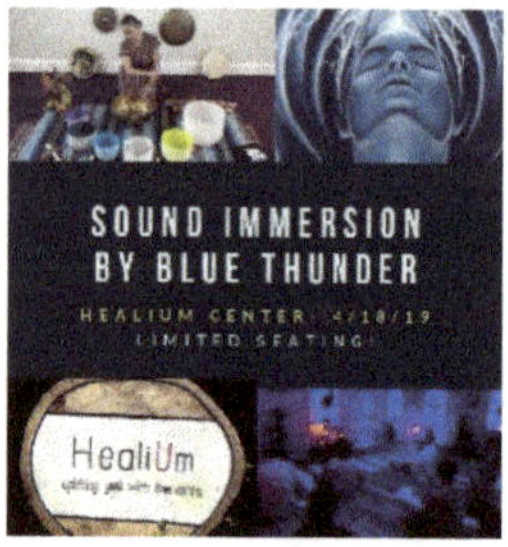

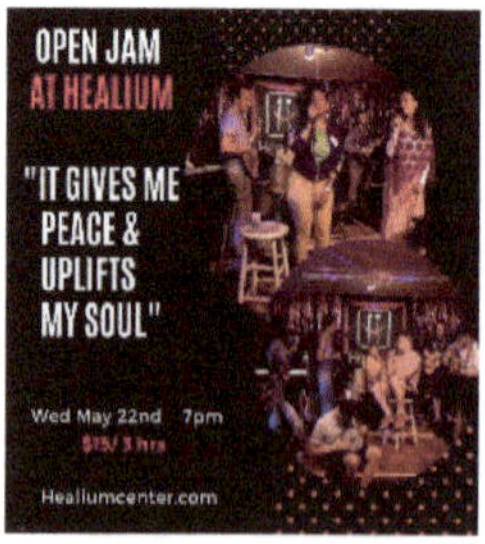

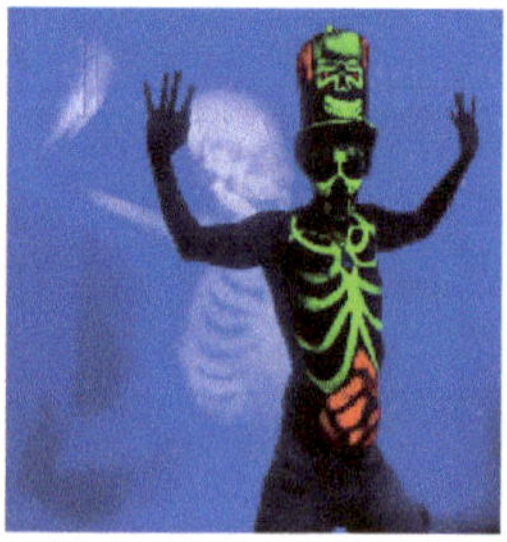

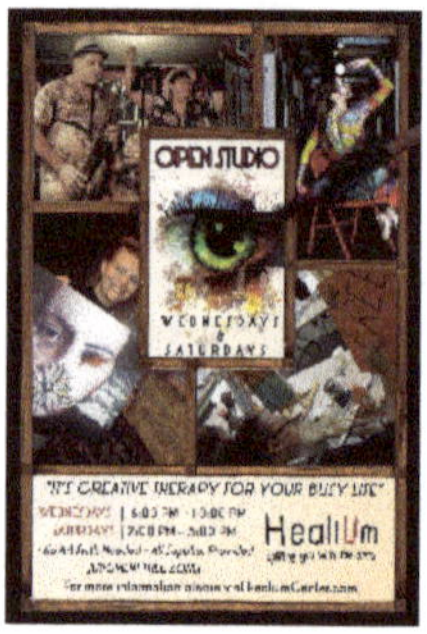

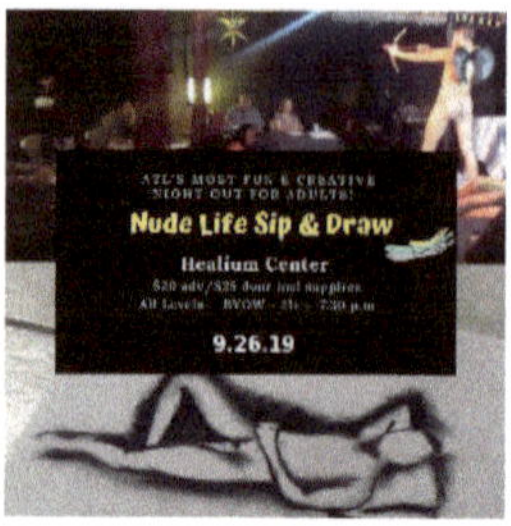

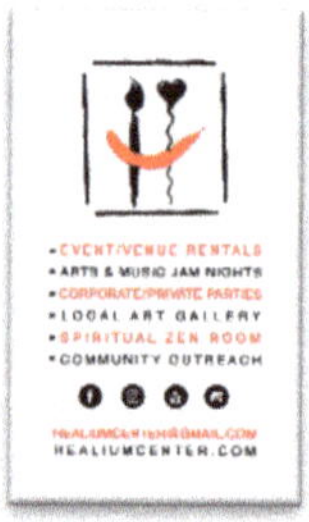

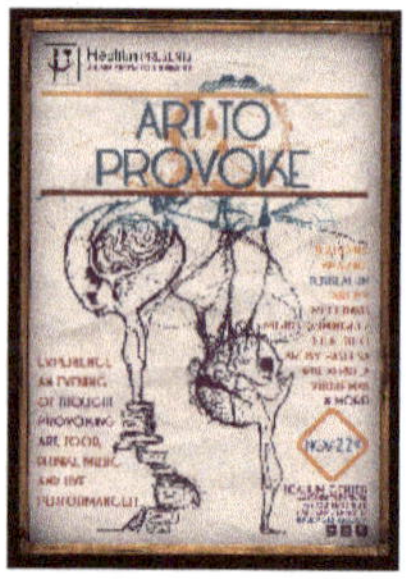

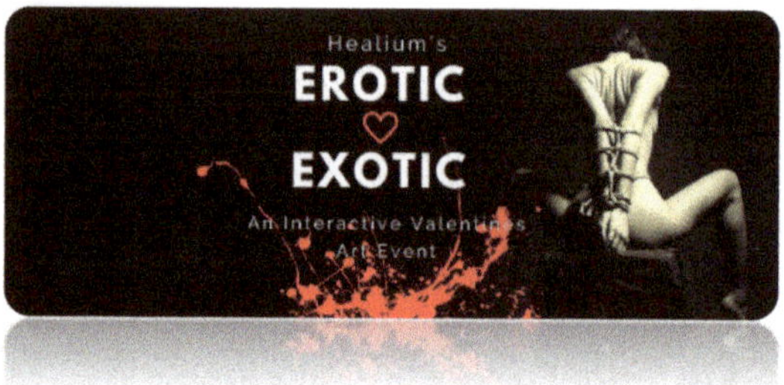

2
THE THREE BEAUTIFUL TRUTHS

FOR ADULTS ONLY

Loneliness is a big problem in America with three out five adults; aged eighteen and over, reporting feeling left out, isolated and depressed, according to Cigna; a leading health insurance provider. When I created Healium Center, it was paramount that our place therefore, cater to adults as opposed to kids. This was a controversial move on my part, but it was done by design. My research indicated that adults were quite underserved in the interactive arts arena. Kids had all the fun and sucked up the attention, while grownups were disconnected and drained from being overworked and thus, lonely. As a first solution, our Center provides a *Creative Playground for Adults,* an unconventional and fun interactive social environment. It allows the parents to keep their flames alive while raising kids; the young adults to get out of their introverted digital-world bubbles; and the empty-nesters to stay young at heart. A second reason for the adults-only concept was to provide a freestyle space where people can receive their creative medicine without the prerequisite of artistic training. To that end, we specialize in a surrealism genre incorporating dark, erotic and controversial works for inspiration and deeper dialogue.

What's more, by restricting our space to adults, we're able to provide edgy events and art installations to open, feed and engage the mind without reservation. The third reason was to create a better alternative to worship centers that are more akin to a creative spiritual wellness sanctuary. By fusing the active and passive activities of the healing and creative arts into one concept, we're able to reveal and fill the Soul like no other conventional place of worship. People feel uncaged, expose their imperfect self without inhibitions and obtain optimum healing results by practicing a pluralistic, as opposed to a dogmatic philosophy. Indeed, all the stories from The Center are examples of adults who often just came to have a good time and left with a memorable therapeutic and spiritual experience. Sometimes they were invited guests, but often they just walked-in to satisfy a curiosity. Whether they came once or were repeat attendees; they left never being the same. Often, the Healium experience is life-altering in a positive way. In rare instances people didn't respond to the out-of-the-box format, or found it didn't jive with their conservative-minded philosophy. For those who took a chance and participated in our diverse offerings, Our Center has worked in the following three ways to shape a pathway toward a more healed life:

1. **The ability to self-care and be empowered without crutches or excuses.**
2. **The power to reactivate our inner-creative as a wellness medicine.**
3. **The importance of maintaining body, mind and soul balance in everyday life.**

All three points are interrelated and important for our self-transformation. I see them as our **beautiful truths.**

The **first beautiful truth** is about being self-empowered, having personal responsibility and blaming no one for our f*ck ups, but ourselves. This involves not being afraid of emotional pain, busting loose of our restrictive boxes and learning to take action:

NO PAIN, NO GAIN

Self-care means having faith in yourself. It involves self-diagnosis through awareness and trusting in your personal power and ability to fix yourself. One of the most difficult aspects of fixing ourselves is knowing how to handle pain. But pain is simply a weakness leaving the body and our way of self-correcting. So, the logic of counteracting our body's weakness would be to give it strength, especially the emotional variety. Yet, we've become a bunch of crybabies when it comes to tolerating pain of any type. In the Western world, we've been brainwashed to repel physical and emotional discomfort with external distractions, drugs and various unhealthy addictions. The fact is, it is in our discomfort, struggle and stress that we grow and become more tolerant, stronger and resilient. Paradoxically, we as a species are at our best and most creative when we are uncomfortable and when we reach the bottom. Just travel to a third world country and observe the hardships and discomfort people endure that permeate their everyday life. Most immigrants from these impoverished countries become successful in developed countries due to this harsh discipline they've learned abroad. In one of my favorite songs by Elton John, "Pain," the lyrics are prophetic for one's healing journey: *"Pain is love, Pain is pure, Pain is sickness, Pain is the cure."* The song's high energy rock beat takes the *no pain, no gain* cliche to another level and helps us appreciate and connect with the flip-side emotion, pleasure. Without guilt, shame or fear.

In order to transition from pain to pleasure, the bridge I love to take is the Divine medicine of the arts. It enables me to dig up the layers of burdensome muck that suffocate my personal growth and overall health. During the course of this book, as we take a deeper dive into the human condition, we will travel through the many layers of our emotions — not just pain. You'll get the sweet with the bitter, the dark with the light and the tears with the laughter. Our lens will focus on an interactive arts sanctuary that attracts a varied and multidimensional microcosm of America.

It's where ordinary adults from all walks of life have come without any predispositions or expectations and left feeling loved, connected and uplifted due to their own intention and participation. Nurses, teachers, IT geeks, architects, realtors, authors, social workers, veterans, surgeons, retirees, singles, parents, college students, etc, have all experienced some form of The Healium Way in action. The Center is ground zero of uniting people through the medicine of the arts. It is where many participants make a conscious decision to surrender to their Spirit and reconnect with their Soul.

BUSTING LOOSE

The doctor in you cannot fully diagnose your emotional pain without looking into the mirror of truth. What I've learnt in my own life is that when we turn the mirror on ourselves, we get a lot closer to discovering our own truths and begin the path to seeing our untapped possibilities. But that's if we want it. Some of us prefer not going there and are comfortable cocooning in our various programmed little boxes. Many of these mind-restrictive containers hold us hostage to self-pity, doubt, shame, fear, ego, judgment, pretense, self-righteousness and other low vibrational conditions. We use these resistant traits as filters to justify sitting in our respective boxes that become the source of our many problems. Instead of staying curious and open to exploring more about what we don't know, we confine ourselves to our comfort zones. Much of it is our own doing, yet a lot of it is not. For starters, we're born already stuck in our particular boxes of race, sex and DNA without much self-determination of our skin color, facial features and preset genes. Simultaneously our life is complicated by being layered in more boxes of cultural and religion-based beliefs and dogmatism, which is compliments of our parents and their family lineage. We step into these boxes without choice during childhood and by the time we're adults we become unaware of their damage to our self- autonomy and personal power. Along the way, we consciously or unconsciously get thrown into a plethora of more man-made restrictive containers filled with programmed behaviors and conformities. Examples of these include organized religion, government and learning institutions, social clubs, political parties, just to name a few. Within these boxes, we mindf*ck ourselves even further by building more little boxes such as special treatments for one group, class or color. All along, we're learning and perfecting how to separate each other, compete and win at the expense of others. These various boxes become our man-made hellholes that we attach to and seldom know how to break free from. For many, the price of breaking out of our self-induced prisons is just too steep. We become good at making excuses and using our various crutches to justify being chained inside. They become our life's pacifiers. The longer we make excuses to get out, the harder it gets – For older individuals, it may be a tall order. So, I'm not going to impose on anyone to try and do that. Indeed. The Healium Way is not a threat to your religious beliefs, political affiliation, sexual practices or tribalist views. Rather, it's about making you aware of what boxes you're in and what impact these various conformities and bubbles have on individual lives. It's also about taking our blinders off by not succumbing, normalizing and justifying our many unhealthy imbalances. It's about how these man-made choices, behaviors and actions may not just be eroding our own Souls, but are detrimentally affecting the collective wellness of our society. The transformational journey therefore is about going inward into ourselves as a solution to our root causes, the good, the bad and the ugly. More important, it is about trying to bust loose from the lower vibrational self-defeating boxes and operating from our higher self.

A good example of busting loose of our respective boxes can be seen along America's road to marijuana decriminalization. Since 1971, cannabis has been sitting in a box labeled Illegal Drug, specifically Schedule One — or the most restrictive category. And anyone who was caught consuming or selling this natural plant was heavily fined and/or put inside of a cage as a form of punishment. As a newly arrived immigrant in the mid-1970s, the last thing I wanted on my plate was to have a stained record of consuming an illegal substance and being deported. So I avoided smoking weed and anyone who was associated with it. In a matter of a couple of years, most Americans went from freedom-loving hippies to fearful caged puppies. A top Nixon aide, John Ehrlichman, later admitted, "*You want to know what the 'War on Drugs' was really all about? The Nixon campaign in 1968, and the Nixon White House after that, had two enemies: the antiwar left and black people. You understand what I'm saying. We knew we couldn't make it illegal to be either against the war or blacks, but by getting the public to associate the hippies with marijuana and blacks with heroin, and then criminalizing both heavily, we could disrupt those communities. We could arrest their leaders, raid their homes, break up their meetings, and vilify them night after night on the evening news. Did we know we were lying about the drugs? Of course, we did.*" This is a textbook example of America operating in its low-vibrational state; specifically the smoke and mirror games played by our elected leaders. These agenda-based political games are part and parcel of a centralized government power all around the world — not just in America. Therefore, I always question authority, no matter where I go. It helps us keep checks and balances on society and bring about positive change. Today, due to people fighting for unfair drug laws and incarceration in America, many states have decriminalized marijuana and Americans are not being caged for consuming or doing business in the medicinal plant. But did we bust loose from the agenda-based cage too late? Of course, we did. There's plenty of evidence that we paid a heavy price by sitting in that fear-based manipulated box for too long and allowing Big Pharma, the gun lobby, Big Alcohol, the DEA, and profit-over-people prisons and corporations to corrupt policymakers to the detriment of our mental wellness and overall health. In four decades, we went from bumper stickers that read "Flower Power" and 'Make Peace, Not War" to "Keep Honking, I'm Reloading," "I'd Rather Be Drinking and Driving" and "Heavily Medicated for Your Safety."

ACTION SWITCH

At any given time, we have three choices available to us: *Doing nothing, doing something* or *doing everything*. The choice you make becomes especially important in the field of self-transformation. The Healium Way is about having a high bar and doing everything you can to improve oneself. Doing everything also gets you to experience life to its fullest; without limitations and regrets. It's about saying more 'yes' to more things than 'no' (although, saying 'no' sometimes is also necessary). On the contrary, unless you're meditating or sleeping; doing nothing to improve yourself shows lack of passion, laziness and apathy, which leads to low self-esteem and mediocrity. And mediocrity is antithetical to our higher self and The Healium Way. Therefore, it is only possible to start *doing something*; in order to eventually do everything. Doing something is the brain's action switch. Make sure you always keep it on. Or else you're wasting your life living in your head. For instance, if you're just going to read this book for entertainment value but will do nothing with the exercises and the Principles, then you're wasting your time. You must start by doing something to advance your personal growth.

The **second beautiful truth** is about reactivating your inner creative and the arts as medicine. It is necessary to be a more healed person and be free of much regret:

ART IS OUR ANTIDOTE

Our inner-creative receptors are wired at birth. We may not be a Michaelangelo or a Mozart, but our creative talents and imagination are embedded in our DNA and gifted to us by our maker to be our self-correcting medicine. I see it as an immune system builder for our mind and Soul. It is no different than the good bacteria and germs within us that help defend against diseases, a bug bite infection, or a physical skin wound. Our antibodies quickly get activated and go to work and help fight the infection.

Similarly, artistic creativity is specifically designed to help us fight our mental wounds and provide relief to many of our brain's misfirings and man-made problems. Think of it as our antidote. It is brilliantly crafted by our Creator because it is available to us to deploy not just for our *pleasure,* but also for our *pain.* And because we're bad at dealing and coping with pain, we must activate this medicine as a part and parcel of everyday life; without needing any artistic training, or making excuses not to interact with it. This deliberate engagement without judgment or predisposition is the main differentiator of The Healium Way. By simply immersing unconditionally in the process of this Divine medicine; we can self-care without seeking external solutions and harmful or addictive chemicals. By allowing ourselves to dive deeper within, we start to acknowledge and recognize feelings that have been lurking in our subconscious, the source of unhealthy behaviors, mental lethargy and inertia. As we look at our inner-creative as a prescription to activate pleasure and heal embedded emotional pain, we find the solution to the problems that are manifesting in the external and material world. Most important, we must take this inner journey without rules, judgment, or fear. Art is the medicinal portal to open dialogue within, so we can cope better on the outside. This is where we have become deficient in the West. In our exterior visible world, we're trained to treat the symptoms rather than diagnose the causal factors that hide deep inside us. We're always looking outward-instead of looking inward. I will give real life examples of how those of us who self-prescribed the medicine of the arts in this manner healed their wounds faster. While the ones who suffered the longest, had not holistically deployed this creative portal within. It's not a guaranteed cure, but it has made a big difference for me and the countless participants at our Center.

THE BRAINWASHING

There's enough societal evidence to point fingers at our mediocre public schools, technologically heavy lifestyles, over-worked schedules and profit over people model for our many imbalances and underusage of our inner-creative. But actually, the bigger culprit is the attitude that we're just too grown up to participate in the arts. Our society has done a good job brainwashing us adults to appreciate art in two main categories; 1*) art as a means of investing and collecting and 2) art as means of spectating and entertaining.* When the arts are mentioned as a way for interacting & creating for self-healing purposes, people are quick to ridicule its value. The key word here is creating. I am not referring to listening to music, going to a play, enjoying a concert, visiting an art exhibition and the like. As adults, we are quite proficient in partaking in many of these social activities for upliftment, relaxation and inspiration. While they all do wonders aspassive and entertainment activities, they fall short in digging out our buried past and healing emotional scars. Putting our headphones on while listening to music during a workout, is a great mood enhancer and stress-reliever, but it does little for unearthing deeper subconsciously embedded wounds. Visiting an art exhibition or museum is great for spectating and appreciating artworks and professional artists; but falls short in discovering the inner-creative genius within us and activating the medicinal antidote within. In order to realize the greater benefits of the arts, one must journey deeper within and step into the shoes of a creative-born individual; You!

THE DORMANT ARTIST

This book will make a lot of sense if you're already interacting with any form of the arts in your life, but even more so if you are not.

This large segment of the Western population is in the domain of what I call the *dormant artist.* It's a paradoxical way of looking at yourself because you are born a creative, talented and awakened being; but along the way have separated yourself from this Divine condition. It's probably not your fault, it's just where you are and what's happened to you growing up.

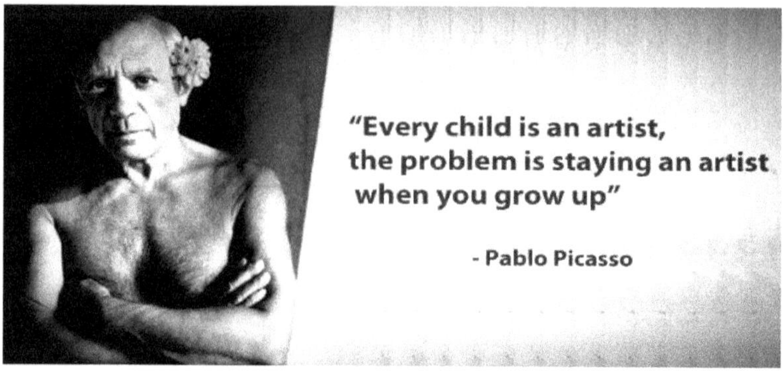

The adult in us has taken on many responsibilities and has weighed us down. If I call you an artist, you'll clam up and let your inner-critic get in the way and start comparing yourself to Picasso or Van Gogh. So we won't. The goal is to remove all the predispositions we've programmed in our mind, to break away from our restrictive pattern of resistance, and to be awakened.

DEBUNKING THE MYTHS OF ART

Most of us have the creative pilot light alive within us, but we've just rusted the connecting wires that ignite our fire. As a result, going from the dormant to the awakened stage isn't that difficult. Notice how I say "rusted" and not dead. Because there's still hope for you skeptics to believe. We know who you are. I've met enough of you in my life, at The Center and in my travels who fit this definition. You're the majority of adults in mostly the Western culture, who've been too busy and preoccupied with life's grind and chase to take advantage of the medicine within. Don't worry you're not alone.

You've probably hijacked your inner-creative and bought into the *societal myths of art,* that we've so often heard people repeat at our Center:

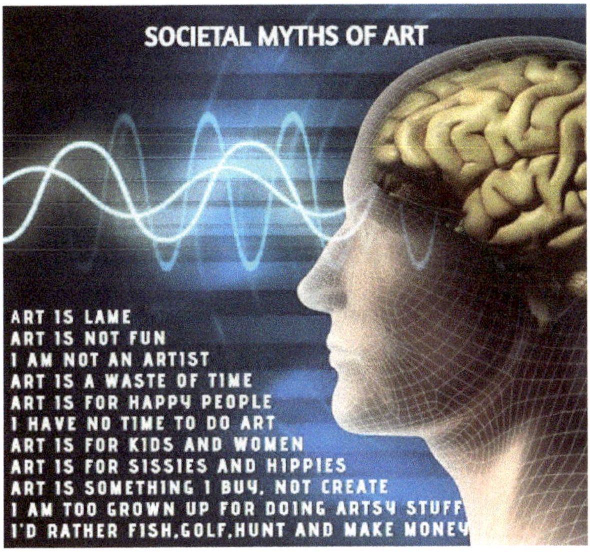

And these are falsities that need to be debunked because they're all convenient excuses that serve no purpose.

OUR SELF-DEFEATING LABELS

The dormant artist is the adult in the room who's great at making excuses, allowing the ego to get in the way of connecting with the true self. Perhaps you've decided to attach some labels to yourself to make you feel important or special. Maybe you've bought into the notion that you're too smart, rich, with too many degrees, sophisticated or even not 'artistic' enough to participate in any freestyle fun and creative activity. Many of you have also convinced yourself that you're too grown up to let your inner child run loose. Your restrictive learning environments and upbringing may have depressed your authentic emotional and expressive receptors. Societal pressures of judgment and pretense may have also sucked the joy out of you. And could it be that your particular religious beliefs have confined you from exploring the non-dogmatic benefits of pure creative freedom?

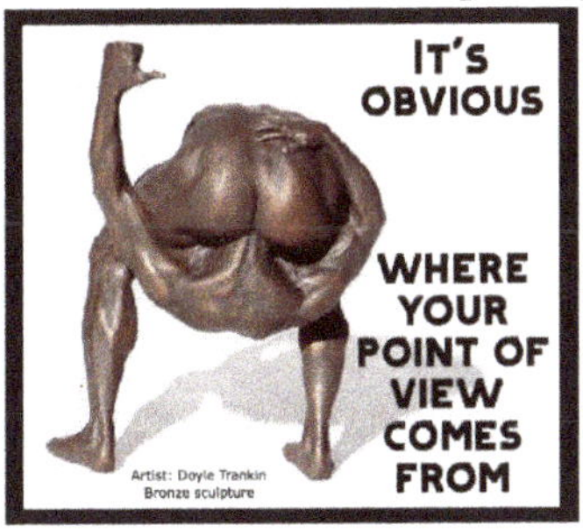

I've seen and heard it all. What we know today is that we rob ourselves of life by being passive spectators, rather than its active participants. Sadly, a lot of this problem has been accelerated in the last twenty five years during the technological revolution. Many of our justifications have resulted in us carrying a burdensome baggage of mind viruses and an ankle bracelet of inflexibility. These viruses have attached to us like parasites and enveloped us in a cacophony of fear and societal programming.

The Covid-19 pandemic, in a round-about way, has made us aware of how a human's weak immune system can fall prey to a destructive virus — and even kill the host. It's a mirror that reflects on our unhealthy imbalances. The pressure of trying to "make it," to pursue the American Dream has beat a hole in our head. We pay a heavy price, yet we just can't admit it.

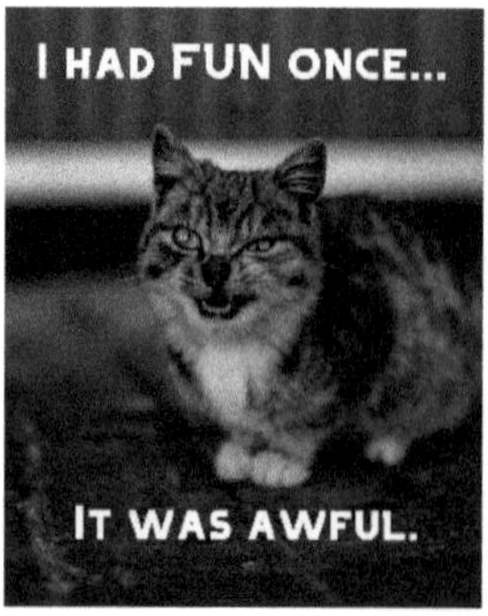

Before we know it, we are a walking wounded adult with open emotional scars, who takes refuge in unhealthy crutches and addictions. If we continue our destructive path, we end up being the walking dead; devoid of any connectivity to our Soul or people around us. We're easily offended and become closed minded. We pop pills like candies, and hang our heads down fixated on our handheld computers all day. It's also easier for us to take on a victim and entitlement mentality. It lets us off the hook for our self-improvement. We can't stand the sight of people having a good time and have turned into bitter and grumpy old farts, full of resentment of others. With our egotistical mind always competing andcomparing. We're never grateful, and rather envious of anyone that is in any way better than us. We become a master of scapegoating and excuses. These are the typical conditions of unhealed people. Often our conscious external-based mind is unaware of most of it, and ironically — that's what's f*cked up about it.

BREAKOUT!

Fortunately, I've met enough of you at our Center, and seen first hand what happens when you break out from your unhealthy patterns of behavior and transition into more healed beings. The lyrics from a song by the Bee Gees, sums it up quite well:

BREAKOUT: *"Don't let the pressure beat a hole in your head. You gotta be a story told, and no one's gonna steal your soul. You'll never do it if you never start. Breakout now!"*

When you stop resisting and just allow love and beauty to permeate your Soul, something amazing happens. You take charge of your own wellness and trust yourself to become your own medicine man/doctor. You self-diagnose your imbalances and take the initiativein removing those labels, covers and chains that bind you. You discover that when you partake in the medicine of the arts on a regular basis byactually becoming an artist, you can be a more powerful healer. A positive cascading effect permeates in every facet of your world. You become a more liberated and joyful person. You rediscover the inner child within, are more flexible in your mind and have more joy in your heart. You realize how your vulnerability makes you stronger. Your ego,judgment and pretenses are less pronounced. You are more humble, empathetic and generous. You become a better team player and a more agreeable collaborator. You stop living in the past and start enjoying the present. Your social skills are improved. Instead of texting your way out of disagreements, you start talking on the phone. In due time, you will look people in the eye and are able to face people head on. You reduce your chemical addictions and medications and seek holistic alternatives. You eat healthier foods and you exercise more. You spend less time glued to "unsocial" media sites or video games. You walk with your head up and smile. You even report how your relationships are real, and reflect upon how you sex life is improved. All this good sh*t happens by your own volition, because you took the extra step of asking the universe to show you a better way for transforming your mundane and unfulfilled life. You have a clear intention to being a more multidimensional, all-encompassing and balanced person. It's amazing how many ordinary people become extraordinary creative beings by just having a flexible and open mind to recognize and turn on their inner artist. Much of it is as simple as getting out of your head and deprogramming societal expectations. I recall a real-estate friend who walked into our Center and told me that he'd tried playing musical instruments and doing art, but wasn't good at any of them. I explained to him that he was probably raised in an achievement-oriented environment, that programmed him to do things that he could only be 'good ' or 'win' at. The epitome of an 'achievement-based' society is America, and this explains why many people have robbed themselves from experiencing their full potential and living life. *"Welcome to a judgment-free place where there's no pressure to be good at anything – so just relax, let go, explore and take risks – and you'll have a lot of fun!"* I told the man.

Check out some examples of first time participants at Healium Center who did exactly that and took a first step towards recognizing the power of their inner-creative self:

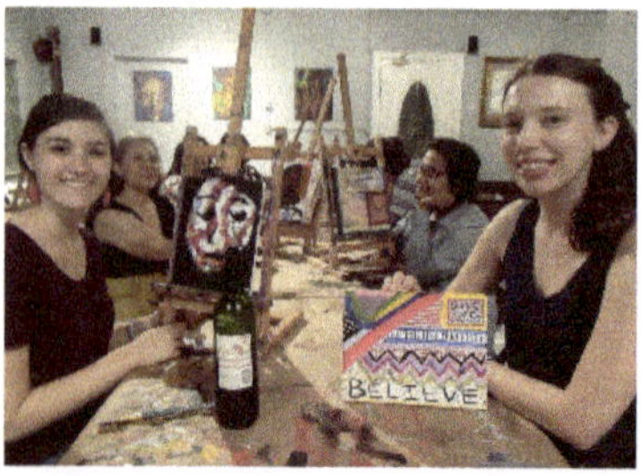

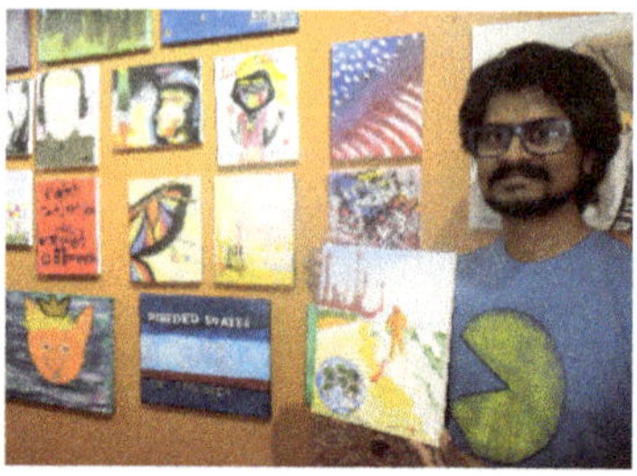

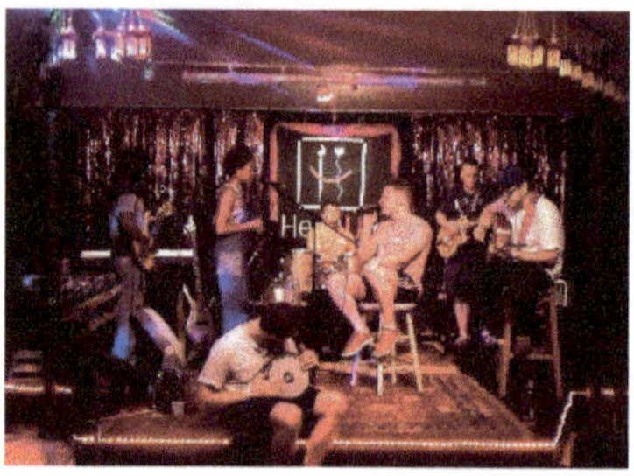

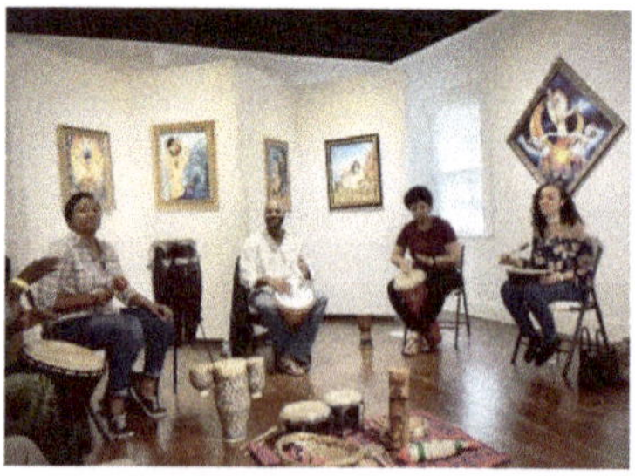

Now, I am not implying that art is a cure-all or that trained and/or professional artists are happier than you are, or stay in healthier balance and have their act together. Artists are flawed and often unhealed like everyone else. Our experience at The Center indicates that quite a few artists actually use art as a crutch. That it's a comfortable justification for their struggle and battle with the many cruel realities that exist outside of their insular, idealistic world. Although some understand the value of struggle, many don't get the memo that it's not supposed to be permanent. By not feeding struggle's hunger, we are not starved for peace. Some artists are self-absorbed with huge egos, and many more are entitlement-minded and needy individuals. I've met them all. I also know those who've come to our Center who are not in body, mind and soul balance, and this imbalance manifests in unhealthy addictions and financial distress. The term *starving artists* becomes a self fulfilling prophecy for many of them who choose a life of creative freedom, over a more Soul sucking "nine to five" lifestyle.

For those who don't mind the trade-off, many of them get trapped into a scarcity mindset and die with a filled Soul but an empty bank account. Lately, I've observed an increase in smart apps and software to digitize art and open new markets and frontiers for artists. Indeed, the future of art and music monetization may look totally different in 20 years, than it does today — with new technology changing the starving artist model into *abundant artists'* one. However, until then, the reality for a majority of artists will continue to be challenging. For the hundreds of career-seeking artists I've met, life is a juggling act between making a living and staying mentally healthy. Very few artists and musicians survive without doing side hustles or drive ride-sharing vehicles. Some choose to moonlight by teaching classes and helping the dormant artists discover the benefits of art and music as a health benefit. Others retrain themselves and get certified as art counselors or art therapists. While the professional term for the creative wellness process is often referred to as *art therapy,* it's a label

I don't like attaching to The Healium Way, as it pigeonholes you into surrendering yourself to an expensive and formal protocol of a more structured way of a *licensed art therapist.*

As much benefit clinical therapy provides to some, it is best utilized under specialized conditions or on an as-needed basis. It is also cost prohibitive for many people. Unless you're experiencing acute depression, severe PTSD symptoms, repeated suicidal thoughts or are diagnosed with chronic mental illness, our model at The Center has proven that you are quite capable of maintaining and caring for your own mental wellness using some simple Principles of The Healium Way. Also contrary to conventional propaganda and television commercials from Big Pharma, you have the power to heal yourself holistically. We are born with this medicine. Yet we're constantly resisting it and wasting it. But why does this medicine slowly dissipate within us by the time we reach adulthood? Moreover, why do most people have such difficulty prescribing it as adults? I will attempt to shed some light on this dilemma — and show you the way to fix it — by deploying the simple but effective Principles of The Healium Way.

The **third beautiful truth** is working to maintain a healthy balance in life, knowing thyself, and demystifying our human complexities by modeling ourselves after nature. This particular truth is the most critical yet difficult condition to follow for many people. By prioritizing balance asa lifestyle habit in The Healium Way, it helps us navigate through life without being yanked around by extreme forces, to stay rooted and grounded amid turbulent and chaotic periods.

THE TREE OF LIFE

Nature is a great teacher and our partner in life. After all, we are our biosphere's primary custodians so it only makes sense for us humans to learn from it, protect it and be in harmony with it. Although as a species we fall short in all three of these departments, we do want to find some similarities with our life's partner. We can learn a lot from the tree, for example. It breathes in what we exhale and gives us life-giving oxygen. It is our tree of life. Using nature as a powerful lesson and the perfect metaphor, the living tree reflects three different types of people. Let's have some fun with this concept:

The Leaves: These are people who come into your life and are temporary. They're just there to provide some shade. You can't depend on them because like leaves they're just there to take what they want for themselves — and then they're gone with the wind.They also are weak and fragile people who sway and are swept away because they don't have minds of their own. Like leaves on trees, there are many "leaves" in our society.

The Branches: These are people who are stronger than leaves, butwho cannot be counted on long term. Because they're rigid and stiff in their ways, they break easily with pressure and stress. If you go through a storm in your life, these types of people are unable to handle it and will break and are fast gone. We meet many people who fit this category in our Western world.

The Roots: These are people who are well adjusted, resilient and grounded. They see the value in growing to improve themselves and are great providers and nourishers. They're also open minded and unafraid to take risks. Selfless, they are there to support when you need help of all kinds. They know they have to be strong as they are responsible for the health of the entire tree. They're not competitive but collaborative. They understand the importance of unity and sharing. These people are low key and don't bang the drum to be noticed. In our over-busy and self-indulgent lives, it's hard to find such people in our society. But we know who they are when we meet them. Because they're beyond the conventional or the ordinary. They practice the art of being extraordinary and they strive to manifest a healed life for themselves.

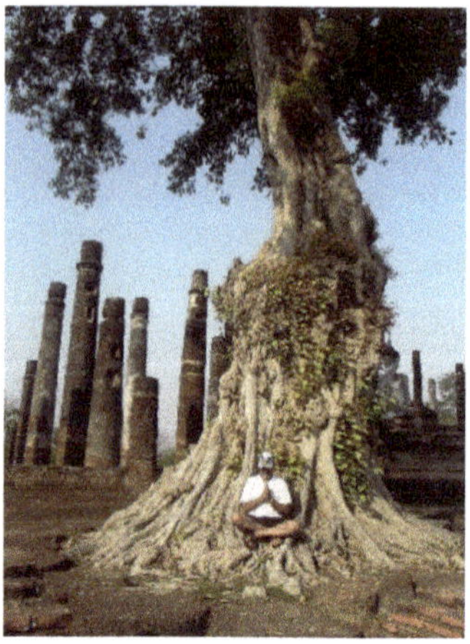

Jim praying on the roots of a Banyan (Bodhi) tree in Thailand

"No tree is so foolish as to have branches fight among themselves"

-Native American Proverb

There are many nuances to these three simplistic human metaphors, but the ultimate goal is to be *The Roots*. This is the high bar for all of us to achieve that is deserving of our Divinity. These are our extraordinary and enlightened people. In this analogy let me emphasize there is no right, wrong or shame in being a leaf or a branch. You have your freedom to exercise your role and if that's what you want to be, so be it.

As a *leaf*-type person, you have a right to your fickleness as much as I have a right not to be around you. But the beautiful concept behind The Healium Way is not to impose or even shame you about the way you are — but rather show you possibilities that exist beyond what you know or don't know. There is comfort in the conventionality of your respective boxes, but if you want to make a change, we're here to help. So if you're a *branch*-type, be a more flexible branch. If you're a leaf, become more aware of your fragility and be a sturdier leaf. Eventually, you'll strive to be a *roots*-type person — and start doing some extraordinary things. This is because you're a powerful being with the capacity to grow, expand and thrive under any condition. By being aware of this truth and having faith in your self- transformation, it will make The Healium Way a lot easier for you to grasp and use in your own life.

THE MYSTERIOUS BLACK BOX

Not surprisingly, we are much more complex than the simplified tree analogies above. Just as every tree is unique and beautiful in its own way, so is each human being. The main differentiator is our more intricate system of intelligence that controls our actions and behaviors: the human brain. This is the mysterious black box that all our other boxes emanate from. And because it has an emotional and logical component, it gets us in trouble and throws us out of balance quite effortlessly. For one, we complicate ourselves to the point of being held hostage in this paradoxical organ, which is both our savior, and our enemy. Within this bi-polar system, the conscious and the subconscious mind plays a see-saw game with our habits, emotions and our entire nervous system. We begin life as cute innocent infants with infinite possibilities, but then get conditioned and predisposed by our respective environments, institutional learning, upbringing and ancestral programming, to list some of the existential forces. Ancestral programming is based on ancient historical beliefs and coping strategies that get hardwired into the next generations' DNA, whether it is relevant to their situation or not. These beliefs may be inherited or learned from hundreds to thousands of years of history and get recycled into our lives. I refer to this phenomenon throughout the book, as it often impedes our self-improvement. During our microprocessor's programming and maturation process, some people grow up to be more mentally agile and resilient than others. What's fascinating is the medicinal role that the creative and healing arts play during our brain's life cycle. Examples include the plethora of studies showing how babies are stimulated by music in the mother's womb before birth and how art activities boost brain activity in Alzheimer patients. And anecdotal evidence at our Center also has demonstrated improved physicality of brain-injured victims with the use of sound-healing vibrational therapy. So, this black box of ours is a highly powerful organ that is gifted to us by our maker for a multipurpose benefit. Its complexity demands that we keep it in a healthy balance by respecting, nourishing and caring for it during our short existence on earth.

WISDOM OF THE TAO

One of my favorite ancient spiritual commentaries on our existence is the *Tao Te Ching* (or Book of The Way and its Virtue in Chinese). It is an often-quoted philosophical manifesto of 81 verses, written by a sage named Lao Tsu. The Tao's genius is its clever use of nature as our guideto practice the virtue of living in balance. I will reference its many powerful verses throughout the book and show how its wisdom is still very relevant even 2500 years after it was conceived. As an appropriate metaphor of *seeing the forest from the trees* (i.e, looking at the larger picture) of our collective humanity and consciousness, we will be looking in detail at the many trees (adult humans) to accomplish our mission.

As we look at this forest, we realize that all the trees are different and unique, as are human beings. Although we're not trying to change this uniqueness, we do want to be deliberate in striving for a harmonious relationship and our coexistence. In this process, each person must do their best to understand and respect self-autonomy and not be hostile for the sake of undermining and destroying others. Although this goal can be viewed as an idealist perspective, it is the virtue of our higher-self and our Divinity, as opposed to a man-made one. You and I are similar in more ways than you realize. For one, we are all made up of energy that emanated from the stars at the beginning of the universe. Secondly, we all come from the same Creator, God, Source, Spirit, or whatever you want to call our maker. And third, we bleed and breathe alike. Therefore, for me it is a non-starter to pit me against any human being, for the sake of separating the connected Divinity between each of us. It's a thought process that does not operate from the higher stream of consciousness. In order to be aligned with my maker's highest ideals, I must simply strive to love and respect everyone as much as I can; be the best at what I do and serve humanity to the best of my ability. I'm sure you have similar aspirations. Or do you? So first, it requires that we detach from the dark and disempowering traits and habits that have our heads hanging low and our Souls tethered. It's important that we not only strive to become positive contributors to society and provide the best life for ourselves and our family, but that we understand the value of self-care and maintaining body, mind and soul balance at all times. Or it doesn't work. Therefore, the onus is first and foremost on each of us to take care of ourselves, in order to provide for the greater good of others. As we strive for this *"One-Planet/One-Love/One-humanity"* coexistence and codependence condition, we must start by bettering ourselves by acting, thinking and behaving like our maker; without any thought of separation. It is the way of the Tao — the way of life.

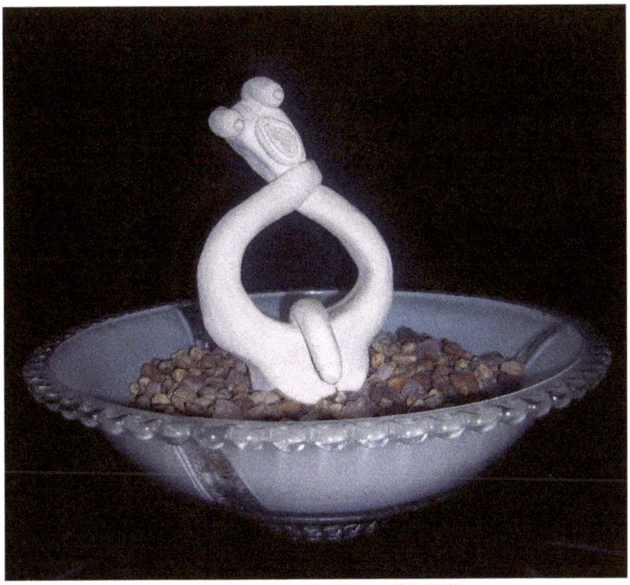

" Human is HumONE"

(Clay, Crystal, Rock). Artist: Jim Peera

3
THE THREE UGLY TRUTHS

"When you change the way you look at things,

the things you look at change"

— Dr Wayne Dyer

Although we have many functional zombies and unhealed individuals walking among us, most of us prefer reading a story or autobiography of other messed-up people, as opposed to holding a mirror up to ourselves. This is why in The Healium Way, we're going to shine some light on our own darkness by looking shamelessly into this mirror of truth. It is here that we will begin opening the Divinity within us, re-activating our powerful creative-selves and becoming our own healers. Our Creator gave us our body, mind and soul but we're responsible for it once we exit our mother's safe and protective womb. And we're pretty proficient at screwing up this balance. But it didn't happen overnight and we certainly didn't get a 'how to' guide marinating inside God's vessel for nine months. Many of our faults, imbalances and transgressions began manifesting in our development stage, and got perfected in adulthood. We've become proficient at normalizing it or sitting comfortably numb in our various programmed boxes, mired by our crutches and excuses. Some of us do a better job than others trying to get out, but we're always looking externally for our internal fixes. For many of us, we come to realize that we're grinding away on a hamster wheel and something doesn't feel right. If we've bought into the consumerism Western model of life, we're getting engulfed by its beastly parasitic burdens of competition and winning at all costs that slowly erodes our Soul from within. Instead of just being, we're constantly doing; never arriving at a place of inner peace and contentment. Life's passing us by, and happiness becomes a temporary illusion of our unsustainable man-made reality. In this physical realm, we get caught up in the rat race without being in alignment with our more spiritual and sustainable nature. This imbalance cleverly traps us into deviating froma higher energy force that keeps us strong, empowered and united amidst any calamity or dark entity. But why?

INVISIBLE IS INDIVISIBLE

As alluded to earlier, we know we're all made of energy matter. Specifically, the visible and invisible world. Our invisible spirit energy operates on a faster frequency and a higher vibration, while our visible (external) energy is on a slower frequency and a lower vibration level. The latter is housed in a temporary shell known as our body. The former resides in the Soul. With this universally accepted dynamic, we accept that our higher and immortal self resides in our spiritual realm, rather than the physical and material one that withers and ceases to exist. Therefore, our aim is to operate on a higher vibration level that matches the permanence of our Soul. This Soul houses our higher consciousness traits of compassion, kindness and empathy, while the lower consciousness is concerned with the self and the survival of our own individualistic success. The higher and invisible self is the embodiment of light and it knows no separation. Its opposite is darkness, which thrives in division. This dualism is also known in Chinese philosophy as yin and yang. What's fascinating however, is how we humans are easily seduced by the dark, divisive and destructive forces. You can call it demon, evil, Devil, Satan, black magic and so on. Although the majority of us are not serial killers or demonic, we are part and parcel of imperfect beings that have the propensity to slide down this deep end at any given time. Carl Jung even identified this dark unconscious side as *the shadow* that we battle within and commonly repress to our own detriment. If it's not reckoned with, it manifests in the physical conscious realm with damaging repercussions. Our dance with the dark side explains the many atrocities and injustices inflicted upon humanity and our self-destructive dehumanizing behaviors. In order to get to the "why" this is so, let's shine a spotlight on the "what."

While existing in this physical state of being, we have to admit to ourselves, as I have done to myself, the *three ugly truths* about the reality of what our human condition reveals about us:

1. **We are flawed beings.**
2. **Each of us is unique, but not special.**
3. **We all harbor some unhealed scars that are keeping us from operating at our higher vibration.**

These three ugly truths are ours to own from the moment we're born. We must be aware of them on our path of transformation. The bad news is that the *first* ugly truth will sit with us until our last breath, while the *second* ugly truth is a reality check for us to understand and accept. The good news is that the *third* ugly truth can be diminished by working on ourselves, deploying The Healium Way Principles in daily life and seeking professional help, if necessary. All of these ugly truths will be exposed in the stories and discussion throughout this book.

A F*CKED UP TRUTH

I've always believed that we are a defective species, and how our human nature is cruel in more ways than we realize. We not only deliberately harm our own species, but destroy our habitat and environment and kill creatures for our own selfish pleasure. We're responsible for some pretty cruel rituals such as incest, beastiality, cannibalism, torture, human sacrifices etc. We can try justifying our immorality as necessary to our survival or blame it all on free will. Whatever it is that deviates us from our higher self, it's something not to be proud of. We must therefore admit and accept that we are all somewhat f*cked up, and do some f*cked up things to ourselves and others. There are various degrees of f*ck-ups obviously, but for our purposes we must call our inexplicable imperfect state of being for what it is: *flawed beings.* It is with this raw truth and humility that we can become *better* human beings. By accepting this fact and not being unafraid of my dark side and perceiving myself as *flawed, not special and emotionally bruised,* it liberates me from being perfect and being afraid of failure in any way. Hence, the bar is set lower and the only way is to go up. In the same fashion, by looking at myself as an ordinary being first, I strive harder to go beyond the ordinary and accomplish extraordinary things. I now have the emotional license to be curious about unearthing my childhood traumas, instead of burying them. I also see myself as a work in progress rather than an all-knowing, fully completed person.

THE SPECIAL TRAP

So I am unique, not special. I don't walk, talk or act like I am. And I don't want to be labeled that way. And neither should a Divine being like yourself. Who wants the pressure of being up on some elusive pedestal anyway? Not me, I'd rather you don't praise me when things work out for you, and throw me under the bus when they don't! I prefer being the unsung, quiet leader whose work and deeds are my legacy. The definition of "special" that I'm referring to has to do with people who think they're "it" — who behave and act like they're superior even when they're just average. It is an ugly truth because in America this word, "special," easily manifests into an arrogant and entitled mindset, which in turn breeds a separatist condition that is antithetical to The Healium Way. The fact is, when you are exceptional in one endeavor, you're often deficient in another.

After all, you're not a superhuman. If you're a well-respected brain surgeon, you have the permission to pat yourself on the back for being fortunate, talented and smart. But to coin a popular Christian term, you're more "blessed" than special.

By seeing things from this prism, it diffuses the egotistic element and supplants it with humility. As a result, we're not boxing ourselves into a *special* trap. This trap seduces us with a temporary pleasure and validation itch that sets us up for a painful downfall — that is twice as painful as the pleasure of the rise.

The higher you rise, the farther you're likely to fall. For every person who praises you, there are going to be those who prick your bubble and wish you ill. I've seen it all too often with famous people, who relish their rise to stardom but cannot cope emotionally when the world knocks them down. Since we're in charge of our own emotions and actions, we must work towards an even-keeled emotional condition that helps us avoid the glitter and gold element of being special. We want you to shape a more sustainable philosophy that keeps you better grounded at all times and is an important prerequisite in the application of The Healium Way Principles.

YOU GOT ISSUES!

The third ugly truth is somewhat difficult for many people to accept, as it reveals our deeper embedded imperfections and exposes our vulnerabilities. No one wants to hear this truth, but it must be told. Imagine opening your email inbox to the voice, *"You got issues!"* I believe that would be preferable to, *"You got mail!",* or some marketer trying to sell you things that we don't need, don't you? Regardless of our ethnicity, economic status or particular state of enlightenment, we all have issues. Many of these issues stem from our undealt traumas and open wounds from childhood. Our molehills grow into mountains internally, until they erupt externally as volcanoes during adulthood. Often these eruptions are our signals of suppressing our emotional pain with external quick fixes and crutches that do more harm than good. Common examples of this include addictive drugs, comfort foods, work, money, gambling, toxic people, alcohol, video games and porn. Some of these crutches manifest in our being verbally nasty with people, or show up as outright hatred and physical violence. But when we acknowledge these flaws, we can begin our journey of truth toward our own self-growth and transformation. By having an honest reckoning with this common form of ugly truth, I believe each of us can turn ourselves around by deploying our beautiful truths as discussed earlier. I know I have. What's more, I've witnessed many people at The Center change their lives for the better by simply facing their issues with grit and transparency. Therefore, these three ugly truths are by design a mirror unto yourself, and a more accurate way of looking at our man-made imperfections through the lens of The Healium Way.

OF THORNS, MUD AND SH*T

I am also not a fan of unrealistic individuals who wake up each morning expecting life to be a pretty crystal vase with mudless, fragrant lotuses and thornless roses; these folks who spend their whole life avoiding conflicts and seeing the world through an idealistic prism. How stressful is that! Without the prickly thorns on a rose's stem, the slimy mud under a lotus or the animal sh*t in the soil, these flowers cannot grow in their natural and beautiful state. So why do we expect our life to be any different? Accepting the harsh reality that life is often unfair, ugly and hard is what makes it interesting — and our journey of transformation into beautiful beings possible. I must admit that we're all guilty of finding ourselves in a tug of war between our ideals and dealing with life's many difficult realities. Yet at some point we must realize that we need to strike a balance between the two paths and face our calamities head on in order to appreciate the joys.

That's the healthier and more sustainable choice that we must encourage through The Healium Way.

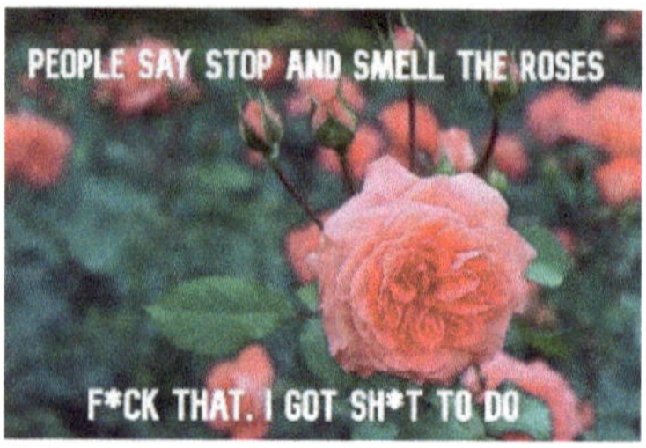

So why do we choose to live in a bubble of falsities while being saddled with crutches, addictions and excuses? It only weakens our coping skills in life. Instead of trying to avoid sh*tty people, complain about sh*t, or pretend that sh*tty people don't exist — we must not be intimidated by any form of sh*t. Once we understand that sh*t is part of life, it's what we do with sh*t, is what really matters. A more healed person reflects on his own sh*t when he makes bad choices; and learns from it. Whereas, an unhealed person enjoys throwing sh*t at others, and never takes responsibility for his own sh*tty actions.

The life lesson: You have to go through sh*t in order to smell the roses. And the sooner you realize this fact, the easier it gets to be the best you. This has been the story of my life, and I am grateful because of it. This is what we are talking about regarding the character of extraordinary, *roots*-type individuals, and what we all must aspire to.

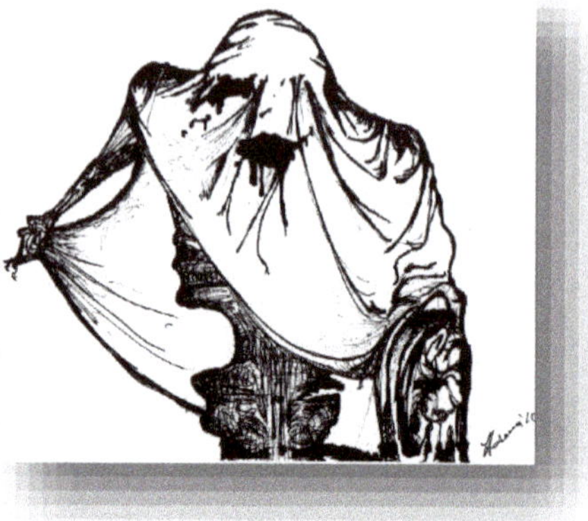

<u>Interactive Exercise</u>

To begin the journey, take a few minutes immersing yourself in the piece of art shown here. It is a powerful exercise to help you open up your creative receptors and start getting into the habit of noting all your emotions without restraints.

On a piece of blank paper, jot down what you feel when you look at this drawing; i.e, your emotions; fear, anger, anticipation, vulnerability, etc. Now go deeper into the piece. Without overthinking or analyzing what motivated the artist,ask yourself what you see. Is the person sad, happy, crying or laughing? What does the face beneath the cover look like to you? Are there tears of joy or sadness? Is it blood, water or other liquid that has soaked the cloth? Or do you see something totally different? Do you see a person who is *covering up* or trying *to uncover* themselves? Write it all down and keep it in a safe place. We will revisit this interpretation later in the book.

Before we delve into the Principles of The Healium Way, it is important to spend a few chapters taking you on an introspective journey of my own lessons in life when I used these Principles effectively. And there have been some pretty memorable lessons that not too many individuals get the chance to experience in one lifetime! The real-life experiences of pain and pleasure noted in these stories will help you breakout of your own self-imposed limitations and discover a life without blame, excuses or regret. The Healium Way will begin to make more sense to you, as I underscore the importance of the arts and self-empowerment through my own lens. I'll expose all the mud under the lotus. By doing this, I will allow you to hold a mirror up to yourself without shame or guilt — and help you get back on your own reconnective path. Some experiences are from The Healium Center and some are personal and quite difficult for me to unpack. But I'm comfortable laying it all out raw and unfiltered because keeping it real is what this book is about. By the time you get to the Principles, in Part 2, you will feel more open and ready to begin implementing them in your own daily life without much resistance and more appreciation.

UNPACKING MY OWN CHILDHOOD WOUND

Since many of our adult manifested issues begin in childhood, I thought it would make sense to unpack one of my own childhood emotional wounds for demonstration. It is a good example of an ugly truth; an unhealed scar that lurked in my past for a long time and that took a while to heal. This wound is healed today, but it was a deep cut at the time that it occurred and could have festered into a dangerous condition, if it wasn't for the medicine that I prescribed myself. In most situations, our unpleasant childhood experiences can be a normal part of our growth and maturation process and pose no long-term emotional damage. But some incidents can be quite traumatic and if left unattended, can continue to inflict psychological pain and collateral damage into adulthood. In a few instances like I am about to share, an emotional wound caused by a tragic situation can only be explained asa Divine-induced catalyst for a person's life purpose and lesson. In this case, it is a revelation about my own shadow. And what a lesson it is.

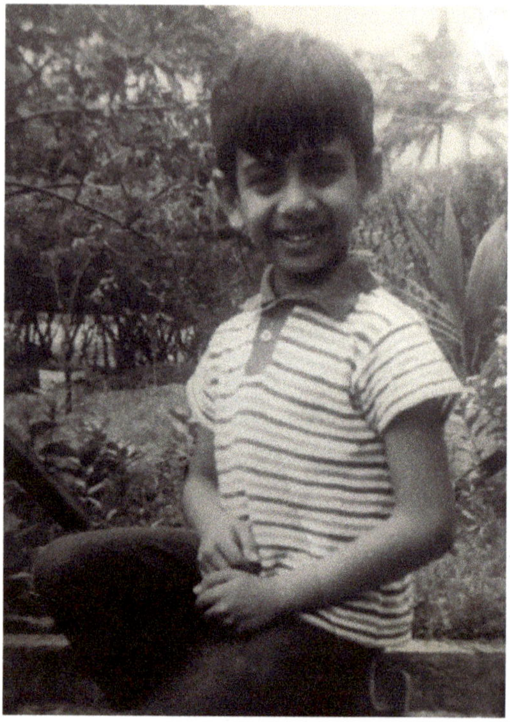

Jim in Africa -1967

4
A Life for a Life

"A brush with death always helps us live our lives better"

— Paulo Coelho

The event I am about to recount after 52 years, still brings shivers to my spine and clouds my eyes with tears. Notwithstanding the details and particulars that have since faded, the significance of the story is permanently etched in my mind. I was around eight years old when this tragic incident took place. Unlike previous childhood traumas, where my grandma or a family member helped heal; this was a trauma with a secret twist that I could not reveal to anyone. And that decision cost me my peace and haunted me for many years to follow. The memory of it would often jar me without notice, as an apparition of a thick eye-browed brown boy with a pensive expression staring at me with a soft smile. His name was Zulfiqar, in Arabic it means 'Clever of Spine'. In the Koran, Zulfiqar was one of the split bladed swords the Prophet Muhammad used in battle. Aptly named for his courage and intellect, my friend was one of the sharpest minds I knew at the Aga Khan elementary school in my birthplace of Dar es Salaam. He was brilliant in math and science and was a straight A student. Looking back, I believe he was a nerdish genius. Zul, as we called him, was a quiet and reserved boy with very few friends and some who even took advantage of him. As a shy and studious boy myself, I befriended him and we protected each other from other taller and more mischievous kids and troublemakers. Often, we'd hang around during recess and share our home-prepared food during lunch. He'd help me with math equations and I'd return the favor improving his social skills with other kids. On this particular day, we got out late from class and were only given about 15 minutes for lunch break rather than the usual half an hour. Instead of going down two long flights of stairs to the playground and eating lunch, we decided to stay on the balcony. We both stood with our backs on the balcony rail and opened our respective lunch boxes. It wasn't long when a lanky African boy who was a known bully came by and began harassing us. He started looking at my lunchbox and didn't like what he saw. So he approached Zul who had packed a sandwich and a candy bar. *"Hey you smartie pants, give me some of that you have there*" he exclaimed to my friend in Swahili. "*Leave my friend alone!*" I replied angrily. At this time Zul was standing to the right of me and beside another boy who was also a troublemaker and watching the commotion with curiosity. It looked like they were trying to trap my friend between them, so I had Zul to switch places with me. We switched places in a matter of seconds. I then advised Zul to close his box and ignore the bully until he left us alone. The bully got hostile and poked me hard in the chest and told me to mind my own business. Zul quickly clenched his lunchbox tightly close to his chest to stop the boy from yanking it. The bully got perturbed and doubled down on harassing him. He began poking him in the chest repeatedly as he did with me and got more aggressive. He then tried to grab the lunchbox with force and as Zul fought back, he used both his hands and pushed my friend with all his might. With my head turned towards Zul and within a blink of an eye, I watched my friend slip through a missing iron rail on the balcony and fall back 30 feet down to the floor below smashing his head on the hard concrete. The incident happened so fast that I remember looking down helplessly, having my mouth wide open, screaming. But I couldn't hear myself. It was as if my ears were shut and my entire body went numb. I was in a state of shock as I watched Zul fall to his death.

It was the most horrific event I had experienced to date in my childhood. As I regained my composure, I heard the sounds of kids screaming everywhere in a state of panic and rushing towards my friend's body. Zulfiqar laid lifeless on his back with his mouth and eyes wide open. There was no visible blood as he had hemorrhaged internally. The bully and I were the only two kids remaining on the second floor staring down at the tragic scene from the balcony.

I was too devastated and angry to look at him, and he was too traumatized and scared to look at me. We were both paralyzed in our own state of grief, as we each processed what had just happened. It was the last time I remember seeing that boy. After I told the teacher that he had pushed Zul, he was permanently banned from school. There must have been a thousand people at Zul's funeral the following week, but I was too devastated to attend. I was told that Zul's parents were more furious with the bully for killing their child than they were at the school for not repairing the faulty rail. I never fully understood that logic, except that it was probably based on racially programmed behavior. The bully was a black African Christian and Zul was an East Indian Muslim. The elementary school was supported by and named after an exalted Muslim religious leader, the Aga Khan. Its image and reputation was at stake. I'm not sure how the grown-ups eventually handled the politics, or if there was any monetary compensation for Zul's parents. As a young boy, I just knew I didn't want the bully to suffer anymore punishment and guilt. No matter how angry I felt towards him, it wasn't my job to punish him for his actions. So I never shared the story of swapping places between Zul and myself with anyone at the time. I didn't think it was relevant, and it would not bring his life back. That little secret was my internal hell to deal with. Why him and not me? I asked God. The missing rail on the balcony was directly on my back that day, but my good friend was the one who took my place and lost his precious life so prematurely. Had I not instructed him to swap places with me, Zul would still be alive. What was that about? I often asked myself.

Not having any experience with Spirit guides to help me reach my friend in his new supernatural dimension, I continued suffering.

DRAWING OUT THE MEDICINE

For a long time, I felt responsible for Zulfiqar's death. I often had nightmares of me falling down with him into a bottomless dark hole. I saw it as a curse, as I could never explain why I was spared that fateful day. The trauma of that incident left me bereft and I agonized with feelings of guilt, sadness and disgust for the next five years. I was suffering internally but for whatever reason I just could not find a way to talk about it with anyone. Then around the age of eleven, I found the medicine to heal my open wound. It was art. I had just arrived in Paris a year earlier from Africa. Our family was evicted from our birthplace of Tanzania and displaced as refugees. My dad chose Paris to be our new temporary home, as one of my uncles was on a business trip there. Somehow, he mustered some money and enrolled me in a top accredited bilingual school near the Eiffel Tower. One afternoon, while sitting on a wooden bench with my classmates in Champs De Mars, a famous park across from the towering landmark, I found myself glancing aimlessly at a beautiful big tree.

From the corner of my eye, I saw a bird suddenly fall down to the ground and die. It immediately triggered that terrible memory of Zul's falling to his death. My eyes dilated and I was speechless. One of my classmates sitting next to me jumped to check on the bird. He shouted and waved at me to come. I walked up to the bird hesitantly. It was lifeless without any blood showing. Its eyes were still open and it seemed like it died naturally. My classmate took out a handkerchief from his pocket, carefully wrapped up the stiff yellow bird and told me to get a stick and start digging a hole. I agreed. While I was digging with the stick, a few other classmates gathered and we buried the bird before the teacher rang the bell for our return to class. After school ended that day and while I was sitting on the train returning home, I took out my writing pad and started doodling and drawing stick drawings. I had never done that before. I wasn't a great drawer, but I simply had to get some images out of my head and onto paper. Apparently, the bird dropping dead from the tree was the catalyst for my artistic self-expression; my closure of internal torment. The first few pieces started out pretty dark in theme with screaming faces of a boy inside of a large black-palmed hand. Another piece depicted a boy's arm being ripped apart trying to save a falling boy These sketches were quite grim and I didn't want my parents to see them so I threw them out before I got home. After that, every day on my 30-minute train ride home I would draw to release my pent-up emotions. Some days, I'd tear up and other days I'd laugh and recall the good times I had with Zul. Art became my therapy. After several days, I noticed my stick drawings progressed into more positive themes. I remember drawing a stick figure of Zul disguised as a body of a huge bird, flying down from a tree with me riding on his back and carrying a sword. Sort of like a warrior trying to save his people.

A LIFE-ALTERING FIELD TRIP

On one field trip, our French art teacher surprised us by taking the entire class to visit a man she called a *"very unique person and amazing artist."* At the time I thought of him as just an old bald man who painted some pretty odd but captivating artworks. He gave us a tour of his place, shared some stories about his work, and told us elementary school kids to never stop creating. His name was Pablo Picasso and I'd never heard of him until that day. Spending about ninety minutes that afternoon listening to this iconic artist talk about his work, forever changed my creative life as I know it. From the day of that visit, I learned to express myself in Picasso's surrealism-style and started to write poetry to accompany my creations. Using that powerful combination of self-expression, I eventually saw Zul's death as an accident, as opposed to it being my fault. And once that guilt factor was gone, it lessened my burden and got me to heal. It was as if Picasso somehow inspired me to look at one of my ugly truths as a beautiful truth. Now instead of working hard to keep the unhealed scar conveniently dressed, I was eager to open it up and release my emotional pain by activating my creative medicines. Slowly but surely, I made progress being my own therapist and healer, and it was life- changing.

But there was still one unanswered question that bothered me. Was there a Divine explanation to how it was that my life was spared?

DIVINE INTERVENTION

I searched for an answer from my maker, but there was no clear signalthat pointed to anything. And then, about 40 years later as I was driving back home from a life-altering property ordeal in Alabama, thatI will detail in the following chapter, it hit me. I realized that a guardian angel was looking out for me, both on that day in Alabama and when my dear friend, Zul, died, in my place during childhood. Both cases involved fighting bullying and injustice. Could it be that it was my Creator's will to keep me here alive so that I would stand up to bullies and fight for justice? Was it somehow Zul's life that had to be sacrificed that day for mine to be worth something 40 years later — such as a life- for-a-life swap? After all, most of my life up to that time had been about fighting hungry wolves and helping the underdogs. Was the African bully boy a serendipitous case of Divine intervention? Were our destinies planned in that way? I am not sure what our maker had in mind, but I do know it was fate that brought all three of God's children aligned on that day. I don't know what happened to that African bully, but I do believe it changed his life forever, as it did mine. In many ways, it was Zul's lesson, as much as it was the African's and mine. Moreover, I now see this tragic episode as a Divine blessing as opposed to a curse. I know I wouldn't be here 52 years later to tell you about it and live to write a book of my life's adventurous journey. So, in the end, I am grateful for that life-altering episode and to my friend for sparing my life in exchange for his — a life for a life.

5
OUT OF THE LION'S MOUTH

"When you lose your sense of fear, you are free."

— John Lewis

I'm a firm believer in destiny, understanding that there are life-changing events that happen in the course of a life for a good reason.

There are also legacy-making experiences where few of us get a chance to make history. So when you are fortunate to be blessed with both of those situations in one lifetime, it is worth honoring the lessons. It is for this reason that I must share with you another transformative event in my life that was a catalyst for Healium Center, and an inspiration for this book. During this period, which was tumultuous and exasperating, I felt like I was inside of a lion's mouth, being mauled and spit out into bits and pieces like a rag doll. The lion in my metaphor, was a corrupt and a racist City Hall in Montgomery, the capital city of Alabama. Alabama was home to events during the civil rights movement, including the Montgomery bus boycott and the bloody Sunday Selma to Montgomery march. As a brown man who's lived in America for more than four decades, I should have known better not to step into a minefield of raw and unresolved black and white segregated quagmire. But as a real estate entrepreneur and a self-made capitalist, I was blinded by the seductive money-making opportunity and stepped willfully into a perfect trap. While I was trapped inside this lion's beastly mouth, its powerful fangs were piercing me with the intent to destroy my life's underpinnings as I knew them. This formidable beast was salivating on my inexperienced ego beast within, and determined to chew me up and spit my bones out, one at a time. I feared I'd lose everything — my family, money, sanity, and even my life. Yet, fate had a different path for me. What started out as a curse turned out to be a sacrificial blessing and I lived to tell the story — once again. I will attempt to summarize for you in one chapter, my five-and-a-half year life-altering ordeal and the significance of this story for The Healium Way.

THE PRICE OF A WRONG TURN

It was early winter in 2005, and while I was a full-time successful real estate investor/developer, one of my brothers and I drove to view an apartment building in Montgomery, about a two-and-a-half-hour drive from Atlanta. It was a cloudy and misty day and as we got to the city, we took the wrong turn and got lost. Soon we drove past four blocks and eight acres of flat land topped with forty cinder block structures that housed one hundred and twenty one-story cottage apartments. They resembled 1960's military housing and were built solid as a rock. My pupils dilated and my brain was conjuring all sorts of ideas to rehabilitate and sell them for a profit.

I called the management company that also owned the property and inquired if it was for sale. The owner wasn't interested in selling, but. I left my contact number and told him to call me if he changed his mind.I didn't hear from him for a few weeks, and I got anxious and phoned him. I must have pestered him a dozen times in the course of two months insisting that he should sell the property to me. In the third month he finally agreed to a price with owner financing. It was a steal of a deal from my viewpoint and I jumped in the car again and drove to Alabama before he changed his mind. He was a short white man in his seventies who many of the black tenants I spoke to referred to as a slumlord. I found out he was a prominent real estate investor who had a reputation for being shrewd and difficult to work with. I ignored allthe negatives of his personality and just wanted to strike a deal. He didn't waste any time with small talk and got down to business. We signed the contract, shook hands and I was elated. I did all my typical due diligence and a month later I was ready to purchase the property. On the day of the closing, I was excited and eager to be the owner of one of the largest pieces of property in the Rosa Parks District. But things took a weird turn. About 10 minutes prior to the closing,the seller called my attorney and told him he had changed his mindand didn't want to sell. I thought it was a joke, but the guy was serious and did not show up to sign the deed. I had been to many closings in my real estate career, but this one was the most bizarre and eerie todate. The seller cited no reasons for his decision and stopped taking phone calls from my attorney. My palms were sweaty and my brainwas restless and heated with anger. *"How can that son of a b*tch dothis to us?"*, I thought. I asked my young white lawyer, *"Not sure whatto tell ya, Jim, but he's not answering. He's changed his mind. I'll try calling him again,"* he replied in a Southern drawl. A couple of hours passed and both my brother and I were getting impatient and frustrated pacing the hallways of the two-storied law office.

Each minute and hour was agonizing as we'd bother the attorney and his secretary for any news update from the seller. Around mid-afternoon, the lawyer finally informed us that he'd just hung up the phone with the seller and had a favorable resolution. He said the seller offered to pay me a $10,000 nonperformance fee to walk away from the deal. I rolled my eyes in disgust and processed the offer as an insult to my intelligence. *"WTF!...So he's got another buyer willing to pay more money!"* I exclaimed to the attorney. Being that Montgomery was a small world, my attorney informed me that the seller's son also was a lawyer and they were playing some sneaky game. Without hesitation, I told my attorney to tell the seller to *"Go to hell!"* and that I would sue him for breach of contract. I really wanted the property and was persistent. Stupidly persistent.

You see, prior to opening Healium, I wasquite a fiery character who persisted the more someone resisted or jerked me around.

THE HANGMAN

Today, I am a lot wiser and simply allow the universe to take charge. But back then, my ego was so attached to this property and I couldn't separate them. My dogged persistence amounted to me being my own hangman, but I couldn't see that. I doubled down on fighting the seller,a decision that would cost me dearly down the road. I paid the attorney some more money to file the lawsuit and headed back home to Atlanta. The following morning the law office called me to tell me that the seller had acquiesced and agreed to sell the property if I paid in cash. He gave me twenty-four hours to come up with a huge sum of money that he knew was improbable and unrealistic.

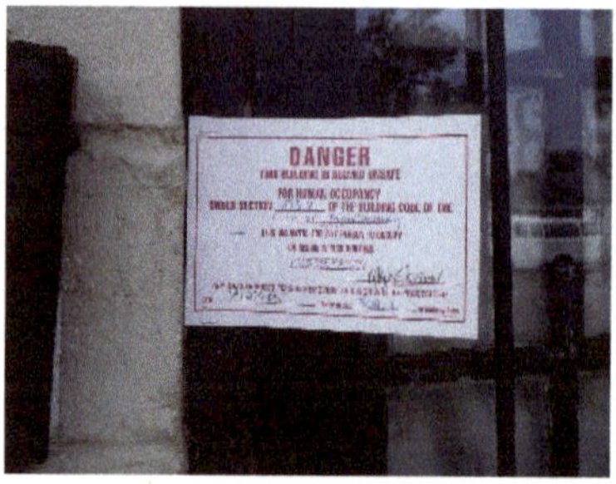

Notice of an unmerited code violation

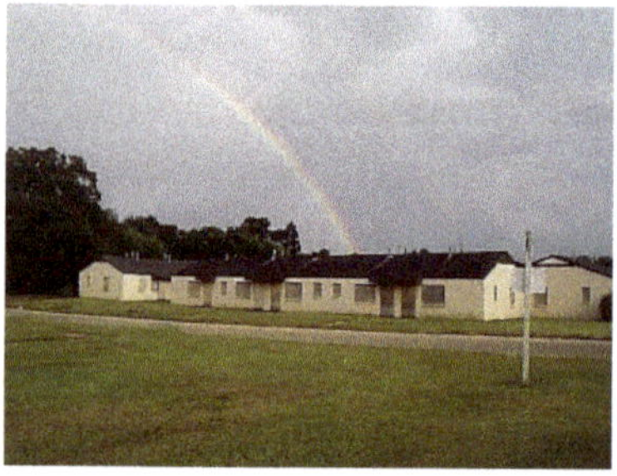

A rainbow casts over a targeted property

Unknown to me, this was a novel but perfected tactic that Montgomery had successfully used with many poor black property owners in this neighborhood. The diabolical scheme is commonly known as "the back door to eminent domain" where the authorities impose a large demolition lien to legally control and eventually steal the land without paying fair market value for it. I know that in the segregated South, legions of uneducated and poor black real estate owners have lost their properties in this way to whites.

THE OUTSIDER

As an unassuming, short, skinny brown man, I nervously walked into City Hall with an appointment to see the mayor. He was a medium built six-foot tall white man in his 40's and wore a white shirt with a red tie. His red-flushed face reeked with a sense of corrupted power and arrogance. My gut indicated this man was trouble. There was no handshake or a smile, just a beady-eyed unfriendly stare. He sat behind his desk and greeted me with a cold stern expression: *"So how can I help you Mr Peera?"* he asked. For a moment, it felt like I was in a lion's den and this powerful man knew he had me cornered for the kill. I didn't waste any time and asked him why the city and his bellicose staff (chief inspector, code compliance staff, council woman and planning chief) were targeting me for no good reason.

He stretched himself back on his reclining leather chair, looked at me with dagger eyes and gave me an unwelcoming reply to the effect that I was an "outsider from Atlanta" who was not welcome to renovate or lease up those apartments: *"Doing business in this city is not a right but a privilege. I'll do everything in my power to see to it that unless you abide by our strict building standards, that you don't open your apartments up. You got the lowlifes and criminals over there. I promise you, that we'll tear 'em down!"* he declared.

What he conveniently failed to articulate is how the city's "standards" were practically impossible to meet, and that he had already fixed it with the judge to order demolishing the buildings. This was the city's plan all along. The "criminals" and "low lifes" he was referring to were my low-income black tenants who were mostly the handicapped and the elderly without any criminal records. Indeed, it was a blatantly racist remark. I took a deep breath, shook my head in disbelief and politely told the man that my group of partners (I had no partners) had invested a lot of money in the property and we could not do that. I suggested to him that if the city had better plans for it that I'd be happy to discuss that with the partners to sell it to the city for a profit. He didn't like that answer and readied to get on an offensive plan of attack.

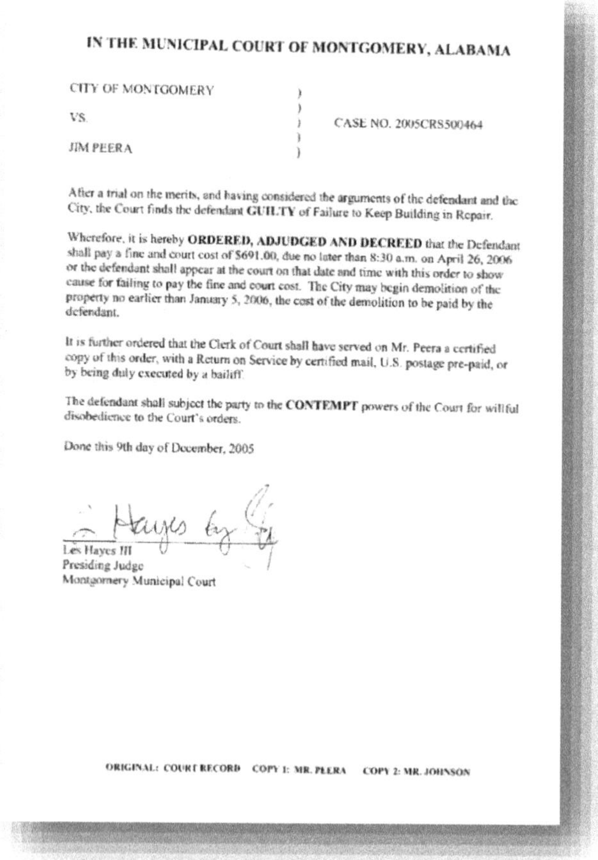

IN THE MUNICIPAL COURT OF MONTGOMERY, ALABAMA

CITY OF MONTGOMERY)
)
VS.) CASE NO. 2005CRS500464
)
JIM PEERA)

After a trial on the merits, and having considered the arguments of the defendant and the City, the Court finds the defendant **GUILTY** of Failure to Keep Building in Repair.

Wherefore, it is hereby **ORDERED, ADJUDGED AND DECREED** that the Defendant shall pay a fine and court cost of $691.00, due no later than 8:30 a.m. on April 26, 2006 or the defendant shall appear at the court on that date and time with this order to show cause for failing to pay the fine and court cost. The City may begin demolition of the property no earlier than January 5, 2006, the cost of the demolition to be paid by the defendant.

It is further ordered that the Clerk of Court shall have served on Mr. Peera a certified copy of this order, with a Return on Service by certified mail, U.S. postage pre-paid, or by being duly executed by a bailiff.

The defendant shall subject the party to the **CONTEMPT** powers of the Court for willful disobedience to the Court's orders.

Done this 9th day of December, 2005

Les Hayes III
Presiding Judge
Montgomery Municipal Court

ORIGINAL: COURT RECORD COPY 1: MR. PEERA COPY 2: MR. JOHNSON

Judge's Demolition Decree.

He quickly got up from his chair, shook my hand firmly and said I was going to regret that decision and rushed me out of his office.

And so ensued a nightmare scenario and a grueling battle between City Hall and me that would test the limits of my strength, courage, resiliency and creativity like never before. Within a few months of purchasing the property, I was found guilty by the City-elected judge and the mayor had successfully engineered my destruction without due process. In this chaotic period, life as I knew it took an ugly turn for the worse and was a daily horrific chain of events. Each morning I'd wake up fearing the harsh reality of confronting a relentless monster trying to devour me. The first attorney I hired in that city (a white man) turned out to be a friend of the mayor who double crossed me and sent me to the gallows (aka, the conspiring city council) to be hanged and executed by the municipal court without legal authority So I had to find another lawyer quickly to appeal the decision. But this time I had to get a black person. I felt that I could not trust a local white man to represent me fairly.

THE AFRICAN AMERICAN

I called the NAACP for help, which it said it would provide for only African Americans who were members of the organization. Well, yes, I was both a native African and an American citizen, and after paying my dues, the NAACP accepted my clever racial claim and agreed to help. I was elated and relieved! The man chosen to take my case was a smart graduate from esteemed Howard University, the Ivy League black university, who was a rookie in law but with a passion to defend minority clients.

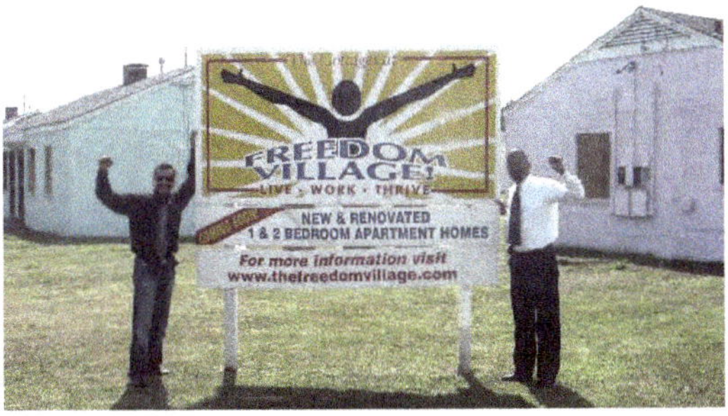

Jim and his attorney at property

His name was Norman and he didn't waste time telling me how he admired "Brother Malcolm", referring to Malcolm X. I knew right away that I had found a champion for the underdogs. I recall meeting him for lunch at a popular restaurant where many white professionals hung out. He wasn't hard to spot as he was the only black man sitting alone surrounded by affluent whites. I felt very cold entering the place as there was a moment of eerie silence and inquiring eyes fixated on me. It was the same feeling I got entering City Hall; spooky and frigid. This black attorney was a handsome newly married man in his early 40s. He was clean-shaven, well-dressed and spoke eloquently without a Southern drawl. I was already a fan. Unknown tohim, he was my only hope as my time was running out. As we spoke, I could feel the quietness around a filled room and people eavesdropping on our conversation. It was annoying and disrespectful. *"Don't these folks have anything better to do than mind their own business?"* I said to myself. I turned my head around and looked people in the eye with a stern face. Almost immediately the nosy individuals got embarrassed, looked away from us and resumed eating their lunch. As we re-engaged our meeting, the attorney quietly revealed to me that he feared for his life if he took the case. It was not what I wanted to hear. I was looking for a fearless fighter. I threw a blank checkbook at him and asked him to write his price, but only if he would fight for me and get me out of the lion's mouth in one piece. Thankfully, Norman was not greedy but rather honest and sympathetic toward my plight, and confirmed my suspicions that I was being railroaded by corrupt officials. He agreed to represent me but warned how the entire City Hall was rigged, racist and too powerful to overcome. He then revealed to me that he was also a religious man and a pastor at a local church. "*I believe in your case and God will punish the sinners,*" he said. But his honest advice to me was to fold my cards before I bled to death financially or was physically harmed. "*They want your property Jim, and they will get it. They've never lost and you don't know who you're up against. They're going to destroy you!*" I told him I had invested most of my life savings in this property and would fight with everything I had in my power, including giving up my life to fight the bad guys. He understood that I was standing up for my moral principles, but he was stunned by my ignorance regarding racism and corruption. Still, he admired my passion and grit.

For a moment, I visualized myself as David defeating Goliath; but I was clueless and underestimated the enemy's relentless war-chest of weapons. I began seeing visions of Rosa Parks' bus ordeal, the events of Bloody Sunday and the civil rights riots before my eyes. It was quite surreal. *"What an idiot!"* I thought to myself, "Why *of all places in America, did I have to buy real estate in the most racist and backward state?"*

THE SAND NIGGER

Apparently, it was a lesson in fate. In the months and years that ensued, being embroiled in this horrific battle, the trauma tested my faith, family, friends and my battle with our legal system. I quickly found out how my real estate buddies were disloyal and callous. My pleas to senators, congressmen and social advocacy groups also fell on deaf ears. I was a brown man stuck in the middle of bi-polar dichotomies of the black and white racial divide. I was not black enough for Jesse Jackson (civil rights activist), and not white enough for Johnny Isackson (Georgia's republican senator in 2007). No one was prepared to stick their neck out for me. Even the ACLU and NAACP were too scared to take on my case as it was too political and involved a powerful City Hall. In Montgomery, the local blacks were too terrified to stand up for me, while their white counterparts were gunning to bury a pesky 'sand nigger'; a term for brown-skinned people that I had never heard until this crisis.

What surprised me even more was the racism and ignorance from the poor black community towards brown people. They associated me with wealthy hotel and gas station owners who dominated the South. I got no sympathy on either side, and the stereotype had me stuck in the middle between two unhealed, hurt and angry tribes. When one kind and compassionate black local businessman named Martin had the heart and courage to testify in court on my behalf, the city punished him by cancelling his government contracts and almost bankrupted him.

By trying to stick his neck out for me, the man almost lost his head in the process.

"*I ain't never seen no one fight the city like you Jim. I wanna be part of that!*" he proudly remarked.

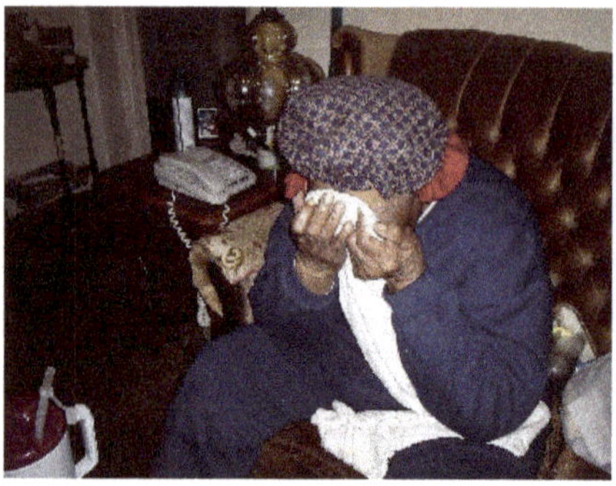

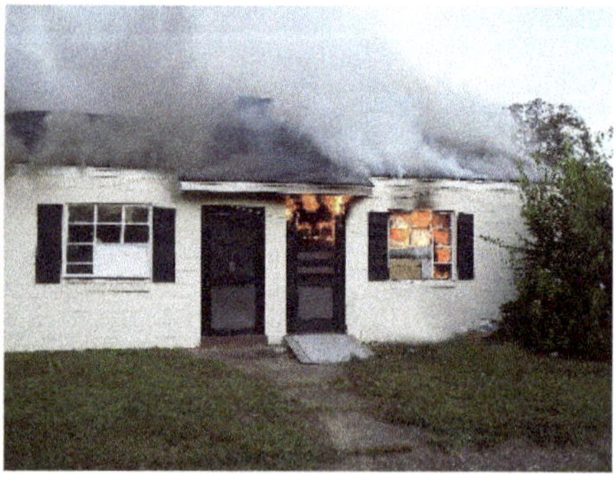

An elderly woman cries over being displaced, as the city torches a renovated cottage adjacent to her.

Soon, I was a plague on anyone who supported me as the mayor wielded his power on disparaging me on radio, TV stations and the court of public opinion. My face was tagged as a troublemaking outsider and the city threatened me with jail sentence and bodily harm if I didn't surrender. Often, I had to rent a car and wear a wig as a disguise when visiting my property in Montgomery. On one occasion as the corrupted bullies torched my buildings, the mayor arrived at the scene with the local TV reporters' live coverage before the fire trucks even arrived. It was a cruel publicity stunt to frame me as the arsonist and villain. The staging was all too obvious and orchestrated. But it worked. Since I could no longer afford the high insurance premiums, I had cancelled my policy before the fires and was forced to vacate all my tenants and to board up the entire property. With no rental income and rising attorney costs I was slowly drowning in debt. The city had me exactly where they wanted me, in a quicksand of hell. During the many court trials, which I hated as they were all a dog and pony show, the city would doctor documents and plant false evidence to try to convict me. They were so wicked and desperate that they rushed to enact new laws in secret meetings to fit their case. During this surreal period, I was sinking into a financial sinkhole without a lifeline. My world was imploding and I felt totally helpless and intimidated by the wrath of a biased legal system and a vengeful City Hall. The stress and emotional toll was unbearable and all consuming. I befriended a couple of kind hearted locals who supported my plight and gave me hope. One was named Jimmy and the other Cash. They never let me forget to fight until I got my hard-earned investment back. I was also fortunate to have a brother who was a pillar of comfort and support during this period and he stood by me the entire way without fail. He'd accompany me to many court trials and sacrificed his time and work to fight the goons with me. We laughed, cried and grew stronger with each blow and setback. Back at home, the story was mixed. My teenage kids had no idea what I was confronting and I did not want them to be immersed in the turmoil.

MAKING THE CASE FOR GUARDIAN ANGELS

My wife on the other hand worked hard to keep the family dynamic and mental health intact. She used her Shamanic healing rituals to enlighten the dark forces that preyed on us with guiding angels and prayers. I specifically recall how she used distance energy healing (aka, Reiki) to keep me safe on my trips to Montgomery and affect outcomes during court trials. I know it worked because on several occasions, my attorney was stunned at the judge's ruling in our favor. *"I can't believe what just happened today Jim, I've never seen the court go against the city in this way before!"* he'd remark. When I returned home with some good news, my wife would simply ask; *"Did you thank your guardian angels today? They were there in court protecting you."*

As a family, we all resorted to many spiritual and creative tools to guide us through the treacherous period. For me, a combination of meditation, creative writing and sculpting were effective in releasing my pent-up emotions and keeping sane. But it was a constant struggle, as I had days where I was so demoralized that I wanted to buy a gun and cause some deadly harm to my perpetrators.

The mind is volatile and susceptible to violence if it's not trained to be calm or stay cool. I learned that lesson quickly. The more I stayed in a creative mode, the better I was able to cope with my inner hostile voice. I was being pushed to my limits and tested at all levels. I even talked to my spirit guides to shine the light on my darkness. And they did. These Divine guardian angels would often protect and save my life from harm. I am very certain of that. I also realized I had to employ out-of-the-box methods to win over this villainous City Hall.

Almost three years had passed and with over a dozen court trials, and we were still at a stalemate. They had unlimited firepower and resources at their disposal and were trying to wear me out financially and mentally. I was hemorrhaging on both aspects but was careful not to show it. Soon I realized I had to stop playing defense and get on the offensive if I had a chance to get out of the lions' mouth. I decided to double-down on my creative ways.

007 IS WATCHING

As an avid James Bond fan, I went into an espionage mode and bought a recorder wrist-watch to tape all the conversations with city officials and court proceedings. Agent 007 would be proud. I also put my private investigator hat on and unearthed the city's records of the past decade on demolition liens and property takings. I recall the day when I walked into City Hall armed with an open records request using the Freedom of Information Act to the city to release 10 years of demolitions in Montgomery. Before I did that, I had called the state's attorney general office located in Birmingham for legal advice and was told of my rights and the city's obligation to provide the information in an expedient time. When the mayor's right-hand man saw the demand, he looked at me in disdain, made a frowny face, pointed a finger at me and exclaimed *"This is insane. You can go straight to hell!"* I looked him in the eye and quietly told him that if I did not get the request processed within 48 hours that he'd be hearing from the attorney general's office. I handed him the attorney general's business card and left. The following day the city clerk called me to come collect the package I requested.

This result shows the power of not being afraid, staying creative and knowing your rights. Once I had the recordings and the demolition records, I was feeling empowered and beginning to see the light at the end of the tunnel. These two creative strategies got me on the offensive to expose the city's sins, racism and corruption against black property owners. I revealed property rights abuses by that city never before seen in the public eye. Besides recording the many racial slurs spewing from top officials, I uncovered an unethical strategy the city used to systematically demolish and steal black-owned properties without proper legal authority. The fraudulent scheme had been used for over a 10-year period and affected some 50 homeowners. All of them were poor, black and the properties were in the same neighborhood as mine.

THE GOTCHA!

This was the smoking gun I needed to set me free and indict the city for its wrongdoing. It was the same blueprint they were using on me. Only this time, they were caught off guard with a property owner who was neither black or poor. In fact, they soon realized that I was a pesky little fighter who only grew stronger and persistent with their continued greed and bullying. I now had the guns pointing at them by potentially incriminating the entire City Hall to face a firing squad of state and federal officials. I sent all the damaging evidence to the Alabama district attorney's office who forwarded it to Washington DC for review. Within a few months I received a call from the civil rights justice investigation panel in DC informing me that they were sending a panel of seven people to Montgomery to investigate this matter Using the open records information, I also contacted all the affected homeowners who had lost their property to this illegal and racist scheme. Many were afraid to talk to me but more than a dozen of them showed up to recount their horrific stories.

It was quite surreal to hear the details of the many experiences of the elderly and poor homeowners losing their property to mundane violations. One woman told me how she had left her house to take care of her dying mother in another county and when she returned three months later, her house was gone. The city had circumvented their own demolition protocols by not giving her (and dozens of others) proper notice and electing to demolish the structures for minor cosmetic violations such as peeling paint, wood rot, rusted gutters and so forth. The way it worked was once the property was torn down, the city issued a demolition lien to the owner that was unreasonably high. Most people could not afford to pay it, which resulted in confiscation of the land. Quite diabolical. The panel heard all our evidence and deemed that the city had abused its power, violated its own demolition laws and discriminated against colored property owners. My attorney soon filed a motion to dismiss the city's demolition case against me and I asked him to separately file a class action lawsuit against the city for illegally demolishing fifty properties. When the mayor heard that Washington, D.C., was involved, he quickly reversed course and got the city's lawyers to make peace with me. But it was too late. The judge soon ruled in our favor and against the city for being "arbitrary and capricious" in its actions His ruling was an unprecedented and historic decision in Montgomery. This City Hall had never been defeated in five decades.

MAKING HISTORY

The judge also said that if our class action lawsuit proceeded, that it would bankrupt the city. So he suggested we forge a deal and make peace. In exchange for me dropping the lawsuit, he advised the city to buy my property for its current market value, which had greatly depreciated in the Great Recession. Although I had lost tens of thousands of dollars and blood sweat and tears fighting this city for over five and a half years, I decided to accept the deal and move on with my life. Afterall, I had been vindicated and accomplished the impossible by defeating a seemingly invincible City Hall.

The following week, my attorney called me to tell me that the judge on the case told him that I had made history in that city. The judge remarked that he didn't recall any private person or entity that had won a large civil rights case against the city of Montgomery since Rosa Parks in 1956. That was heavy!

That weekend, I created this art piece:

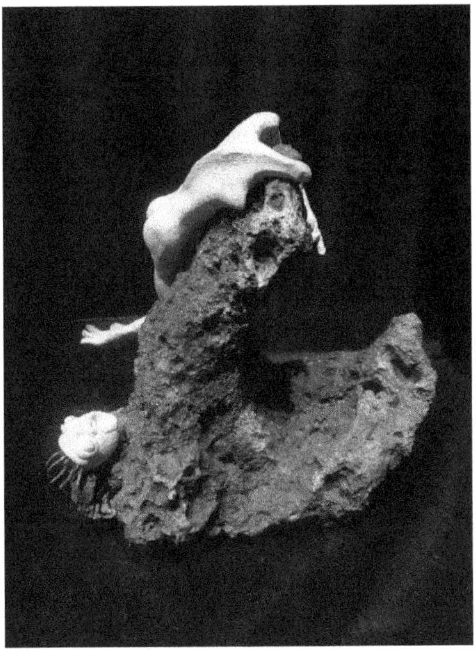

"Out of the lion's mouth"

(Clay & Rock) Artist: Jim Peera

The Alabama ordeal was quite a scary but remarkable experience and it changed my life forever. For one it turned me into a social justice warrior, and secondly it tested me in ways I'd have never imagined. I'm certain Rosa Parks and John Lewis would be proud. It made me stronger, smarter and more resilient.

More important, our victory helped better protect the disenfranchised black property owners in Montgomery. Although at the time I saw the calamity as a curse, it was undoubtedly a blessing in disguise Was it serendipity for a little brown man to be placed in the heart of a racial battlefield of the deep South and expose the corruption and injustices on the poor blacks?

Or was it just a coincidence? I believe without any hesitation it was the former. It was a case of Divine intervention and I was the lucky one to sacrifice a part of my life to right the wrongs of that city and its bullying tactics. It was my John Lewis moment. If I had any doubt about my faith in God before this experience, this incident reinstated it. Although I was mistakenly dismissed as a weak and non-threatening brown David who would fold through intimidation and pressure, a formidable Goliath City Hall was brought down to its knees. It was a team effort and I am humbled by the experience. The lessons learned from this ordeal have made me wiser than ever and are worth noting. For one, it demonstrated how bullies and corrupt players fall by their own weight and die by their own sword. It confirmed for me how light cancels dark forces. Another important lesson: the value of having holding power. By paying cash and not having any debt on the property, I was able to fight and wear out my enemy that attacked me with formidable firepower and resources. The power of saving gave me the power to my freedom. Quite frankly not many investors would have lasted five and a half years with borrowed money. They would have been foreclosed or gone bankrupt. The most interesting lesson however was spiritual. I was thrown into the lion's mouth to be an instrument of truth and transformation. And all the pieces fell into place in Divine order. By being short, thin and unassuming, I was not perceived as a threat. By not being white or black, I was able to see things without a binary or myopic ancestral filter. By being somewhat ignorant of the racial history in that city, I wasn't afraid to face and tackle the white elitist good 'ol boy network. By losing my sense of fear, I was free to fight and win at any cost. By having faith, I had the strength to keep going. Not only did my case change the demolition and property rights laws in Montgomery but it helped correct the imbalances of political and social power in that city and give renewed hope to black property owners. Interestingly, it also earned me a lot of respect there. After the incident, many of my adversaries in City Hall complimented me for "fighting a great fight." In a twist, I was actually invited to run for council. *"We'd love to have you on our team out here, Jim. Come move to Montgomery."* one person remarked. How crazy and surreal is that! Today, 11 years later, although racism and inequality still exist in Alabama, the city of Montgomery elects a significant number of black public officials who work to protect the rights of black property owners and businesses. This sea change would not have been possible without being victorious in my case and in all our combined efforts, sacrifices and struggles. The trials and tribulations of that experience taught me a lot of lessons including the dangers of feeding the ego, the prevalence of government corruption, the resurgence of white supremacy, the pervasive black-plantation mentality and the role of greed and power in racism. It also revealed America's ugly side beneath its mask of superficiality. Everything had changed since Rosa Parks' bus incident; yet nothing had changed. The force of racism as a divider and social injustice is still alive and well in our country today, as our fight for peace and justice demands creative and unconventional solutions — for a better tomorrow

My exit wounds were so deep and painful that after it was over in 2010, it took me another four years to have the stomach to revisit Alabama. When I went back, I was respected by both whites and blacks alike who thanked me for standing up and speaking truth to power. While many people would consider this once-in-a-lifetime experience their life's legacy and retire, for me this incident served as inspiration to redirect my life on a more spiritual and altruistic path, which manifested two years later with the creation of Healium Center and sowed the seeds for The Healium Way.

6
THE TRUTH LAB

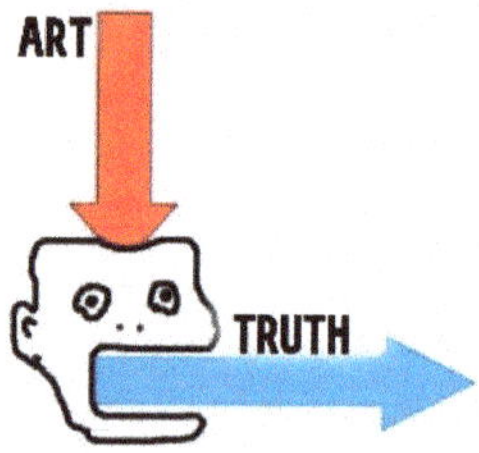

"Artists are the gatekeepers of truth"

- Harry Belafonte

According to the Cato Institute's recent study, 62 percent of Americans are afraid of speaking their views in public. This does not surprise me, as we've witnessed people's fear and apprehension hold them hostage to voice their honest opinions. The problem has been exacerbated in the age of technology and political polarization. A lot of it is a result of escaping from online attacks by groups with specific agenda, that can ruin innocent lives and thriving businesses without merit. Sometimes it's avoiding being targeted by "cancel culture", the phenomenon of promoting the "canceling" of people, brands and even shows and movies due to what some consider to be offensive or problematic remarks and ideologies. Often, it's avoiding being easily sued by someone who takes offense to some hard truths; a reality that is exacerbated by our litigious society. Sadly today, many Americans elect to silence their voices and hide their true feelings.

But silence through fear or indoctrination leads to catastrophic problems for the wellbeing of our species. North Korea and Russia are two good modern-day examples of this practice that deprives Divine beings of discovering their full potential. Lucky for us, we Americans are fortunate not to be caged up and punished for speaking our minds and freely expressing our views. Not yet anyway! It is our reality, at least for now — and a very valuable asset that we must not take for granted or waste and strive to keep for a very long time. Inherently, we humans need a healthy and unrestrictive emotional, intellectual and creative outlet to function properly. It is necessary for keeping a check on our imbalance. It's also important as flawed beings that we become proficient at being better observers of ourselves: the good, the bad and the ugly.

In this way we will be able to extract the truth within each of us so that we don't normalize living in a tempest of lies, cover ups and bulls*it. Interestingly, art is a truth serum that is an amazing outlet to help bring to the surface our authentic selves. This truth serum accomplishes this task by opening our dialogue deep within, as well as throwing open the doors of communication with everyone around us. We know this fact because we've seen how art works its magic and reveals people from the inside out, and helps unite people at our Center.

Many of the Principles discussed in Part 2 of The Healium Way come from observing almost seven years of actual behavior of some 6,000 Souls from all walks of life. It comes down to just you and me — regular ordinary people — who are striving to get better and become extraordinary. And we get there by mining what's already within us and doing things in context with our Divinity. In order to do this, we must step out of our respective unhealthy bubbles and partake in the medicine of the healing and creative arts. As an all-welcoming but unconventional creative public space, our Center has accomplished this well. It has revealed and witnessed human behavior and emotional intelligence in its naked form — stripped of all its falsities, pretenses, boxes and labels. I call it a creative *Truth Lab* —with our sanctuary becoming a litmus test-research Center that uses the creative and healing arts to expose our unfiltered and true self. This Truth Lab is not a specific area where we put people under a microscope as experiments as much as it is a figure of speech to underscore how art always tells the truth. What's more interesting is how we've taken the *ugly truths* and made them more bearable, using The Healium Way philosophy of activating the *beautiful truths.* We also stress how the journey of this transition is an opportunity to observe our flaws for what they are — and how we can best address them. While our Center has served a very important purpose of connecting, uplifting, empowering and inspiring ordinary people, the Truth Lab has revealed a lot about individuals on a personal level that would not have been possible otherwise. On the downside, we discovered that most Americans are fickle, gullible, impulsive, compulsive, lack the discipline and patience to take self-responsibility, want quick fixes, are individualistic and think they're more exceptional than anyone else on the planet.

But you probably already knew that. On the upside, we discovered that those who made the effort to remove social blinders, filters, labels and unhealthy distractions from their lives to be transformed into more beautiful, and more balanced human beings So the transformation from ordinary to extraordinary is real and possible in every one of us. I've witnessed it countless times. Our ubiquitous unhealthy distractions, such as social media and handheld supercomputers (aka, jail phones) are the primary causes of many imbalances in the 21st century. It's not because they're necessarily bad inventions. Rather we abuse them and allow them to rule our lives. Therefore, the quicker people reduce their attachments and dependence from these man-made distractions, the smarter they become, the easier it gets to reconnect with their wandering and caged Soul, and the more we find improvement in people's mental health and overall stability. Using unconventional workshops, thought-provoking art installations and multifaceted events at The Center, a more transparent and holistic dialogue is activated.

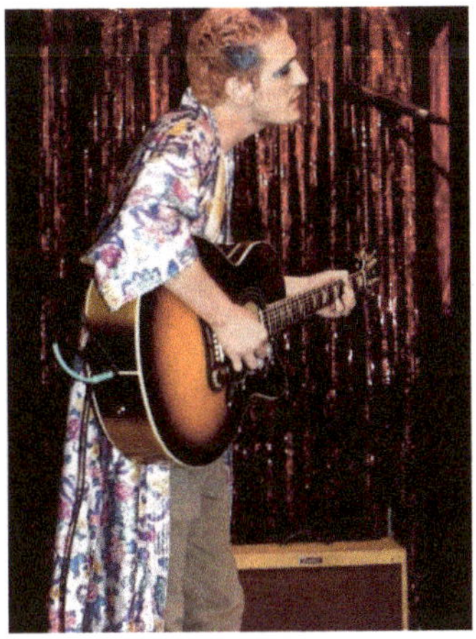

A musician performs at

***Queer Youth Fest* at Healium**

As we pry open the boiling hot pot of controversial issues such as drugs, sex, politics, religion, race, etc. the steam is allowed to cool off and settle, allowing an honest and a reservation-free discourse to take place with respect and tact.

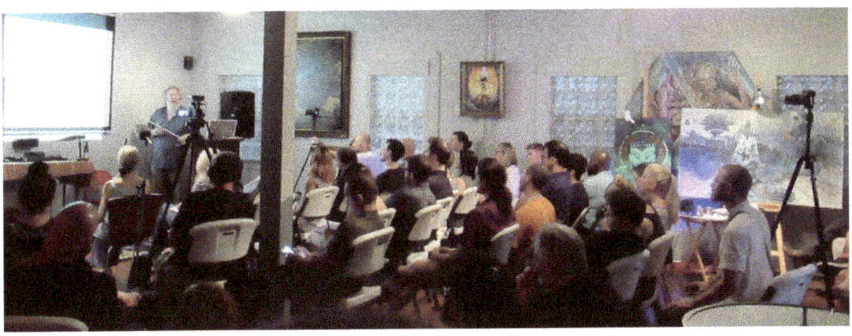

Seminars and debates at Healium

By allowing the freedom of self-expressionto be without rules or judgment, people confess their transgressions and f*ck-ups openly and fearlessly. What's more, as a "safe place" for the LGBTQ community, The Center provides a refuge for the marginalized and ostracized individuals to open up in ways not possible in other restrictive environments. Total strangers are free to trust and confide in each other and share their life stories cathartically. Often there's a beautiful interplay of exchange that occurs among diverse sets of individuals with opposing views who come together to agree to disagree. Since there are no confining rules, the conversations that are integrated with art and spirituality take on a rich and fluid meaning with depth and unabashed intensity. Sometimes what you discover in these unfiltered interactions is far removed from what you'd unearth in conventional polls or surveys. Let me elaborate on some fascinating observations at this creative Truth Lab.

HEALIUM PREDICTS TRUMP

One of the eye-opening revelations of the Truth Lab came during the 2016 presidential election. There were a lot of heated debates at our center a few months prior to that Election Day, and we discovered some disturbing patterns of behavior. Many musicians and artists surprised us with an early warning that Donald Trump had a good chance of winning. While many national polls indicated Hillary Clinton would win, I was getting a different signal from many participants in both their words and their art. Shockingly, most were liberals or progressives. We knew that suburban conservative whites were backing Trump, but we didn't know the extent of the anti-Hillary silent majority. Far too many people were comfortably numb, lazy and ungrateful for what they had. And this segment of the population wanted to disrupt a good thing. Some even wanted a revolution, not really understanding what that word meant in real terms. Interestingly but not surprisingly, many of these disruptors were millennials (including my own kids), who told us they were either not voting at all, or would vote for candidate Bernie Sanders, who wasn't the Democratic nominee but a far-left favorite. When I told them that by abstaining in their vote Trump would win, they scoffed and some even championed a civil war. I was extremely perturbed but felt unheard.

From an intriguing perspective, the art that I was observing at The Center was showing a more accurate gauge than the sophisticated national polls. It was all disconcerting, but it was revealing the uncomfortable truth in an unconventional manner.

UNSKINNED

Our Truth Lab has also revealed a community's true colors. And what it exposed wasn't so pretty. It cracked open and exposed the fear, fragility and fickleness below our thin skins. When I say "skin", I am referring to the acts of ugliness based on our skin color. We're speaking of tribalism turned racism in all forms and colors; black, white, brown and yellow. Interestingly, our flawed human nature shows its true colors when exposed to our Divine attained human color. When one color engages in micro-aggression and separatist ways against the other — all other colors manifest the same exclusionary behavior against others. It's a nasty cycle of contagion. We first experienced this flaw of human ugliness with a local community of the "Western Kirtan" movement. The mission of the traditional Eastern Sanskrit-based chanting and reciting practice is devoted to healing and attaining peace. In fact, *"Kirtan"* means '*to cut through separation*'. But when a predominantly white community with lost self-identity attaches itself (often cultishly) to an East Indian philosophy the result is far from healing or cutting through separation. The result is divisive and slices and dices with its ugliness. It manifests into tribalistic behavior against non-whites (like myself) with unapologetic disdain and envy and reveals the hypocrisy of a territorial mindset. As an East Indian, this perverse behavior was quite disturbing for me, as my Center appeared to be 'not white enough' for their white-washed version of an East-Indian based practice. How f*cked up is that? On the opposite end, we were ostracized by another separatist mindset with a symptom of similar identity crisis. This was a black-only movement that didn't believe in mixing and matching diverse points of view, while imposing on outsiders a religious-based radical black power and Afro-centric philosophy.

Apparently, we were not 'black enough' for them. On further investigation, I discovered that many of these folks had never even been to Africa, but deemed themselves 'experts' of African culture by reading books and pontificating to those who didn't know any better. When I told them that as a native African, I knew more than they did about the country, and that their version was bastardized and Westernized to suit their self-serving agenda — they were offended and stopped coming to our Center. I was fine with that and remember telling one man that his ignorance wasn't my problem. Not surprisingly, he got offended and never returned. Once again, Healium revealed people's true colors, their unhealed condition and exposed the bullsh*t beneath the surface. On the brown and yellow spectrum, we often discovered another thin-skinned minority mindset that succumbed to the ego of being too special, sophisticated and overeducated than their black and white counterparts. These were my people — and I was not the least surprised! They exposed their ignorance and racism by assuming that black people with dreads came from the ghetto and were drug dealers, and that white people with tattoos were uneducated rednecks. Some of those critics were from my mosque and I felt like removing the deeply lodged sticks from their derrieres and saying, "Get a life!" So the Center's embrace of diversity and pluralism gets a lot of push-back from tribal, ignorant and separatist mindsets, which is a disturbing revelation of where America is heading as a society. On a business community level, it showed us how competition trumps collaboration and how white-owned businesses were shamelessly favored.

At closer inspection, The Center also revealed how white privilege and gentrification has sowed the seeds of division with unfettered hostility against non-whites. I will elaborate on the many examples of this ugliness in subsequent chapters. All in all, our Center becomes a truth mirror on our flawed humanity. The more we've tried to unite people from diverse backgrounds, the more we find people's need to segregate and manifest low-vibration behavior.

So for sure, we believe our Center proves that God made us all different skinned to test our self-defeating shallowness, our ugliness, our fears and our ignorance.

GO AHEAD, GET OFFENDED!

What the Healium Truth Lab also demonstrates well is how hypersensitive and self-righteous a lot of us are. Much of that flaw derives from not having a reality check on life, by taking it too seriously or being in denial of any negativity. This mentality is displayed when attendees get offended by a poignant marketing flier, a controversial art installation, a particular art piece or even my off-the-cuff remarks or jokes. As a person who likes to keep things real (notice my use of expletives and humor in this book to underscore my points), I do find myself sometimes offending some people. In many past cases, I had to walk on eggshells in an attempt to not offend LGBTQ or religious individuals. But that approach is antithetical to The Healium Way — so I doubled down on humor where I was the butt of the jokes, and that reduced the sensitivity. I figured if I get people to laugh at me, they'll be less likely to not laugh at themselves and their own opinions. And it worked. We also don't pander to those who are prone to be offended. We openly post our intolerance to this low-vibrational condition on our walls. It is a product of our many imbalances.

The fact is, I often see offended people as ones who can't be themselves or handle the truth. When we choose to take offense, we make a choice to weaken ourselves and create the same destructive energy that offended us to begin with. Not surprisingly, our Center reveals that the unhealed are a lot more easily hurt than the healed. Therefore, the prescription to fix this condition in my opinion is not to retract and reduce the "offenses" — but rather to get creative with them. Once we shift people into a more healed state, the less annoyed they are likely to get. Because it's no longer about others, but about themselves. Therefore, we double down on surrealism, and political and erotic art that cantend to disturb touchy people.

This in turn opens thought-provoking dialogue, which in turns opens a multitude of healthy emotional releases and begins the healing journey.

The openness we display at The Center also provokes the taboos and exposes the restrictive "small minds." To address that, I increased the controversial art in our galleries and put up a sign that reads, *"If it offends you, it's art."* And it has worked wonders. People now stop fussing and just smile when they're uncomfortable with any work of art. After all, how are you going to argue with that statement? Because art is not the problem — you are.

MONTANA IS THE MIRROR

The Healium Truth Lab also divulges America's inherent bipolar character that ferments its imbalances. The quick to the draw, see-sawing habit between two opposing poles breeds extremism and excesses that manifests into a short-sighted and a self-destructive way of life. Many films have been made about this unhealthy condition in our society. Yet we don't seem to get the memo. One of my favorite movies is Oliver Stone's masterpiece, "Scarface," starring Al Pacino as Tony Montana. In Pacino's most memorable role since "The Godfather," he plays a Cuban refugee-turned cocaine kingpin gangster, whose American Dream boomerangs into a self-destructive lifestyle engulfing everyone he touches. The life lesson of this movie is theprice one pays for feeding the ego and extolling greed. *"Nothing exceeds excess more than excess"* is one of my favorite lines in the film. In an odd but cathartic way, Scarface puts a mirror up to ourselves showing what can happen to any of us when we succumb to the excessive worship of money and materialism. Then we're off in a tailspin of other imbalances without discipline or boundaries. The creators of the film's iconic character give us many clues to relate to our own climb up our symbolic and peakless mountain, starting with the main character Montana (Spanish for mountain). A classic scene has Tony's face buried in a mountain of cocaine on his desk —

signifying the epitome of excess and addiction. That scene is a bone-chilling reflection on our own dangerous climb up the incline of wealth and power that all too often prefigures our ultimate downfall. By observing the pitfalls of our excesses via the lens of fiction, we are reminded of our own fragility and price of not correcting those imbalances. Otherwise, like Tony Montana, we too will self-destruct and take everyone else down with us. In real life America, we see a scary parallel of excesses in our own communities, with friends and families succumbing to unhealthy imbalances. I don't think balance is even part of the American vocabulary. They certainly didn't teach it in any school or learning institution that I've been part of. The American way is more about unbalanced extremes: *work hard and play hard, take it to the limit, bust your balls, get rich quick, more is better, swing for the fences,* and so on. That is not a message or a philosophy about staying even-keeled and being satisfied. This inverted value system has resulted in many inequities and imbalances in our society. The statistics are jarring and show clearly how the nation is on a collision course with its social and economic ills. For example, studies show that more than 70 percent of Americans are overweight of which 40 precent are considered obese. America's mental health is also in peril. Around 20 percent are diagnosed with some mental illness, although if we add anxiety, stress and depression — the numbers are much higher, with drug companies raking in billions of dollars in peddling their pills for all the ills. If you just landed on American soil for the first time and turned the television on, and noticed the volume of pharmaceutical commercials being bombarded at you — it would make you think the inhabitants were drug addicts. And you wouldn't be totally incorrect, based on our opioid crisis and societal pill-popping culture. In most countries that I've visited, drug commercials are banned on television. But in America, the profit-over-people system allows the powerful corporations to have free reign over the airwaves and sell anything they can get away with — with little or no accountability. Dangerous drugs with life-threatening side effects are sugar-coated with a fast-talking CYA (cover your ass)10-second warning narration, camouflaged with peppy jingles and actors skipping and dancing in joy. And Americans eat it up like candy, even though the medications may kill them before their ailment does. Over time, our society has come to normalize this zombie culture that fails to fix the root causes of our actual emotional pain, and actually worsens it.

America's economic inequality gap is at unprecedented levels, too. Its top 10 percent have 10 times the income as the bottom 90 percent. There's also an ugly bipolarity of unprecedented homelessness and food-insecurity crisis in America. According to Feeding America, each year 72 billion pounds of food goes to waste, while 50 million people struggled with hunger in 2020. And when America feeds its people, it stuffs the bellies with junk and non-nutritious food. For those unlucky to be incarcerated in overstuffed for-profit prisons, most of the food supply is essentially unfit for human consumption. I've spoken to quite a few ex-prisoners whose tales are horrific. When they're released back into society, these Americans are not only mentally unhealthy, unhealed and unsociable, but they're physically out of shape too. America's societal imbalances reveal not just where we are, but where we are headed as a country. Our priorities need to change as a people — to treat ourselves with respect regardless of our status, race, religion, or sex. When we fix our ills and imbalances as a society, it is easier to be inspired to do the same for ourselves as individuals. The fact is, we must teach ourselves the value of balance. Because too much or too little of anything is not a healthy recipe for our survival. That is why our Truth Lab provides solutions to educate and engage people in the rebalancing process. In order to make sure people who attend our events don't become a statistic, we make our sanctuary a place of inspiration and positive action. We provide yoga, stretch and dance workshops to help their mind and body find better balance. We help them improve their mental health with drum circles, sound meditation, freestyle jam and paint nights. We inspire them to eat healthy by cooking gluten-free dinners that are affordable, international in flavor and prepared by local retirees and professional chefs. We open their mind with thought-provoking art, movie nights and unconventional educational workshops. We uncage their Soul with spiritual and metaphysical offerings. We encourage controversial dialogue with creative self expression such as spoken word and poetry writing. We inspire people to be their own doctors and self-prescribe Divine self-healing medicines while reducing the man-made chemicals that are killing them. Getting back into a healthier balance is not about shaming people as much as it is about getting creative and demonstrating better alternatives for our overall well-being. It's about looking at Tony Montana, and declaring, *"F*ck you, Tony, I ain't gonna end up like you!"*

FREEDUMB

The Healium creative Truth Lab also makes us aware of our incompetency as a society. Our preconditioned rigid boxes are its culprit, and we see its effect everywhere from our pocketbooks to our polarized politics. Legislatively, we see it manifest in a relentless tug of war between our dysfunctional government and dangerous partisan politics. Ideologically, it is demonstrated in our conditional freedoms for the few on one hand, and our inability to lead effectively on the other. In this pretext of freedom, we see how in periods of crisis (as the Covid-19 pandemic), people with a self-serving agenda can use the precious gift of freedom to be reckless and even inflict harm on others with justification. This condition is called *freedumb.* For example, while writing this book many Americans politicized the health crisis and have suffered and died in disproportionate numbers in contrast to our global counterparts. And deservingly so. The fight was over wearing masks to protect each other from spreading the virus. Now, how complicated of an issue is this for my fellow Americans? All people have to do is use their common sense to know that anything that covers the airway passages will reduce contaminants from flowing into the air. It's not rocket science.

Yet, we have to politicize it, fuss and fight and wave the freedom flag into people's faces and justify not wearing face coverings. In fact, we have to show our defiance by hating and resorting to violence to those who wear masks. That's not only selfish, reckless and totally un-American, but it reveals our deviation from common sense and seduction with silliness.

America's *Land of the Free* model has been hijacked by the land ofthe spoiled, the selfish and the stupid — and paid by the poor, the marginalized and the underserved. Sometimes it all overlaps and has a boomerang effect, as excessive freedom without guardrails leaves many people in the dust. The results of our collective incompetence are quite stark. According to John Hopkins University, as of this writing, I am soberly reminded how the United States recorded 1,200 times the deaths per capita as Taiwan, a tiny island in Asia where a united coordination of smart leadership and public sacrifice has almost eradicated the virus. The fact is, our freedoms are superficial at best and our greatness is indisputably overrated. The American young capitalistic model is not lifting all boats — as the tide doesn't rise equally on all shores. Our system is rigged with many unfair laws and practices that favor the few at the expense of the many.

At Healium, we bring many heavy subjects such as these to the forefront; using art and interactive events to create the necessary awareness by questioning rather than providing right or wrong answers. The most effective art asks questions, with the answer lying within you to interpret. That answer is usually the healing one. By presenting the controversies and harsh realities without any agenda in a creative format, we are able to open a healthy dialogue for people to think for themselves and reach their own conclusions and solutions.

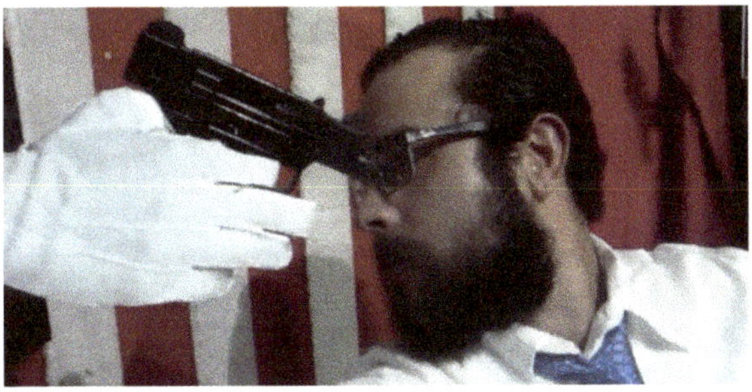

2016 Healium art installation on power and police brutality

With two-thirds of Americans living paycheck to paycheck, according to a CNBC report, most folks also do not have the financial wherewithal to travel abroad and experience different cultures, as do people from other developed countries, such as Canada or Europe. This lack of exposure to diversity shows up in ignorance and unapologetic hostility toward immigrants. As humans, we fear what we don't understand. So at The Center we try to bring the world to the people. Not surprisingly, what we find is quite sobering. While most people are easy to bitch about America's many problems, from immigration to racism to economic enslavement, they're unwilling to stick their necks out and help solve them. Instead of being the change they seek, most are quick to find excuses, such as not having the time, the money, interest or empathy. Instead of joining hands to work together and collaborate with people they don't understand, we find that most people are highly competitive and want to benefit themselves. It's the "I matter" instead of the "we matter" mindset.

No matter how the excuses are justified, the overall apathy and individualism of Americans is having a boomerang effect on our society as a whole — and it's our own sh*t to fix.

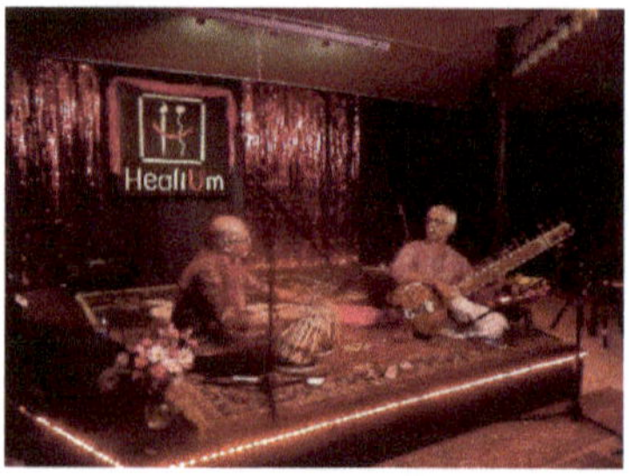

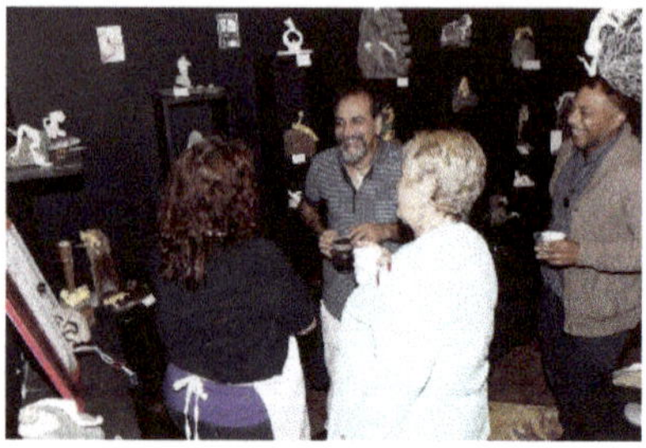

Showcasing Indian tabla & sitar music.

Opening the mind in Jim's 'Forbidden' Gallery.

AWAKENING THE CUBICLE MIND

In the summer of 2017, I got a call from a supervisor at Emory University in Atlanta that was quite revealing. The woman reached out to our Center wanting for us to design a summer program to help employees at her finance department open their minds and expand their creativity. She mentioned how the workers were losing their imaginative spark and were becoming monotonous in their tasks. As I prodded deeper, she revealed that the problem was due to their working environment — specifically, being stuck in a dark and dingy room in cubicles eight hours a day. "*I've heard great things about your Center, and I believe the Healium experience is exactly what we need to awaken and inspire the employees. We've tried other art and motivational type programs, but they haven't worked that well. Our only condition is that you bring Healium to Emory. Can you help?*" she respectfully asked me. I assuaged her concerns and agreed to help. Soon I teamed up with my wife and daughter to help create and facilitate a four-week *Lunch and Healium* summer program for the 150 or so university employees. We customized a 'Healium-on-the-Go' session for Emory that included meditative storytelling with sound healing, freestyle painting, clay sculpting, drumming, poetry, creative outdoor group activity and dance. The response was overwhelmingly positive from the first day, as the busy-minded employees slowly but surely loosened up, engaged in the various activities with passion, and had limitless fun, *Healium-style!* People said they had not experienced such judgment-free and authentic fun since they were kids. Many thanked us for reigniting their inner child and later reported that they were sleeping more soundly, with improved sex and mind clarity, thanks to the 90-minute sessions. The supervisor told us she noticed that workers' stress levels were lowered, they laughed more together and their creativity and productivity had significantly improved. The Healium Way had awakened the cubicle mind successfully!

ASK BUT DON'T EXPECT

Wherever we deploy The Healium Way Principles, we notice that the Truth Lab reinforces the power of the mind. Specifically, by demonstrating that those who have the clear intention to *open* their mind, do the work to shift their life into a more joyful and healthier balance, will reap the best results. But those who don't will stagnate, suffer and imprison themselves emotionally and creatively. It's the *Ask and you shall receive* Biblical mantra that I honor, i.e, that you have the onus to obtain desired results in healing, blessings, good health, prosperity, love, etc. It is important to be clear about what we as the receivers desire from the givers, if we're ready to create a more healed life for ourselves. In the larger scheme of things, our maker is our ultimate giver. Before we can ask this invisible entity to grant our wishes, though, we must practice having clear intentions in everyday life with regular people and circumstances. In my own life, I try not to be shy to ask anyone to do me a favor, give me a better deal on something, or throw in a free gift. It's my subtle way to test people's level of generosity and sincerity, especially when I'm spending money with them. So if I'm buying $500 worth of tires from a tire shop, I'll ask the clerk to throw in some cheap goodies such as key chains, car fresheners, pressure gauges and such, as a goodwill gesture. I usually get my "ask." But if the clerk refuses or makes an excuse that he can't honor my wishes, I know that shop is not in alignment with my values and I can elect to not give them more business, write bad reviews, or simply ignore it. I have the power of choice, recourse and punishment at my disposal. The proposition of "asking" in the business of self-transformation is slightly different however — as the giver being the Universe (Spirit, God, Source, Almighty, Invisible Force, Higher Power etc.) is not a punishable entity. Therefore, the alignment can only be unconditional. If you ask the Universe to make you healthy from an injury, but you remain sick, you can't blame the bad result on this invisible force, can you? There's no one to bitch or complain to! But what you can do, is have faith that your intention to heal yourself will eventually manifest in a positive transformation. The trick is to look at the big picture without being bogged down in the details of "Why" or "Why Not."

More often than not, this is where we disconnect with the higher self. Because our intention becomes about satisfying a "demand" and expecting a certain conditional outcome — as opposed to being an "ask" that is free of any expectations or having an entitled mindset. When we do this right, there's no excuse to be disappointed and bother God with all our daily problems or unmet needs. We quickly discover that our maker doesn't owe us anything and we have to hope and pray for the best — as hope is a powerful motivator in human nature. Using this approach, we have a clear and positive line of sight that is in alignment with our higher spiritual version of ourselves. But no matter what, there can be no progress unless you make the "ask" commitment. This is critical. Those workers at Emory who had the best time and positive results made that commitment, with a clear non-conditioned intention to improve their unhealthy and imbalanced state of being. They were the ones who were ready to explore, take risks and let loose without predispositions. They understood that as facilitators of the program, we were merely giving them the tools to help them get there. As a result, they also did not complain if they didn't find any benefit.

Because their transformation and their connection to their higher self was in their hands, not ours.

IN-MAN-TRA

You can say that these folks used a certain key for their ignition to start their engine and drive to their desired destination. I like to call this ignition key, *IN-MAN-TRA*: *INtention—MANifestation—TRAnsformation.* The most important part is intention. Without this self-motivational desire, nothing ignites the spark to manifest our goals to transform ourselves. But intention slices both ways, with dark and light energy. An example of dark intention is someone who uses the various tools as a physical weapon or even a metaphysical one, such as black magic, to harm others. To keep it simple, our discussion of intention focuses on the pure light version, not the dark one. It is this higher vibrational realm that powers The Healium Way. You bought this book because you had an *intention* (not just curiosity) to improve on something within you that you didn't like or wanted to change. Intention in The Healium Way is about being ready to get off our butts for self-discovery, growth and personal healing — and matching it up with our actions. For some of us, the trigger for such action-based intention could be the loss of a loved one, an illness or a divorce. For others, it's losing a job, dealing with economic hardship, being in a bad relationship, or experiencing other setbacks. I've encountered many attendees at The Center who suffered from depression, but were sick of poisoning their minds and bodies with addictive chemicals, and became motivated to find healthier alternatives. Once they were ready to detoxify, they followed through with a plan and stuck with it. Others came close to taking their own lives and turned around using a more spiritual approach to healing. Whatever the catalyst is for you, your readiness and commitment is required to manifest a better life and transform from the ordinary you into the extraordinary you.

Now, meditate for a few minutes and think clearly about the intention you want to set for yourself at this time for your own change — as we will be revisiting it later in the book.

The Principles presented in this body of work, when used consistently, are a powerful prescription to combat loneliness, reduce depression and anxiety and increase connectivity with others — regardless of artistic ability, brain characteristics, political affiliation or other human labels and nuances. The Healium Way is also relatively inexpensive and easy to put into practice wherever you are in the world. There is little barrier to entry. You can deploy it at home, in your travels, at work or at an institutional level. The beauty of the arts is how it reveals and exposes us from the inside out. And the charm of The Healium Way is how it inspires each of us to experience limitless possibilities within us, devoid of any crutches, resistances and excuses. So here's to all our clear and true intentions!

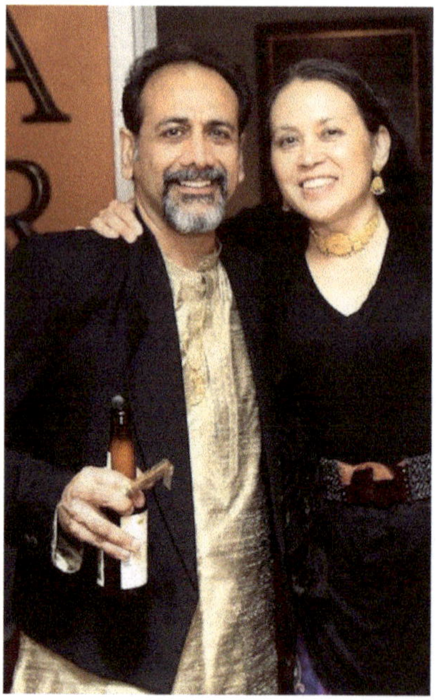

Jim with wife Donna

7
GROWING PAINS

"Creativity is intelligence having fun"

- A. Einstein

Our paradoxical universe clearly demonstrates the natural duality of our existence, destruction and creation. It's the circle of life. Each of us must allow our destructive habits and programmed behaviors to perish in order to grow new and healthier ones. In this context, creation is the higher purpose. By being creative we not only survive in our hostile environment but we thrive. Creativity is our most innate and abundant resource for solving our problems. Yet as adults, we've lost touch with it and have supplanted it with a robotic mindset, low vibrational thoughts and even destructive habits. For the most part, freestyle creativity has been suffocated during our childhood and adolescence, via our deficient learning institutions, tech-heavy lifestyles, the busy grind and a plethora of other environmental factors. As humans we'll need to reignite our raw and spontaneous creative spark, or else we'll slowly die from within. In order to manifest a healthy creative mindset, it's important to undo the conventional thinking that is resisting its expansion during adulthood. Much of that conventional thinking shrinks our mind and emanates from our own self-defeating programming during our growing-up stage of life. Instead of seeing ourselves as creatures of unlimited possibilities, we carry a burdensome stick of doubt and resentment. Somehow, we've forgotten that we all started out as winners. You were once a feisty and resilient sperm that beat a million others to overcome obstacles inside of your mother's womb and became the joy of creation. Your beautiful and unique life form miraculously developed into an intelligent and emotional being that was abound with creativity. So if at any time you believe that you're a loser, that's your misguided man-made perception of yourself. Not what your Creator had in mind — or the truth. As babies we were all risk takers, fearless and without any inhibitions. Our innocence was pure and untethered. We didn't operate on logic, so our creativity was raw, untamed and needed no explanation. But then during our growing pains stage, we began our creative descent. If our parents or our learning institutions got too protective and restrictive, it strangled our ability to freely activate our creative receptors during adolescence and into adulthood. We also became a product of our environment, conditioned by our upbringing, surroundings, culture, friends, beliefs and modern technology.

At home, we were constantly told what was right and what was wrong, and got rewarded for conforming and taking orders — but got punished for asking questions. At school, we were disciplined into obeying the teacher's rules and were told not to raise our hand to question the books or the subjective teachings that were dished out. We got brownie points, stars and awards that we probably didn't deserve. But it boosted our ego, made us happy and gave us a sense of being special. But were we really happy and so special? Or were we living in the shadows of our parents and societal pressure? The truth is, I discovered that most middle and upper-class parents wanted to make up for their own unfulfilled childhood, so they enrolled their kids in every extracurricular activity they could find. Most were probably exhausted being yanked around from piano lessons to karate classes to soccer games to Sunday church. During the summer break, these parents spent more money putting their kids in various camps, where they got judged, graded and reprimanded for having fun that wasn't tied to prescribed activities. Over time, the kids' playtime slowly decreased, they got more competitive-minded and were encouraged to grow up fast. The rule was to always follow orders like robots and seldom question authority, even if the orders were bad for them. In school, instead of writing essays and poetry, they punched true/false questionnaires. Instead of spending creative time outdoors, they cocooned indoors and were fixated on their handheld computers. Instead of creating pieces of art, they worked on destroying their opponents in competitive sports. Eventually, the grown-up kids showed no interest in doing freestyle creativity and shut down their emotional receptors altogether. They couldn't spell, write, read, create dialogue, play any musical instrument or create any artwork from scratch. As they grew into adults, their low-attention-spanned busy brain got them in deeper trouble, and they lost their creative spark altogether. It was a heavy price to pay, but it was too late. They resigned being held hostage in the various boxes of confinement — some of which they were indoctrinated into, and others that were self-inflicted. Could this kid have been you?

ESCAPE FROM ARTCATRAZ

In this past generation, many American students probably have a similar story to tell if they attended any public or faith-based private schools. That is because America forgot to prioritize not just its financial education, but also its freedom of self-expression for its future generation.

I remember the period when I noticed a difference in both my high schooled kids' creative spark. It was starting to extinguish, and I did not like it. For one, I noticed that art was being reduced or eliminated and being replaced with competitive sports in the school's curriculum. And secondly, the closed-minded art teachers had an absurd and rigid system of actually grading art in the same fashion as the other subjects. To my surprise, most parents didn't resist or even care to question this protocol. To their children's detriment, their silence resulted in teachers legally pumping more neurotransmitter stimulants into their kids that numbed them and helped dim their youngblood creative spark. I experienced this reality firsthand, with both my adolescent children in Georgia's public school system. And I wasn't going to be a pushover parent. My son was a smart and gifted kid, but according to the public school he attended, he was characterized as inattentive and disruptive. The teacher conveniently diagnosed him as having Attention Deficit Disorder (ADD) and was anxious to dish outan addictive prescription called Ritalin, a popular drug for his non existing condition. But besides ringing the cash registers for the drug companies, something was not ADDing up on our side. Why was the school so anxious to medicate my son instead of putting him in a more creative and challenging environment? My deduction was that it was far simpler and easier to do so, which is a condition of conventional and ordinary beings. We saw that disciplinary action as a huge red flag, and immediately got him out of that toxic box and enrolled him in a private school. It was a smart move, and he flourished creatively by reigniting his artistic flame.

My daughter, a gifted surrealist artist, got failing grades in her high school art class because she did not conform to the conventional realism-style art that was required by the teacher. She was attending a top-rated public school in the suburbs of Atlanta. But there was nothing to top her disempowering art story. One afternoon, she came home from school in tears and threw a handful of her surreal drawings in her trash can; *"I am a terrible artist and I keep getting D's and F's by my teacher for not obeying her assignments!"* she cried. *"Obeying what?"* I asked her. Since when did art become an obedience-based assignment that punishes with vile words and hands out grades? What evil artistic creation did my daughter create to deserve such demoralizing critique? I angrily thought to myself. But I knew the answer, it was the system — not just the grading teacher. Without hesitation, I picked each one of her black and white drawings from the trash and ironed them out. I had never seen such thought-provoking and raw emotion executed so beautifully and powerfully on paper. I remember tearing up when I saw her works.

Her art was deeply captivating and very unconventional.

Two of my daughter's drawings that were given a failing grade in her high school art classes:

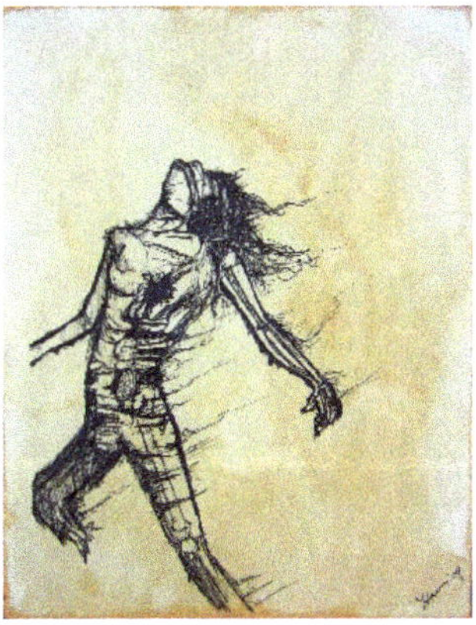

"Birth"

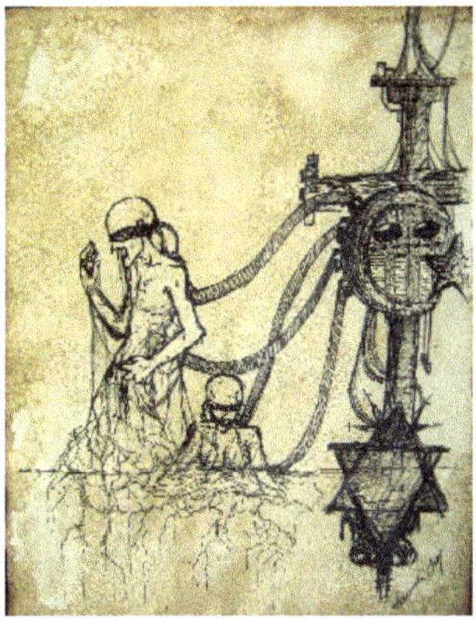

"Adam & Eve"

(Artbyhaseena.com)

I realized at that moment that she was a self-taught creative wunderkind, who was ahead of her time. Shame on her public-school teacher for not encouraging my daughter to express more freely and elect to demoralize her with failing grades. Even worse, I wondered how many students had been ostracized and degraded for exercising their creative freedom in this fashion? But I knew it was a hopeless case to plead to a closed-minded teacher and her matching public - school protocols. So my wife and I pulled her out of that toxic box and enrolled her in a private home school. We thought it would solve the problem. Unfortunately, it didn't make a lot of difference there either. Her art didn't sit well with the conservative Bible-thumping Christian teacher, who was disturbed by my daughter's edgy and dark-themed works. Both teachers' definition of art was seeing rainbows and butterflies wrapped up nicely in a bow without much thought or substance.

What the teachers totally missed is how my daughter's thought-provoking drawings and songs were her emotional therapy. It was her medicine. But they were operating from a predisposed curriculum that preferred students to be brainless robots rather than free thinkers. While my daughter was releasing her growing pains holistically, her teachers were pumping unhealthy and addictive medications onto other students and even onto themselves. It was quite dismaying to see the future of America disintegrate right before our eyes! But as a family, we refused to conform, being numbed and dumbed down by subjective rules and conventional wisdom. I doubled down on encouraging both my kids to continue their creative endeavors at home without limitations and not to deviate from their unique and powerful styles. It was the right advice and they both have grown up to appreciate the power of uninhibited self-expression in their adult life. Our kids were lucky to have escaped the restrictive lynching and imprisoning of non-judgmental creativity. You can say they escaped from the prison of *Artcatraz* just in time. They were fortunate to have open-minded parents and not have their creativity bound in a straightjacket.

Unfortunately, most parents don't have the financial wherewithal to do what we did, or have the courage to disobey the zombie and closed-minded protocols dished out to them. And this leaves us to beg the question:

How many millions of American kids have fallen prey to being strapped into the mind-conformity of the *Artcatraz* schools?

THE RISE OF THE MACHINES

When you layer the excessive use of smartphones and the addictive lure of social media into the mix — the problem of raising kids with a healthy balance is even more challenging. Today, most American students have outsourced their creativity to robots, virtual games, software and sophisticated apps that reside in a supercomputer in the palm of their hand. As much as technology has made it more efficient and speedier for kids to be innovative and smarter, its ubiquitous use has also rusted their holistic, creative and emotional mechanisms. It's not a healthy balance. You can make a case that it was all planned by design. Numb them, dumb them, and choke these kids' holistic creative receptors so that when they grow up you can make them feel less mediocre by getting them addicted to smart machines that will do all their thinking and creative tasks. We supplanted the "work hard" ethic with a "work smart" mantra, but it is all bulls*it, because America is not much smarter today than it was yesterday.

It just has an illusion of being so. Yes, there's been incredible progress and sophistication in most things we do. The digital revolution is a game changer for our civilization, and we're able to accomplish some pretty mind-boggling feats in a nanosecond. And although there are many highly intelligent programmers and software engineers who are behind the microchips and interface, America's nerds comprise a small percentage of our population compared to the high school dropouts and the small minds who appear to be smarter than they actually are. Examples of this are the plethora of apps and software that require little or no effort, skill or talent, but make you feel smarter than you actually are. In the music business alone, what took someone a couple of years to learn to play certain instruments just a generation ago, can now be taught in a matter of days on a laptop computer with self-tutorials.

Art and music have been digitized to turn any computer savvy person into a musician or an artist by pressing buttons on their portable machines and learning the pre-programmed sounds on sophisticated software. You don't need to have a good voice or much talent. My own son (who is actually quite a talented songwriter) created some amazing beats and symphonic tracks using such technology without having serious musical training. He played violins, drums, guitars and even sang hip- hop like a pro using auto-tune voice program.

For sure, he created some incredible sounding mixtapes and songs that could have never been possible in my day. I believed the kid had a musical career. In fact, so did he! But as much as he tried, he couldn't monetize his music, as everybody else was doing it too and giving away their music for free. It's the classic case of getting into a career with little barriers to entry. Today, for a few hundred bucks anyone can be a music producer or even a DJ who carries the power of a multitude of musical bands in a metal briefcase. Just like any commodity, it has little pricing power. I know computer technology is valued in the arts because it's easy, fast, and it is the future. But I caution that excessive use of such machines robs us from activating our raw talents, imagination and free spirit. We need to feel the emotional connection with real musical instruments and hold a paintbrush and smell the aroma of paints when we create our masterpieces. Putting this technology in the hands of exceptional-minded Americans is also a self-defeating proposition, as it makes our kids feel they're more special than they are. To be sure, the rise of smart machines does give small minds false hope. In one way, our civilization seems to be evolving beyond our comprehension. But in another way, could we be falling into a devolutionary and degenerative trap of sorts? We are at a critical crossroads for our species to get into a better balance that preserves our emotional intelligence, inspiration and innate creativity. We can't make the mistake to "out*source*" that to machines. We need to keep connected to our Source by keeping our Soul alive and inspired (in-Spirit) holistically. Listening to a live mariachi band or a musical band fills the Soul in a way that a DJ just can't. And we must not get trigger-happy and substitute computers for humans. Hopefully, we don't turn into emotionless humanoids implanted with computer chips in order to feel pain, joy, love, or be artificially aroused to have sexual satisfaction. That reality is closer than ever today, but would upend our ethos as our maker intended — and sadly, it will be all justified and self-inflicted in the name of progress.

THE RISE OF THE SMALL MINDS

Our state of adulthood is a product of our upbringing during childhood. So it's important that we don't f*ck up raising our kids, as it will boomerang back on us parents and more importantly, on our future. When a society punishes our kids for their freedom of self-expression, elects to grade and judge art, and then suppresses their emotional receptors with drugs, we're asking for trouble. Because as adults, our coping skills are weakened, our imagination is constricted, our voices are silenced, and we become pill-popping zombies by choice. When we reward our kids with high-sugar, high-salt and high-fat junk food diets, we see the effects manifest into high rates of obesity, diabetes, bad eating habits and overall mental malaise into adulthood. Garbage in, garbage out. When we don't teach kids proper life skills and fail to prepare them for the harshness of the real world, we produce a generation of thumb-suckers and crybabies. When we don't train them to be financially savvy and entrepreneurial-minded, they become enslaved to low-paying jobs and struggle to attain any upward mobility. When we don't spend enough quality time with them and pacify them with computers, we turn them into robots without any social skills. When we uplift them by posting huge yard banners for finishing high school, we lower their standards for attaining higher education. When we fail to prioritize our children's education, mental wellness and overall balance as a people, we shrink into a society of small minds — stuck inside a big box of couldas, wouldas, shouldas — known as present-day America.

MIND THE GAP

Modern America's infatuation with kicking kids out of their parents' nest prematurely is also a self-defeating mindf*ck. This agenda is definitely not helping the adolescent grow into a financially, mentally or spiritually healthy adult. By the time our children are 18 years old and considered legal adults, our society throws them out of the door to stand on their own two feet — whether they're ready or not. According to the National Institute of Mental Health, the human brain is not fully developed until the age of 25. That is an eight-year gap during which a lot of young adults act like fish out of the water. I've seen enough of them at our Center. So why does America even do this? It only encourages the creation of ungrounded and unstable individuals, who develop an unrealistic and entitled view of life when they're fully grown up. We need to do a better job minding this crucial gap. Sure, they toughen up and become more independent-minded, but due to the lack of adult supervision, deficient mental and financial societal support, they stagger and stumble, getting into some nasty habits and pitfalls.

If these young adults somehow make it whole, and are mentally undamaged past this stage into adulthood, most of them have no concept of what being in healthy balance looks like. In fact, on one end, their role models are the personification of materialism and greed that is marketed to them by money-hungry credit card and payday loan companies. On the other end, our own government hands them a financial noose to hang themselves with college debt. They learn no other value except *profit over people*.

In contrast, when we look at the lives of people in many Eastern societies, there is a sharp difference. Young people in those countries are not pressured to leave their home before they're mentally and financially ready to do so, which occurs typically around their mid to late 20s. While spending more time at home, they get ample grounding to practice the core values of their parents. They also get a better foundation and it shows in their academic drive, work ethic and spiritual connection in life. I'd argue that these young adults have a better sense of gratitude and respect for their parents, too, and that they are more inclined to be caretakers of them in old age. It is rare to see an Eastern-raised person elect to send off their aged or sick parent(s) to a nursing home, as is common with their Western counterparts. This positive karma has a cascading and often lasting effect generationally and permeates into all facets of their ethos.

The extra effort of parental nurturing and guidance shows up in a larger societal framework by producing the likes of the Dalai Lama, Mahatma Gandhi, Nelson Mandela and Mother Teresa. The more these young people were taught to increase their human capital output growing up, the more they were rewarded for their own inner peace and wellbeing in adulthood. After all, we reap what we sow.

So can we find the right balance to successfully deal with our growing pains? Can we become a society that produces less whiners and more mentally and financially stable adults? Can we not perpetuate an environment that helps people fall through the cracks during the eight-year brain development gap? Look at your own children as examples and reflect on those questions. If you're a young adult, ask yourself how you could have benefited from staying home longer. The answers will lie in each of us, taking the time and making the effort to prioritize our growth so we can reduce our pain, individually and collectively when we're adults. It is as much about *minding the gap,* as it is about mining our collective resources to achieve that shift.

Chapter Takeaway:

What did this chapter do for you? Inspirations, lessons, comments? Look upon your own experiences in school and growing up at home. Take some time here to reflect and jot down anything you would do differently for your own kids or grandkids — and then meditate for a few minutes before moving on.

8
HURT PEOPLE, HURT PEOPLE

"One does not become enlightened by imagining figures of light, but by making darkness conscious"

— Carl Jung

During the third month under Covid-19 quarantine, I was preoccupied worrying about the pandemic's effect on people's mental condition. According to a CDC and Census Bureau poll in April 2020, the percentage of U.S. adults with symptoms of anxiety and depressive disorder increased to 42 percent, from 19 percent the year earlier. This large increase in such a compressed timeline indicates Americans' poor coping and adaptability skills, as well as our misplaced priorities. By pushing a profit-over-people agenda, America has successfully induced a mental health crisis on its own people that is dangerously out of hand. Unable to cope and adapt to a new normal, individuals who live hand to mouth and are mentally fragile, unhealed and dangerously armed, are venting their frustration with hostility. And hurt people will hurt other people. But you can't put out the fires of your own ugliness by throwing flames onto the beauty of others. Or can you? Sales of alcohol, guns, sleeping pills and depression medications jumped by double digits during the crisis. Americans felt steeped in such problems as racism, the pandemic, polarized politics and financial distress. Today, the country's unreckoned ugly and dark past is surfacing at a rapid rate, and it's revealing its inequities, disparities and imbalances like never before. Perhaps we have to hit bottom and will rise again as a healthier and functional society. I am often wondering, when an uncivil war is imminent with half its people misguided andthe other half in disgust. Is a mass revolutionary event the necessary catalyst to shake out our dark faculties and shift us into light? Based on our anecdotal evidence at our Center, I don't think most Americans are mentally fit, resilient or ready to handle such tectonic changes and put themselves in the line of fire for their country. People bark more than they're willing to bite and/or sacrifice their own life.

We've also become too comfortable, lazy and passive for our own good. Yet we can't continue spewing out bitterness and vile on people who don't think, look or talk like us. A fractured nation is a weak nation that can ultimately only repair and rebuild itself by respecting its own inhabitants, no matter what creed or color. It is alarming but not surprising to witness a superpower's spiral, especially its tribalistic hostility and micro-aggression behaviors towards non-whites. Having spent more than four decades as a brown immigrant in America, I've seen its good, bad and ugly side from many perspectives. From the Iran hostage crisis during President Jimmy Carter, to George W. Bush'sdebacle of the Iraq invasion, to the engineered xenophobia under Donald Trump and everything in between, I've experienced my share of the ugly American treatment of immigrants and colored people.

I always thought I'd be judged by the content of my character, not the color of my skin. But, boy, I was wrong!

AJIM

As a brown man in a white-dominated world, I've had to work harder and smarter than my white counterparts to overcome many obstacles and stigmas to succeed. I even gave myself an American nickname to blend in with the white-dominated world. I've noticed how Anglicizing my name to Jim (from my Arabic birth name of Azim), has opened more doors and reduced stereotyping in the American Bible belt South. I didn't set out to sell out my identity or culture but rather chose to adapt to a rather ignorant Southern demographic by adopting an easy nickname, especially when it was often mispronounced and I got tired of explaining where it came from. It was also to test a valid theory that we humans are quick to judge others on any excuse we can find. Not surprisingly, the new *Jim* got less harassment and more respect. So how did you go from Azim to Jim, you ask? It happened purely by accident at a restaurant. My wife and I went out to a Korean restaurant and when asked to give our name for the waiting list, my wife gave the name Azim. When the table was ready, the Korean waitress who had a thick English accent and could not pronounce the "z" in my name shouted on the speaker phone, *"Ajim, Mr. Ajim, party of two, your table is ready!"* I looked at my wife with dilated pupils and a big smile and she said *"That's it honey. The nickname we've been looking for is Jim!"* And so Jim it was. Some of my justification for Anglicizing my name stems from being raised in a white colonial-ruled Africa that subconsciously devalued and degraded dark skins, made a mockery of our culture and tried to *whiten* us. What's more, I was rejected in many home and car loan applications in Georgia and had to hide behind my wife's name (Donna) to get an apartment. I also found that I was treated unfairly by many Jewish people after disclosing that I was a Muslim. In fact, my entire highly successful carpet-cleaning business, which at the time had many wealthy Jewish customers collapsed, in the aftermath of the 9/11 tragedy. I felt falsely stereotyped as an Arab, which during that polarized political climate translated into being a potential terrorist. One client went so far as to suggest that I needed to change my name to "Jim Peeraberg" to stop the Jewish clientele attrition. I was stunned and simply shrugged off the uncouth remark. This shows how shallow and judgmental humans can be sitting in their man-made seats of power. It's interesting how once a discriminated and persecuted minority (like Jews) become successful and powerful, they carry a self-righteous stick of hypocrisy to justify their racist and aggressive behaviors on other minorities. I found it to be a discomforting double standard to wave the flag of anti-Semitism on one hand and stick the middle finger to your Abrahamic brothers on the other. In my particular case, they knew I was a Muslim before 9/11 and loved me without judgment or predisposition when I did business with them. Yet after the attack many clients did a 180-degree turn and dropped me like a hot potato. I was now on their enemy list and couldn't be trusted inside their home. Overnight, I went from being a hero to becoming a zero, and from being a friend to an enemy. Untruths and rumors spread within the Jewish community, and I eventually had to shut down my 10-year-old thriving business. After this incident, I could definitely relate to how the Palestinians got abused and imprisoned in their own homeland by Israel. To be fair, it's not just Jews who have repeated the sins and atrocities of their perpetrators onto other people. Modern examples of this inhumanity include the Chinese against the Uyghur, the Africans against their own competing tribes, the Hindus against Sikhs and Muslims, and the Syrians against the Sunni Muslims. It is yet another tragic reminder of our flawed humanity and unhealed condition as a species.

WHITE-EVER

It's funny and rather revealing to have some of my white friends comment how 'embarrassingly white' they are. Sometimes it's an off-the-cuff remark comparing our two different cultural habits and appreciating my Eastern *collaborative-mindedness and mutual-sharing* positive traits. A good example is when we go out together on social outings. Instead of ordering separate plates at a restaurant, I suggest we order plates to *share* together. Instead of splitting the check, I'll pick the tab and suggest that they reciprocate the next round. Rather than seeing things as mine and yours, I show them the benefit of *ours*, and the value of *togetherness*. I tell them that it's how most of my foreign friends and I have been raised.

Not surprisingly, most of the time their new awareness results in them preferring it to their self-centric upbringing. Small character and behavioral differences in individuals say a lot about people and a society. Often, it's a sign of larger value differences that can clash and stir trouble — specifically with skin-tone stereotyping. And for this reason, it's fascinating to comment on the reality of America's "melting pot" misnomer. Contrary to fabricated propaganda, America is far from being a well-assimilated melting pot. As a young society, it is showing much immaturity and hot temperament akin to a confused and idealistic teenager. In this way, America's demographic resembles a combustible mixture of oil and water that's not mixing well in a burning pot, with immigrants being the oil surfacing to the top by way of color. Although America is built by the blood, sweat and tears of immigrants, there's a caste-like social behavior that often feels like two separate standards that are always in play based on skin color, within the colored and immigrant community— one for the lighter-skinned, and one for the darker-skinned. The programmed white-supremacy colonial mindset is to blame. I experience its judgment and stereotype as a brown skin American all the time. Many darker-skinned immigrants like myself don't get the same respect and equal opportunity as the lighter-skinned immigrants who blend more seamlessly into the white culture. I seldom hear of Europeans, Israelis, or Russian immigrants being labeled as rapists, gang members or lowlifes who take away America's jobs. It's quite an interesting dichotomy of a people that differentiates and segregates immigrants by skin color. Despite us "coloreds" having to work harder to rise to the top, many are having a tenuous time mixing with the majority of the country that sees us as outsiders or a threat to their white sovereignty and supremacy. Most of my white friends explain it away as part and parcel of human nature. While my colored friends see it as an extension of a white privilege mindset that's mired in insecurity and jealousy. In translation: You're doing just fine as Pedro the

Mexican roofer living in an apartment with six other people and riding on the back of a white man's truck. But when you're Pedro, the successful owner of that roofing company living in a high-end home and driving an expensive truck hauling white workers, now you're a threat and a hated (and targeted) immigrant. How healthy or normal is that type of behavior for a melting pot society? In some way us colored-skinned people have become trapped by trying to *whiten* ourselves to assimilate and model the white man's programming of superiority. Instead of being proud of our dark complexion, we've bought into the white-colonial mindset of lightening our skin and trying to avoid being in the sun. From Japan to India to Africa, this mind virus has permeated its people. It's become a self-induced mindf*ck. The darker-skinned folks are trying to be white with bleaching creams and white mannerisms, while white people are busy colorizing their skin with tanning lotions and listening to rap music and getting skin cancer in the process. *White-ever!*

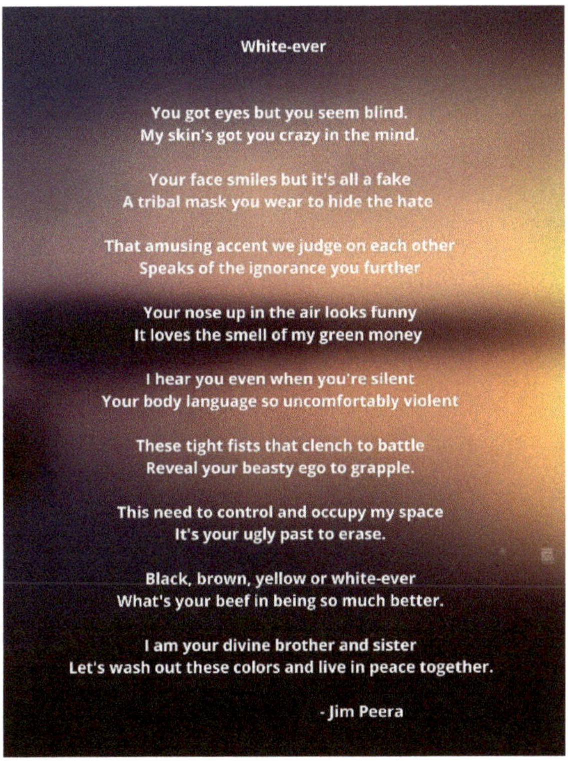

White-ever is a term that supports the idea of dismantling the programming of purity and white superiority. This programming manifests in pretty ugly ways by separating and stereotyping humans all across the globe. In Bollywood (India's Hollywood) for instance, the lighter-skinned actors are cast as the heroes, the protagonists and the beautiful. While darker-skinned actors are favored for the roles of the ugly villains. Perhaps they learned that stereotyping from Hollywood and the British powers that ruled them. So in this context we're all responsible for giving credence to the idea of white supremacy. We want to question these man-made flawed behaviors and hypocrisy. But racism is pervasive among colored people too, as it is not just based on race and color, but many other factors including religion, culture, status, ideology and power. We need to reverse this self-defeating stereotype programming by dismantling the entire notion of pure-blood superiority as it propagates the purity nonsense that separates people based on their color or creed. Could the Creator be showing us a path to the beauty and benefit of mixing our color palettes as a society?

THE BLEND IS YOUR FRIEND

Is it possible that much of the world's racism problem may be contained by blending all skin tones and cultures as the solution? Could *the blend be our friend,* where our maker may be pointing to a much more mixed racial composition for the survival of humanity? Mixed marriages are relatively new in America with only about 17 percent of couples being interracial, according to Pew Research. But the trend is growing in popularity and is not a hot button or as stigmatized as it was just a generation ago. In my case, my wife, a Filipino-American woman, and I married nearly 40 years ago, and our interracial marriage definitely went against the grain against our own respective families' wishes. Not surprisingly, the risk and the blend has definitely paid off, as our offspring are a lot more worldly and open-minded compared to their pure-bred counterparts. Different is not justgood — it's better. So I'm very encouraged by humanity in general to self-correct its racial differences by intentionally mixing and blending with one another. But a word of caution to all those who've not yet undone your white race is better, smarter or prettier mantra. As we intermarry and have mixed complexioned children (such as mine),we're going to have to undo the colonial definition of beauty or we'll create a generation of stuck up and arrogant fair-skinned adults. If we make the necessary corrections now, America's mixed couples and their offspring may actually help reduce racism across its society and the planet. Xenophobics, purebreds and haters will be confused and conflicted enough not to fuss, fight and fear trying to uphold the ancestral notion of staying imprisoned in a box of purely white, black, brown or yellow color. We'll all be impure, and that will be perfect as it won't offend any particular race. How beautiful and Divinely inspired!

TO PROTECT, PRESERVE AND ADVANCE

Contrary to divisive rhetoric, immigrants also are more a fountain rather than a drain on the American economy. The facts show that immigrants are a positive contribution to the whole and we pay our fair share of taxes. I know I do, and I'm not alone. According to the IRS, immigrants, including those without documentation, pay billions of dollars in taxes to federal, state and local governments every year. Immigrants paid $405.4 billion in taxes in 2017, including an estimated $27.2 billion in taxes paid by the undocumented. This is in sharp contrast with the likes of Donald Trump and the billionaire class, who are openly dodging the system and not paying their fair share of taxes. The truth is, the American economy would collapse if immigrants had an exodus from our country. Immigrants now make up 70 percent of the farming economy and more than 50 percent of the technology workforce in America. During the Covid-19 pandemic, more than 70 percent of the essential workers were immigrants.

Ironically, this positive contribution to the American economy gets conveniently overlooked by both the haters and the privileged whites. It's a mindf*ck that most whites don't know about because they've taken their privilege status for granted. Is it therefore fair to surmise that due to ancestral programming, manipulative rhetoric on America's airwaves, right wing media, and clever propaganda, that a good portion of white America (from the elites to the poor) seems to consider the white race as the only legitimate occupant of America, and all others as an imposition? Let this question soak in your brain before you answer it. I use "imposition" to underscore that when we say that Americans have a "tolerance" for people of all colors and faiths, we're actually revealing that we're "putting up" with them. It's not offering them a welcome mat, or giving them a 'coexist' bumper sticker. As we dissect this white superiority complex that is resentful towards colored people (especially the successful ones), you get an even uglier picture. There's a colonial-power mindset of territorialism and Anglo-Saxon privilege that really underpins racism in America.

Could it be a fear-based philosophy of the *protection, preservation and further advancement of the white race* at the expense of the collective human race? If this proposition is true, it's scary and concerning. A prevailing, exaggerated narrative claims that whites will be a minority race in America in the near future. Although America is definitely browning, it is far from making white people extinct or an under-class. So stop bitching, crying and wanting sympathy, y'all. This fear-based rhetoric only fuels the flames of hatred, violence and division. Instead of "otherizing" people and being ugly towards them, we Americans should be inspired by each other's uniqueness, strengths and talents by celebrating the beauty of all our differences. Until white people come to grips with their own insecurity and stop seeing colored people as subservient or as a threat to their survival, racism will continue to infect and divide America and be an ugly stain on our humanity for some time.

GREEN WITH ENVY

This white supremacist dynamic has been revealed to me during my climb up the ladder of financial success. The more successful I became or appeared to be, the fewer real friends I had, especially white ones. I attracted a lot of animosity and envious people whose intentions were disingenuous and highly competitive. When I was a struggling young student studying fashion design, no one saw me as a real threat or had much envy toward me. I had a handful of quality people I could call true friends. I owned nothing but in a weird way it was liberating. As I got more successful, I didn't really change as a person but my world began to shrink. I noticed a lot more resentment and jealousy towards me, and I couldn't understand why. I was generous with my moneyand wasn't a dick, yet I felt stifled by my relationships and attracted alot of enemies. Most disconcerting to me was how my financial success invited a lot of haters and greedy sharks. Much of that happened through the lens of racism and jealousy. These two ugly beasts have been on my back since childhood. I've experienced the wrath of a black populist despot named Idi Amin in Africa, the corrupted white good old boys in Alabama, and the poisonous venom of America's 45th president — all in one lifetime. The latter problem is the most dangerous, of course. Because when America sneezes, the whole world catches a cold. Racism, authoritarianism and right-wing populism have been exacerbated across the globe during and following the Trump era, as many countries are freely indoctrinating their peoplewith the white supremacy poison. If history teaches us anything, we should know this is how empires fall by their own sword and actions. Personally, I see racism as a human flaw that's rooted in our man- made malignant condition. First, I see it as a psychological cause of hurt and unhealed people; and secondly, as a weapon of power, money and corruption. This helps to explain the many genocides and atrocities in human history. Unfortunately, unless we practice empathy and see racism as a dark ugly cancer on our entire humanity, we're not getting rid of it.

But we must not deny it, normalize it, or feed it, as we're all guilty of participating in some form of prejudice as a people. The healthier option is to have the capability and courage to arrest it early on before it metastasizes into its full-blown ugly beast and ravages our respective communities, our nation and the world at large.

THE UGLY WHITE LIBERAL

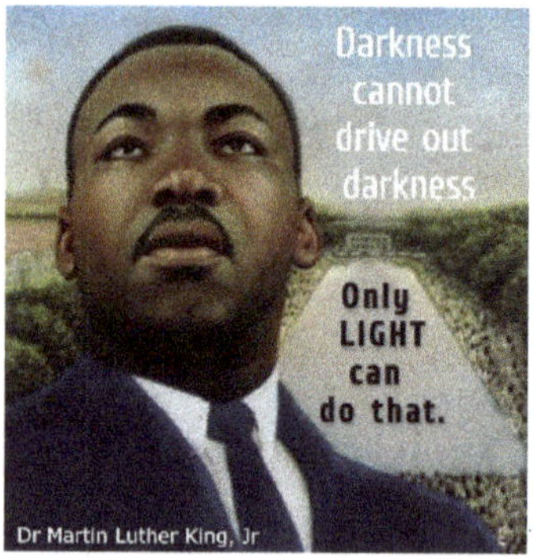

I am quite vocal about how the affluent, white-dominated neighbors displayed their unwelcoming mat when I opened Healium Center in Atlanta. To my surprise, the detractors were liberal whites. But it didn't matter. I was treated like a second-class citizen who was constantly interrogated and harassed by envious neighbors upset that a non-white person had purchased the large historic church property. I heard their tribalistic voracity circulate through the grapevine and thought it was just fear and ignorance of a new owner. But it was more wicked. It was the ugly head of racism as seen from the lens of white privilege. In The Healium Way of dealing with ugliness, we don't look away from it, but we look straight into it and expose it for what it is. When we opened The Center we'd experience regular police visits courtesy of the neighbors' unmerited complaints. I was so perturbed that I visited the local police precinct and threatened to file an injunction against the city if they didn't stop harassing us. As flustered as we all were about why we had such unfriendly and antagonistic neighbors, we needed some confirmation of their behavior. We got plenty of evidence that revealed a combination of fear, ignorance and jealousy, all stuffed into one sinister package of racism. On one occasion, I overheard a person at the neighborhood meeting plainly state to me that if I didn't have a black church as a tenant above my Center that I'd have a better chance of success in that white-dominated community.

He was dead serious, and it confirmed to me that the neighbors were downright racists. The neighborhood association continued giving me the dirtiest looks each time I attended, as we continued experiencing the cold shoulder from our neighbors. But this racism didn't always come in a straightforward package. Because a lot of people don't admit or realize that they're racists. One day, we actually had a chance to test out a common phenomenon known as 'implicit bias': that occurs when we have attitudes towards people or associate stereotypes with them without our conscious knowledge. Unlike explicit bias, this condition gives racist people an excuse not to come clean with their ugly actions. Instead, it reveals a racist person from the inside out. The opportunity to confirm that our neighbors were in fact racist came to us when we had set up an outdoor artist market. On this day, I noticed how all the cars and pedestrians would rubberneck at our market but would not stop. I had my suspicion as to why this was happening as I noticed that all our vendors that day had one common trait — they were all black. So to prove my point, I asked all the six vendors to step inside the building and leave their booths for an experiment on implicit bias. As we congregated inside, we all had an instinctual feeling that the test would confirm and reveal our hypothesis. And it did. Within a matter of about 15 minutes, white people began stopping by and walking up to the unmanned booths. It was quite disturbing but not surprising.

We had to remind ourselves that we were still in the segregated and unhealed South, a place where it is common for people to be fake and artificially smile at your face one minute and stab you in the back the next. They call it Southern hospitality; I call it Southern hostility. It's where a convenient pretentious mask is worn on the exterior that hides the disdain for you within. All of us looked at each other with a sad *"Aha, I told you so!"* glance, then took up The Healium Way-style of doing things and greeted the newcomers with love and compassion.

UNHOLY SH*T

Implicit or explicit, all bias is a form of a separatist mindset. And a separatist ideology breeds hate, and hate turned ugly and antagonistic against any race, religion or gender is not Godly. If you're a religious person, you'd call it all a sin. So the fact that one of the pastors at our church atop of our Center would tell me stories of persistent ugliness from the neighbors was not surprising. He'd complain how he was being confronted by neighbors on noise and parking issues during regular church hours. He also recounted how they'd bring their dogs to defecate on the front steps prior to Sunday morning service and give him dirty looks. That's quite some *unholy sh*t,* I said to myself! These were the same affluent white neighbors who put up yard signs around their homes that read "Black Lives Matter," "Coexist" and similar messages — a contradictory exterior cover to cleverly hide their inner racist character. All this ugliness and hostility was quite unwarranted because the church had been built more than 110 years ago in this location and had precedence over all the other properties. The history of this neighborhood reaffirms how over a period of two decades it got gentrified and replaced by affluent and mostly white privileged homeowners. Indeed, this was a classic case of territorial and tribalistic behavior, with symptoms of deeper unhealed scars. In all my encounters with the neighbors, I have always felt a certain bitterness, rage and sadness in them. In the Trump era, xenophobia and justified antagonism toward colored people got normalized to dangerous levels. What is quite odd but revealing is how 99 percent of the residents on our block have never even entered our building to check out what we did. Yet they were quick to judge, hate and ostracize us. We invited them with open arms, but they returned with a closed fist. For a well-respected and agenda-free community arts center, this un-neighborly conduct is quite abnormal. Of the handful of neighbors that have entered our space, most roll their eyes, make no attempt to participate or greet anyone and walk right out. A group of regular participants mentioned to me recently how they noticed the more they laughed and had a good time, the more the neighbors hung their heads and got upset. I told them I'd experienced this behavior with them all the time and how this just reveals symptoms of unhealed and unhappy people. "*How can they possibly give out what they don't have!*" I explained. In fact, this point was proven to us at our Center recently. A nosy male neighbor in his 60s who drops in occasionally for a few minutes to feed his angst admitted the truth. He walked in with his usual disgruntled face and started bitching about a handful of issues from Trump to global warming. I asked the liberal white voter what Democrat candidate he thought should replace Trump. He looked me in the eye and with an angry voice pointed a finger at me and said: *"It doesn't really matter. It's people like you that are the problem. You make things worse by preaching your happy bullsh*t and everything's gotta be fun and that artsy fartsy crap over here!*" I reminded him that I made a special sign outside our entrance that read, ***Warning! This is a Happy Zone*** for people like him. He rolled his eyes, turned his back, hung his head and walked out the door. He had just revealed his unhealed self, something he shares with most of the neighbors.

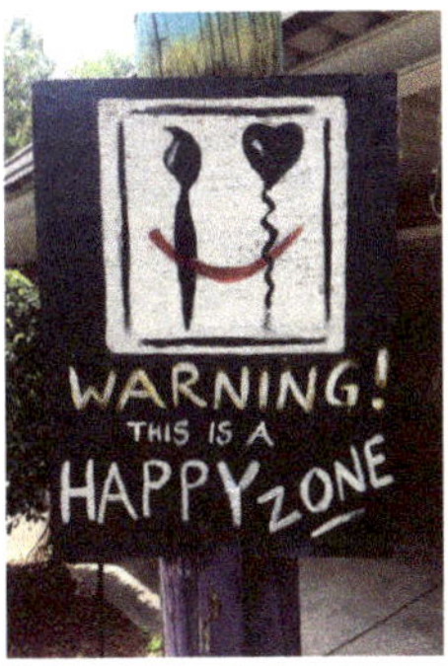

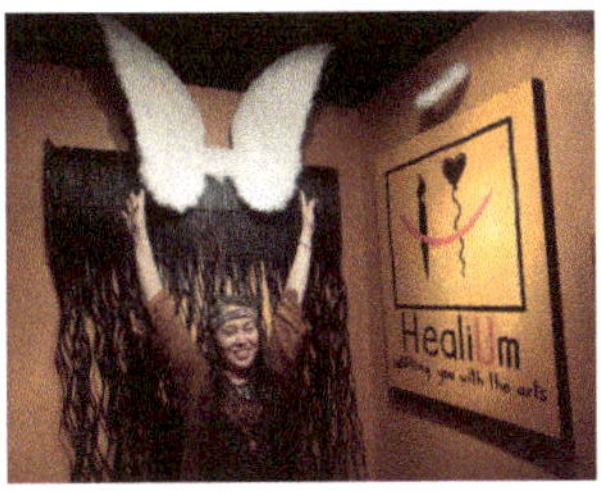

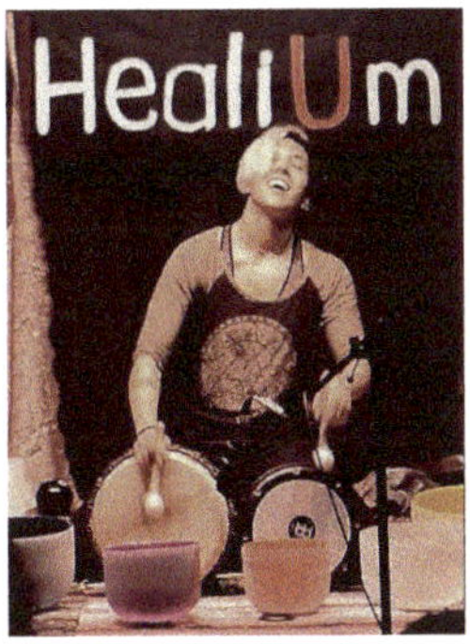

GO HOME, YOU PAKI!

As an immigrant who's lived in the American South for half my life, I've had to swallow my pride, toughen up, fight for justice and stay cool in the process. It's a delicate balancing act that I learned early on in my boarding school years in England during the 1970s. It was a period in Britain I can't forget, as it unleashed white power racism on immigrant Indians and Pakistanis with vengeance. They labelled all brown skins as *Pakis* even though I was from Africa. There would be numerous occasions where I'd be harassed by a group of far-right radical whites yelling, *"Go home, you f*ckin' Paki!"* They'd throw rocks and sticks at us and provoke us to fight them. But no matter how ugly and violent the skinheads got towards us, we were always advised by our elders and professors to ignore them and not retaliate with violence. My English teacher in boarding school, Mr Williams, loved Gandhi and often quoted his famous words: *An eye for an eye makes the whole world blind.* It changed how I dealt with rage and fury. Williams' advice to me was to fight only defensively when necessary and to use words rather than physical force in any confrontation. Those wise words have stayed with me and have helped me survive and thrive as a stranger in many strange lands: England, France and America. When I analyzed the many ugly incidents that resulted in unjustified provocations of hatred and racism, I came to the conclusion that the individuals who perpetrated the abusive behavior were basically unhealed people with unresolved issues. This phenomenon inflicts damage not just on individuals, groups and institutions, but can penetrate and instill harm on an entire society.

We are seeing this play out on a global scale today as populist leaders across the world are inflicting tribalist and segregative policies in their respective countries to dangerous levels.

ONE TRIBE

Tribalism is as old as prostitution, but it's more wicked as it feeds on fear and ignorance that breeds racism. As much as we all love to support and defend our own tribes, technically there exists only one tribe: the human species. Let's see 'Human' as "HumONE'. It's the only one proposition worth defending.

But we complicate life by our affiliation with organized social groups, rigid attachment to our comfort zones, and grouping with like minds. It's an oxymoronic formula, as it seems to unite us in one way, yet sows the seeds of separation in another. We conveniently turn a blind eye toward one of our *ugly truths* — the need to be special. This is our first mistake and it is how our divisive mindset is born. It is a philosophy that starts off quite harmlessly, as individuals form groups boasting a particular belief system or their loyalty and allegiance to one another. But this *tribal* mindset becomes dangerous as it soon grows into an exclusionary proposition. Clubs, gangs, clans, cults, secret societies, many organized religious groups, etc are all forms of this separatist thinking that soon attaches labels on its followers and brands itself as "exclusive" or "members only." With this type of setup, no matter how benign the tribe, it is vulnerable to unleashing more vitriol against individuals or other groups of people it considers *outsiders,* or not a part of its circle. It doesn't take much for that group to then go into a discriminatory mode and practice racist and malevolent acts. And defend its position by cleverly justifying it. The catalyst is typically envy, greed, fear, competition and resentment. I've experienced this condition with all types of groups from brown people to white people to black people — and not just in my community but all over the world.

THE ISMS

Religious persecution and systematic racism have existed since the beginning of our civilization, and are part and parcel of our dark human condition. In these modern times, a lot of our darkness has been magnified and brought to light because we are living closer to each other, intermarrying, and have a supercomputer weapon to propagate and broadcast bigotry at our fingertips. Today, cellphones are exposing human ugliness in real time, and the browning of a culture is creating an unmerited fear that is unleashing some pretty harsh vitriol across the globe. When this fear is combined with economic inequities, fierce competition and corporate domination, we are seeing the rise of many *isms* at play; capitalism, socialism, consumerism, corporatism, populism, extremism, exceptionalism, isolationism, tribalism, terrorism, colonialism, sectarianism, racism, fascism, and the newest kid on the block, Trumpism. Interestingly, all of these 'isms' are about our imbalances. For instance, Trumpism has penetrated our society well because we have the perfect storm and underlying conditions at play. A psychologically imbalanced, unstable and unhealed narcissist has met an unhealed people, who are fragile, destitute and ready to drink up his magic potion and take orders to hurt and kill their own fellow humans. It sounds like I'm talking about Adolf Hitler or some foreign rogue dictator in a third world country. Sadly, I am talking about an American-born and raised billionaire named Donald Trump, who became the 45th president of the United States of America.

The former president's brand of divide and conquer is nothing novel. It is a playbook that has been deployed successfully by despots and egomaniacs for centuries. Its precept is based on fear, hatemongering and separation that feeds off of the weakness and desperation of its prey. When it works, it reveals a lot about its victims. By getting almost one half of America to despise the other with pride and justification, Trumpism is America's litmus test. America under Trump was a prime example of witnessing humans operating at a low-vibrational energy. Fortunately, The Healium Way can help us see the forest from the trees. Every symptom has a root cause, and it reaffirms the *hurt people, hurt people* premise. Trump's sociopath and narcissist tendencies originated from his dysfunctional relationship with his father that manifested in an unhealed traumatic childhood. This is a well-documented fact. While growing up, he was too preoccupied with feeding his oversized ego and spent more time working on becoming a real estate mogul rather than working on himself and sewing up his open wounds. Over time, he believed in his own bag of lies and his self-serving ways of enriching himself.

He became a master of his own deceit and realized that he had the talent, the charm and the "gift of the gab" and bombast to catapult his wealth and his brand beyond his wildest dreams by using the vehicle of reality television and politics. Reality television turned him into an entrepreneurial star and politics was a vehicle for him to reach further for the stars. As a highly insecure person, he was able to use these platforms to attract enough Americans who shared his dark and unhealed side — and prove to his now-deceased dad and to his family that he was not a loser and could rule the world. The Trump rise is a profound lesson in our society's own unhealed wounds and misplaced priorities. Using a village metaphor, let's look at Trump as a person who discovered two camps of people that he found useful for his playbook. In the first camp, he discovered a fertile soil of poor, uneducated and disgruntled white people who desperately needed a good excuse to vent their anger onto colored people for their problems. In the second camp, he found a group of people who hated to play by any ethical rules and were money worshippers. When he pieced the needs of both of these people together, he sensed an opportunity to fill their respective voids. He quickly discovered his weapon of choice to help and appease the two camps: the age-old *divide and conquer* tool. By pitting people against each other and dividing them by class, race, gender, religion, etc; a power-hungry leader can fast track his way to accomplish his diabolic mission. In order to burn the flame of separation and chaos, a leader needs to light the spark with the most popular ignition method known to man: fear. Once the people crank themselves up with fear, the sparks of internal rage and hurt take over to cause harm toward a camp that opposes its tribe's belief system. For Trump, these two components were already fermenting in his blood, and were eagerly waiting to be activated on his opponents. And so he did it in the only way he knew how, by hurting and pouring gasoline over the rest of the people who *did not* belong in any of those two camps. It's a win-lose game that Mr Trump often plays and openly writes about in all his books. But who ultimately wins and who loses in his one-way street game plan? Only time will tell.

Whatever happens to Trumpism, Donald Trump's story is America's perfect *hurt people, hurt people* example for us to learn from. It will be studied by historians for decades to come. But what we do as Americans today, will determine our fate tomorrow. So let's deploy The Healium Way of creating a more healed outcome for ourselves at this critical juncture. First, let's take a flip-side approach. By looking at Mr. Trump and his separatist movement as a blessing, rather than a curse on America, we have a chance to put America back together again. It's difficult for many of us in the non-Trump camp, but shifting our mode of thinking into a more positive and "forest from the trees" perspective, is actually the needed catalyst for change. It is how we can transform from an ordinary mindset into an *extra*ordinary one, and make some positive progress for the sake of everyone's mental health and peace. It's the *do I want to be right or do I want to be happy?* moment of truth. When we shift into this mode, we immediately stop hating one-half of America. By not hating people, we're able to have a clear mind and be better observers of them. When we're better observers, we're able to properly assess disparate points of view. Soon we're able to open a dialogue and listen to others' pain and concerns without predispositions or judgment. We may not agree with them, but we're not writing them off as terrible people or as our enemies. That is a major shift. Interestingly, the "other" side starts changing its perspective too and pretty soon each side begins to see commonalities that exist in ALL the camps and becomes slightly more empathetic. It may not be a seismic shift of perception, but it is enough to stop the worst of the hate-mongering.

This baby-step shift is all it takes to put a tourniquet on America's bleeding Soul and have us individually operate as a slightly more healed American, as opposed to a chronically hurt American.

THE GENIE IS OUT

By allowing an unhealed person to covet the world's most influential seat of power, the 45th president of the United States' controversial throne was akin to handing over car keys to an inebriated person; it was a terrible and risky proposition for America. The exit wounds and PTSD (post-traumatic symptom disorder) on Americans will be deep and could last generations — because the poison of the hate- mongering he's unleashed is not easily going away. The window of opportunity is rapidly closing to put the Trumpism genie back in the bottle. The psychological damage alone will be enough to derail the nation's imbalances and divisions into a deeper bog of chaos, especially when the hurt has been successfully scapegoated and weaponized instead of being healed. As the disinformation bubble keeps insatiably feeding the fragile and the unhealed followers, the facts also get dangerously distorted and the ugliness gets magnified. All this further weakens and will tear apart a divided people for some protracted time. When hurt people are left hurt without resolution of past traumas, the open scars can manifest feelings of betrayal, not being loved and insecurity. Many of these people will simply get proficient at numbing the pain and inflicting collateral damage onto others along the way, often unknowingly and without taking ownership of their deeds. You simply can't give out what you don't have. This is why when we put unhealed individuals in a state of power such as a police officer or a president, we experience the wrath of their rancor on innocent and peace-loving people across all demographics. These behaviors show up in the form of bullying, greed, infidelity, dishonesty, deception, hatred, misogyny and racism. Many of their victims are the *leaves and branches* we discussed before, and are easily manipulated into "sheeple." Sometimes the victims are simply defenseless and outgunned, as we've seen in rising cases of police brutality on colored people. The dark behaviors of unhealed people are always justified defensively and often displayed by traits of victimhood, projection, manipulation, resentment, jealousy, denial and the like. In some ways, we all know someone in our own circle of relationships or family who exhibits such conduct that detrimentally affects us. Can you relate to these types of people?

CAUSE AND EFFECT

Personally, I have four older siblings who display some form of these low-vibrational attributes to varying degrees. They may not be aware of it but I notice it and have been affected by them. It's my life's lesson that I'm sure will relate to others who've had similar experiences with their siblings. I have three brothers and one sister whose behavior toward me has not been normal or typical of East Indian-close knit families. It's been a dysfunctional and patronizing relationship at best, being resentful and jealous of me for most part of my life. So while writing this book, I asked myself why did this condition exist in my own family? How is it that the youngest of five kids that my mom bore just happened to get the most disrespect, ridicule and crap thrown at him? Especially when I'm not a dick, but am kind, loving and have extended my generous hand each time they've asked for it. I first thought it had to be that I was the youngest, but that excuse was too easy and cliched. It's also inexplicable when all my efforts to fight for unity and get them to experience my Center failed. Using The Healium Way as a litmus test, I knew there was a deeper answer to my question. Since nothing happens in life coincidentally, but by Divine design and our own creation, I knew there was a cause to the effect of this unhealthy condition. The Sanskrit translation of this phenomenon is called karma.

Karma is about taking responsibility for our own actions and life. Often, it's the consequence of past actions that can be programmed into us subconsciously — known as ancestral karma. Similar to ancestral programming (a Western term) discussed earlier, it is where hereditary traits and characteristics have compromised your physical, emotional and mental health. Typical examples of the harmful type include drug and alcohol addiction, domestic violence, racism, scarcity-mindset, fears, and so on. More important however, is the opportunity for healing, balancing and having positive karma in the present. In many ways it is a balancing act that offers us chances through life circumstances, situations, and relationships to learn important spiritual lessons. For me, the answer appeared as clear as daylight while I was writing the prologue of this book. By starting this literal journey with the story of my mom's mental breakdown encapsulating that fateful day, it puts into perspective how each of us must have the courage to cut the unhealthy cords of low-vibrational behaviors and elect to break unhealthy karma. As I started to look at the forest instead of the trees, I realized that I was looking at the wrong thing all along to justify my emotional pain of not having a normal relationship with my siblings. Could it be that the sibling dysfunction was not about me but about them, and related to their own karma? Is it possible that all my siblings are a product of hurt and unhealed Souls, and I just happen to be the trigger that is a convenient scapegoat to dump their pain on? More important, that it is not up to me but up to each of them to bring themselves to a place of self-awareness, and hopefully, their ultimate self-awakening? Indeed, as adults, we have one of two choices: to continue expanding the unhealthy karma or to break it. By electing to expand it, and engage in low-vibration actions against others, we risk passing the toxic baton down to our own offspring with more collateral damage. By choosing to break the programmed karmic loop and shifting into a positive gear, we can begin a healing process that is long overdue. Obviously, The Healium Way is to do the latter and strive for inner peace.

Interestingly, the awareness and reckoning stage is the hardest part of breaking this karmic padlock, as the catalyst and cause of pain is often old and buried in the depths of the subconscious and unhealed mind. I'm not sure how far back or deep it goes in our own family tree, but I can pinpoint my birth as the source of most of my dysfunctional and divisive relationship with my siblings. It's quite a fascinating story to unravel for my own peace and closure, and will provide a lesson for many of you who may be experiencing a similar sibling dynamic.

THE PRICE OF DOING NOTHING

There's a 10-year gap between me and my next sibling — a brother who I am closest to and the sibling I trust the most. The fact is, as an accidental arrival, I seemingly fu*ked up all my four elder siblings' childhood memories and deprived them of their youth. At my birth, they were aged between 10 to 16, and as teens they had growing pains due to the lack of much-needed parental attention. Since my dad was always working and traveling abroad, that put the onus on my mom to give that parental attention, but as I detailed in my prologue, she was incapable of proper mothering. She became a mental wreck after giving birth to me, and suffered chronic episodes of depression and mental illness for many years. During this critical period, the kids naturally experienced some ugly episodes in the home and processedit by experimenting in their own "hit and miss" ways, and by clinging on to my grandma and uncles for love and support. But that was little consolation. It appears that my mom and I soaked up all the attention in the family, and they felt abandoned. Sixty years ago, there were no therapists to talk to, or freestyle self-expression tools that were commonly prescribed for emotional release and pain.

In fact, the doctors who made house calls either gave you antidepressants and sleeping pills to numb you, or put you in a straightjacket and sent you to a cuckoo's nest for electric shock treatments. Yesterday's parents weren't the parents of today, either. They were tough, unapologetic and didn't take any cry-babying from their growing offspring. Most of them punished their kids with sticks, rulers, paddles and anything they could find under the kitchen sink. Without any computers or televisions to keep them occupied, many children simply resorted to releasing their pent-up emotions by getting into trouble in order to get their parents' attention, albeit in a negative way. As they grew older, these unhealed adults conveniently unleashed their emotional pain onto their respective relationships, including their own children. Instead of trying to get professional help, they camouflaged their internal rage by scapegoating their way out.

In our case, my elder siblings continued to blame my mother for not being a loving and caring mom during those years after my birth. But that excuse vanished the moment she was widowed at the age of 52. They were mature adults by then, and couldn't dump their unhealed scars on a fragile and mentally unstable person. So the attention focused on me. And when I was younger, immature and struggling, I could take their emotional abuse. But when I got older and had a family, and was successful on my own terms, the resentment, jealousy and condescending mindf*ck that I got from them was enough. I had to retreat from that toxicity. They never tried to get any help, despite my repeated calls to them to do so. As I see it, it is no longer my problem or a guilt trip to own — but theirs to unpack. Today, as senior citizens, all of my siblings are each comfortably sitting in their own dark "coulda, woulda, shoulda" boxes of their own karma. But the price of doing *nothing* is steep, with the prospect of vultures looming over your charred Soul when you're six feet under. What's even worse is passing and expanding the pain and unhealed scars onto the next generation.

BLOOD IS THINNER THAN WATER

Fortunately, I elected not to choose that path with one sibling who went rogue on me some 20 years ago. It was my life lesson and a classic *hurt people, hurt people* story worth recounting for anyone with unhealed siblings. It involved one of my brothers who felt my parents neglect more deeply than the others, and his story demonstrates the collateral damage of an unhealed person onto himself, his blood relatives and his own nuclear family. My brother held a grudge on my mom since my birth, and then blamed her for sending him away when he was a teenager. He avoided revisiting the incident with my mom and kept his relationship with her quite superficial. He didn't have the heart to call her Mom, and always addressed her by her first name, Sheru. For his own comfort and justification, he weaponized that story and bubble-wrapped it into his unhealed mind. He believed that he was not smart enough, not loved enough and labeled himself a black sheep of the family. He carried that proverbial monkey on his back for years. Despite being a perfectly capable and street-smart kid, he magnified his story of betrayal and neglect, and rebelled with resentment. As a popular ladies' man, he could have prolonged his footloose and fancy-free bachelor life, but instead decided to settle down and got married in his early 20s. Soon he had his first son and added two more kids raising a family in England. All along he was in a competitive race with all of us, trying to prove to the family that he was not a loser. Being a street-smart entrepreneur, he became a master jeweler and was financially successful before the age of 40. We were all proud of him. He bought expensive toys, took exotic vacations and spoiled his wife and children with the same. Each time he waved his status flag on us all to show he had made it. He hung around egotistical people and became a product of his unhealthy environment. His world revolved around money and his obsession with it never satisfied him. The higher he climbed his elusive mountain ofgold, the more he looked up to more wealthier friends and felt envious, lower and tarnished. When any of us siblings excelled and showed any financial success, he'd get jealous and tried to beat us down with ugly remarks and even enjoyed cheating us. He displayed many insecurities and manifested a materialistic and competitive character. Instead of spending his time and money on therapy to healhis festering emotional wound, he chose to dress it up and numb it with more material pacifiers. He worked longer hours and fed his ego with more investments and unhealthy distractions. His self-absorption with money and competitiveness was damaging his relationship with his own family, but he wouldn't admit it. Instead of spending quality time with his kids, he numbed their pain by spoiling and showering them with expensive cars, toys and superficial things. On a few occasions, I warned him that his teenage daughter was in need of therapy, as she was desperately trying to get his attention by being promiscuous with men two to three times her age. Here was his chance to be a better father and stitch his own childhood wounds, but he ignored all the signs, and conveniently wore his denial and defensive hat. This type of self-absorbed and delusional behavior is a classic sign of hurt people. To everyone's detriment, this hurt Soul would hurt many Souls in his life's path from friends to relatives to his own blood. As a low-hanging fruit, I was the perfect scapegoat for him to skin next. He proceeded to cheat me out of some money that I had invested to help him get out of a financial bind. It was a catalyst that revealed his true colors as an unhealed Soul. He justified the deception and made me look like the antagonist. Since the elders in our East Indian culture are "always right" and are seldom held to account, it wasn't too difficult to sway most of my family members. Using his victim and entitlement tactics, he successfully launched a vengeful attack against me and manipulated his way out with some clever projection tricks. My sister, a *leaf*-type personality, joined in feeding his dark side, and convinced all of the other siblings to do the same. I was left dangling alone, feeling sick to my stomach and scratching my head without a viable explanation. I remember saying to my wife at the time that money isn't the root of evil, it just exposes the worst of unrooted people. My siblings had just revealed their unhealed selves. To make matters worse, my mother, who knew I was right, kept silent and did not have the courage to speak up for me. That was disappointing for me, and came close to reopening our past wound together, but I chose not to go there. I was smart enough to know that my mom was incapable of taking sides as she was mentally fragile and still mourning my dad's passing. She could not give out what she did not have. After this latest missed opportunity to heal my wounded family, I took the high road. I dismantled my egotistical self and proceeded to break the cords of toxic karma. I chose to relinquish the ordinary mindset of quarreling about money, of being right and, instead, chose the path toward peace. The Healium Way of being extraordinary. I didn't look back at that dark episode again and just forged ahead into the light. To this day, my brother and I have been estranged and my sister and I have never regained our closeness. The unfortunate incident left an indelible scar on the entire family dynamic, proving that hurt people do hurt people and confirming the ugly truth — that when it comes to money for flawed beings, blood is thinner than water.

THANK YOU, WAYNE

In seeking the path of peace, we eventually gravitate toward a direction of universal truth. One of the truths of unresolved emotional pain and suffering is being attached to something. In my case, it was about expecting a particular outcome, an apology from my brother for his deceptive actions and from my family for enabling him. But that was unrealistic, especially given that I was the youngest in the family. Being an empath, I suffered even more and had to change my idealistic thinking for my own sanity. A good omen during that time occurred when I met the late American author and motivational spiritual speaker, Dr. Wayne Dyer. My wife and I were treated to a beautiful warm and long hug from him that still resonates in our hearts today. He aptly reminded us in the audience of the power of forgiveness. One of his principles was to understand that there are no justified resentments. He went on to instill in us how, *Once you change the way you look at things, the things you look at change.* Wayne's masterful advice helped me look at the bigger picture, the forest instead of the trees, and shift my thought patterns from a place of weakness to a place of empowerment. When I applied a non-attachment prescription with a dose of forgiveness with all my siblings, I began the necessary healing and Soul-cleansing process. Soon I worked on transforming myself from a hurt person to a healed person. I stopped asking "why" and got out from the muck of victimization and onto a recovery path of unconditional forgiveness. It was my responsibility, not anyone else's in the family. I forgave all my siblings and mom, and journeyed on to a higher path on my own terms. I did it for my own peace. It wasn't easy and it took a decade to stitch up my deep-seated wound. But through patience and the application of The Healium Way Principles — activating the healing and creative arts (sculpting, poetry, meditation, sound healing) and exercises of detachment and forgiveness — I have released many dark emotions of this episode and brought them to light with love.

I also came to the conclusion that I couldn't accuse anyone of being bad. This would be a judgment call and counterintuitive to The Healium Way. In this context, there's little credence to labeling someone as "bad" or "good." It's more complex than that. People often do bad things to other people, but their actions are more a symptom of other darker underlying causes on their end. Since we're all flawed beings, it's best to look at people as healed or unhealed. And within this definition there are less healed and more healed beings. Through this lens, we can see an unhealed individual manifesting the bad, the dark and the ugly attributes, in different ways. Sometimes they crave attention and are unintentional in their low-vibrational actions. This type of person just needs a jolt of awareness to show them the light. But sometimes they're intentional and want to test the limits of their darkness to feed their selfish beast within. Sadly, my brother chose the latter path. We can blame it all on being imperfect humans. Even elevated spiritual beings were guilty of testing the limits of their dark side at some point. The difference though was that they transformed themselves from being ordinary to extraordinary by their own good intentions, right choices and positive actions.

Today, I accept that family incident as a valuable lesson that made me stronger and more resilient as a person. As a natural fighter, it was difficult for me not to put on my boxing gloves to defend my position. But for the sake of not causing a bigger rift in the family, I chose to close the chapter and am satisfied with changing my own thoughts and sending love their way. In the end we are all responsible for our own pain. Since we only have control of our own actions, we have a choice to take the higher road to fix it, or wallow in conventional methods of conflict resolution and suffer. What I know from my own trials and tribulations is that I prefer to not ignore or hide the demons under the rug, but face them with courage and tame them with unconditional love. It helps me sleep well at night, not harboring any resentments, and know that I will not die with the hurt still in me. It also reinforces the power of losing the battle but winning the war. In this case, it reminds me of the powerful words of another Bee Gees song:

"I surrender, but I'm victorious in defeat." So hurt people, hurt people, but healed people, heal people. And I feel empowered being among the latter group.

In the 79th verse of the Tao Te Ching, Lao Tsu eloquently reminds us that resentments don't come from the conduct of the other party but rather survive and thrive because you're unwilling to end it with kindness, love and authentic forgiveness. He writes; *"Someone must risk returning injury with kindness or hostility will never turn to goodwill."*

79th Verse of the Tao

After a bitter quarrel, some resentment remains.
What can one do about it?
Being content with what you have
is always best in the end.

Someone must risk returning injury with kindness,
or hostility will never turn to goodwill.
So the wise always give without expecting gratitude.

One with true virtue
always seeks a way to give.

One who lacks true virtue
always seeks a way to get.

To the giver comes the fullness of life;
to the taker, just an empty hand.

Chapter Takeaway:

What did this chapter do for you? Inspirations, lessons, comments? Draw upon your own experiences in America, especially if you're an immigrant or colored person. Have you dealt with many hurt people and acts of undeserved hostility? Take some time here to reflect and jot down on a piece of paper anything you would do differently with hurt people (including those in your family) moving forward — and then meditate for a few minutes before moving on.

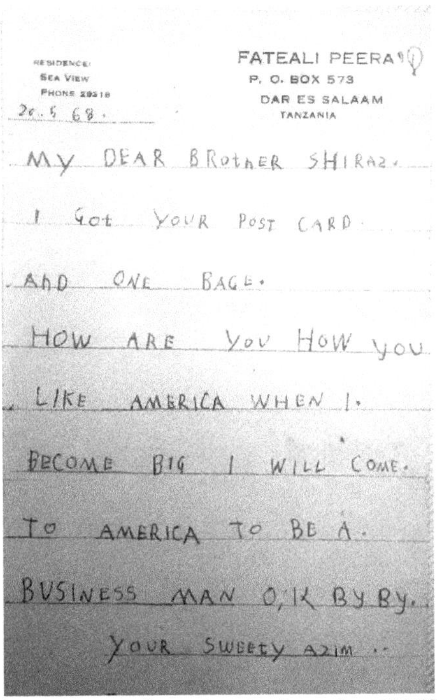

RESIDENCE:
SEA VIEW
PHONE 29318

FATEALI PEERA
P. O. BOX 573
DAR ES SALAAM
TANZANIA

20. 5 68.

MY DEAR BRother SHIRAZ.
I Got YOUR POST CARD
AND ONE BAGE.
HOW ARE YOU HOW YOU
LIKE AMERICA WHEN I.
BECOME BIG I WILL COME.
TO AMERICA TO BE A.
BUSINESS MAN O,K BY BY.
YOUR SWEETY AZIM ..

Jim dreams of coming to America (1968)

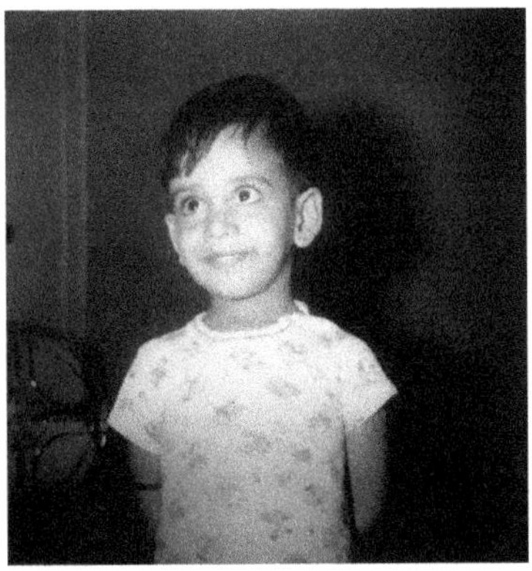

Jim in Africa (1964)

9
THE BLAME GAME

"To move the world, we must first move ourselves"

— Socrates

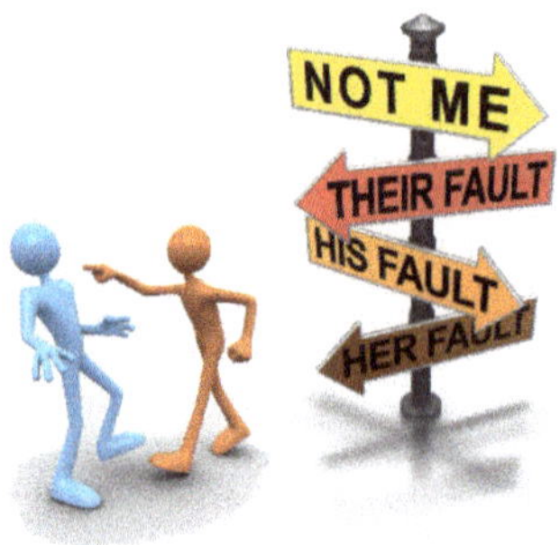

With the Covid-19 pandemic devastating the global economy as of this writing, it's clear to see America's finger-pointing at China and everyone else except itself. Having put up an exaggerated image of being exceptional and "the richest and strongest nation in the world," America finds itself in an inconceivable position: a self-imposed empire of illusion taking responsibility for its own leadership failures and admitting its lack of preparation and serious blunders in a crisis. Because those actions would admit faulty governance and indicate vulnerability. And vulnerability is weakness. So instead of taking that path, our leaders chose to distract us by passing blame and avoiding responsibility.

Sound familiar? Welcome to what most Americans are good at: *the blame game.* This scapegoating tactic becomes a self-defeating proposition in our own personal growth and progress. Because personal responsibility is in short supply these days, and we are less and less prepared to own up to our own mistakes and choices. With a nationalistic and quasi-tribalistic societal mantra of *God Save America* embedded as its ethos (as opposed to God save the world or God save our humanity), it's far easier for a diehard pure-blood white or black American to blame a hardworking successful immigrant for stealing his job than to retrain himself in the workplace. It's also a lot more convenient to blame any leader at the helm, than to admit you didn't participate in the voting process.

WE, THE IDIOTS

America has come dangerously close to testing the *I the King* autocratic leadership, as opposed to the *We the people* democratic ideology on its turf. How quickly the seeds of authoritarianism were sown into our republic during Trump's reign reveals a lot about America and how it has coped. At our Center alone, we saw people reporting increased levels of depression, heightened sleep apnea, anger, anxiety and many other psychological issues. Our attendance also dropped as many simply stopped socializing and were afraid to go out in public due to the rash of violence against colored people and the LGBTQ community. With the most powerful leader in the world distorting facts and spewing lies (more than 30,000 recorded during his term), many people have also simply divorced themselves from the news media altogether or adjusted to their new demoralized reality.

As a baby boomer, I could surmise that a combination of a young generation's weak coping skills and the existence of the internet as a news dissemination portal is to blame for this particular condition. Or is it more complicated than that? As we dissect the period between 2016-2020 (The Trump era), we learn a lot about ourselves as individuals and as a collective people.

How about not blaming Mr. Trump as the cause of our individual or collective pain and suffering? Because that lets us off the hook. Yes, history will judge him harshly, as it should, for taking America to the brink of fascism during his tumultuous tenure and unleashing the country's Pandora's Box. But Trump was simply an opportunist who delivered on his promises of divisiveness and hatemongering that revealed America's true colors. He laid out his cards as he was going to play them and half the people bought the deck. In truth, Trump was an accelerant and a symptom that exposed the fissures of America's own fickleness, fragility and fear. Some would call him a truth messiah. Because here was one man who used and abused his power seat for his own personal gain — yet revealed many ugly truths about our people. Using a salesman metaphor, there needs to be a reciprocal relationship to sell you anything. Specifically, salesmanship involves some form of convincing, persistence, manipulation, exaggeration and creativity. In effect, I'll say you're a pretty good salesman if you can convince a handful of people on your block to buy your snake oil potion, promising an elixir of immortality. I'd consider you to be a great salesman if you could get an entire village to do so. I'd also call you a master salesman, if you were able to manipulate and convince 900 disempowered people to drink a lethal grape punch and commit suicide — as Jim Jones did for his religious cult in Guyana in 1978.

But when you've got 63 million American people in 2016 who bought your package of xenophobia, sexism, lies, division, bullying and racism and put you in office — and an additional 10 million more (73 million Trump voters) who doubled down for you in the 2020 presidential election, despite your egregious mishandling of a deadly pandemic, in my books you are beyond the realms of salesmanship and manipulation. You're a mastermind shrink who just exposed America's open wounds and pierced it deeper and wider, with a big smile, a middle finger — and profited from it at the expense of all its 330 million people! You're what many liberals have called Donald Trump: an evil genius. If we viewed these 73 million people as being *consumed only with self-interest,*' we would call these folks idiots.

Because to the Greeks, the term *idiot* in a classical context means exactly that. As the originators of democracy, the Greeks considered an idiot to be highly dangerous to the function of democratic governance. They reasoned that if enough of a society was consumed with self-interest and individualism, a society would cease to be a democracy. The truth is, America is not only a product of all that, but it is also a purveyor of masterful marketing and propaganda that feeds the appetites of idiots. Our radio waves, cable news, internet, social media and so forth are all responsible for the rise of 21st century American idiots. So thank you, Mr. Trump, for showing us how f*cked up and idiotic we are as Americans — and are about to expand our idiocy, if we don't change our trajectory as a nation. But make no mistake, the f*cked up are not just the one-half of us that revealed and acted on our unhealed wounds, but the other half that pretends the wounds don't exist.

In a sacrificial way, Mr. Trump has woken many Americans up from our comforted malaise of sitting on our butts. By unapologetically normalizing division and hatred, and pitting one person against the other, he inadvertently incited the better angels in America to rise up to face our responsibilities and fight for our common ground and higher ideals. In this fashion, can Trump's firehose of pain on one-half of America become the needed medicine to awaken and potentially fix America's ills and dysfunctionality? Only time will tell. Because we have a long way to go in terms of accepting and coexisting with people we don't currently understand.

PAINTING DALI'S AMERICA

The question to ask ourselves therefore, is how badly have we eroded our allocentric (other-focused) virtues of generosity, kindness, humility, beauty, courage and empathy for each other? And supplanted these virtues with egocentric and nihilistic vices — that are eroding our ethos and exploiting our lowest vibration. It is this truth that we must grapple with. In order to become smarter beings, we cannot sit comfortably in our self-righteous bubbles and be quick to draw a line in the sand with anyone we don't agree with, or who looks and talks differently than us. We've got to be better than that.

For example, if you're in a shopping mall sitting beside a person who is eating a chicken biscuit with iced tea while you're dipping an almond biscotti in your soy latte, do you automatically judge and assume you're somehow more sophisticated, smarter and better than that person? Could you even start a conversation? Would you care a flip if that person vented to you about having a bad day or made small talk? I've observed too many similar situations living in the deep South that suggest not. In fact, you'd probably move away from that person altogether and send a derogatory text to your friends about that person. You'd be quick to point out that he was weird or intruding on your privacy. Of course, the unsophisticated Southerner is not making any light conversation with you either. Having endured half of my life inthe most segregated portion of America, I believe the new 21st century South is a microcosm of the nation as a whole: blacks, whites, browns, LGBTQ, liberals, conservatives, the young, the old, techies, artists, poor, wealthy, religious, atheists, etc. It is America encapsulated in a rather opaque bubble. The apparent diversity is camouflaged in a deep-rooted white conservative right-winged self-interested value system that is clashing with liberal progressivism and multicultural assimilation. Therefore, the canvas I've had to work with for more than three decades living in Georgia, paints a pretty accurate but grim picture of what America is right now — and more important, where it is heading. It's becoming more akin to a dark surrealist painting by Dali rather than a colorful garden by Monet. Our social behaviors and predispositions are an indication of our larger problems. Once you add color, gender preferences, attire, religion, party affiliation and so forth, the prejudices become even more pronounced and magnified. Instead of smiling at someone who looks and acts different from us, we'll give them dirty looks and make negative assumptions about them. We'll judge people on their accents, instead of being curious about their origins. In due time, we'll make a habit of creating false narratives about people who are different from us. Eventually with the help of social media, we become tribalized and justify our disdain for these outsiders or weird-looking people who don't fit our own profile. In essence, we begin the process of our own undoing by separating and justifying these divisions that weaken us individually and provoke social unrest. And it can start with just one person at the mall who plants the seed of ignorance and discord, or an egotistical person who's self-consumed without any respect for anyone else. We are quick to complain at our neighbor's odd-looking newly planted tree, but fail to look at our own stiff and dying oak tree. Even worse is to contemplate the decline in health and biodiversity of trees in our entire landscape. At the core of this rot is our own unhealed past traumas, open wounds and internal demons that we don't prioritize to address. Eventually, we get proficient at denying the source of our ills and learn to defend our vitriolic symptoms. But why?

UNPEELING THE BANANA

When did we as Americans lose the ability for critical thinking and succumb to such levels of idiocy? Was it a culmination of our societal decline due to our imbalances such as mediocre education, consumerism, greed, workaholism, corporatization, outsourcing, drug addiction, unreckoned racism and so forth? Or have we always been so shallow and stupid, and it simply took a charismatic reality TV star and demagogue to unearth it and throw us over the cliff? If you're like me, you're dumbfounded but not surprised at our decline. Why were Americans more fixated on watching "Living with the Kardashians" reality show, instead of asking why they'd waste their valuable time doing that? Perhaps America loves trash and sensationalism because it can't look in the mirror and deal with its own reality. Often, we are given messages and lessons by smart and powerful people in real life — who we make fun of, but fail to learn from. As an example,

I was saddened more than I was shocked of a respected president getting caught with his pants down during the Bill Clinton/Monica Lewinsky scandal. To me, it clearly revealed an imbalance in his marriage. But most patriarchal-thinking Americans blamed his wife and the young intern, Lewinsky and soon turned the incident into a White House reality/comedy TV show. Men in my gym's locker room were giving the president a thumbs-up pass (as a privileged white man), buying *Monica kneepads* and made fun of it all. Perhaps the narrative in the women's locker room was less sexist, but as we *peel the banana* (pun intended), President Clinton's incident was exposing some hard truths about America. For one, it wasn't the obvious sensationalized dynamic of power, ego or sexism at play, but a more serious issue affecting millions. The Clintons were pointing the mirror of truth at American couples. It revealed the fissures of marriages and relationships due to workaholism and overdriven ambition of both spouses — irrespective of status. The symptoms show up as reduced intimacy behind closed doors, dishonesty, double personalities and infidelity. It demonstrates how people fail to look at their own transgressions and disequilibrium in their own house — but are quick to judge the imbalances and flaws in others. So our biased human values have been disintegrating for a while and how we selectively forgive some and blame others has a lot to do with our own character and self-motivated agendas—that we may hide, but can't run from.

If you're a diehard fan of Trumpism, you must dig deep within yourself to expose the dark truths of your own unhealed past that have made you fragile and fickle akin to a *leaf*-type person. Is your view of the world so narrowly mired in conspiratorial theories that it distorts the truth and facts and blinds you to suit your idealistic reality? Or is it that you're just too gullible and uneducated? Perhaps it's a convenient filter that has you programmed via patriarchy and ancestral behaviors of attachment. Maybe you're justifying living in an alternative universe because you're trapped in the world's most individualistic bubble — and you just don't know it.

BUBBLE TROUBLE

Individualism will definitely germinate scapegoating, and seduce us to play the blame game. Unlike a majority of other countries I've traveled to in the world that practice *collectivism,* where unity and selflessness are valued traits for a common goal, *individualism* is only about the rewards and benefits of the self. It's *me* as opposed to *we.* And it is a pervasive modus operandi in America. But you wouldn't know this fact if you have not traveled overseas. Sadly, many other countries are adopting America's unsavory habits and ideologies, with the *me* movement valuing profit over people. I see this toxic model result in inflated prices and lowered quality of service in many tourist destinations where Americans frequent. Mexico, Bahamas, Costa Rica and Caribbean Islands are good examples of this. On the flip side, there are many more countries in Asia and Africa that don't welcome this philosophy. Therefore, if you're raised in an individualistic country, have never been around the world — and think you're hot sh*t because you're American or emulating to be one, your bubble world mindset will quickly get you in trouble. Especially, if you want to transform yourself from ordinary to extraordinary. Because you'll be viewed as egotistical, spoiled, selfish and so on. That's not a sustainable condition; you are an immovable object facing the irresistible force of mankind's evolutionary progress. Today, we're living in tighter proximity and interdependency than ever before. Therefore, sitting in our little bubbles of individualistic self-interest becomes a self-defeating trap. We're going to have to learn to live with each other, take a two-way street approach and get along. Shining a mirror on our trappings and doing a character autopsy may not be pretty, but it's necessary to our livelihood, not as an idealistic tribe but as a realistic American who is part and parcel of this dynamic experiment called America. It is also humbling knowing that we attract what we are, not what we want. If we only worship someone because they make us money or magnify our dark energies, but do terrible things to our fellow humans otherwise, it will have a negative karmic boomerang effect on our own self. Whatever goes around, comes around. More specifically, those unhealed Souls are likely to attract people who will use us for money and inflict pain and suffering unto us. It's the law of attraction at play and it is an inevitable outcome. So buyer beware — there are no refunds or exchanges with your toxic purchase!

CRAP IS KING

Using his masterful tactics of scapegoating, President Donald Trump, the unhealed and damaged Soul who was voted in by many unhealed and damaged Souls, also cleverly used his bully pulpit to incite conspiracies on half of America with great success. From anarchists, to the conspiracy theories of the white supremacist ideologies of McCarthyism, to the race-bating of the KKK, to the QAnon deep state — the blame game thrives and survives in 21st century America. The QAnon far-right conspiracy theory cult has attracted tens of millions of American followers as distrust of institutions and truth grows amongst the radicalized. Thanks to a divided society and a broken system, it appears Americans love unearthing dirty laundry and feeding the mind with garbage and fabricated lies. It's the prevailing thought that crap is king and the government is the enemy. But the government is us and not some alien entity from Mars. It's the members of our churches, book clubs, titty bars, private enterprise, gyms and so on. It's not a perfect institution, but we need some body of law to balance America's freedumb pendulum. Unless we want anarchy, we need a fair system to keep our greed and laissez faire mindsets in check. The paradox, of course, lies in having a governing institution that is in itself corrupt and usurping its powers and being a watchdog. Perhaps the future of governance lies in a decentralized model led by not just one or two parties, but by a more diversified, more efficient system of structure with agenda-free method of control without doctored influences.

The reality is, that finding fault with others makes people feel less f*cked up about themselves. It's textbook scapegoating. This insatiable appetite for dark and despicable fodder is manifested by disinformation and disseminated freely by the sensational-driven media. It has been fed into our brain for decades disguised as news and freedom of speech, but it's at best *infotainment* and highly toxic for our wellbeing. The pioneer of this trend is the National Enquirer tabloid that started luring Americans with its uncredible crap back in 1926. Today, the internet, cable news and talk radio are its heirs. But *crap is king* more than ever. By fabricating stories and redefining facts for the entertainment consumption of the fragile and the ignorant, these media powers are seducing Americans like never before with the dirt they are digging up on others. Especially on those who are more successful and smarter than them. With the instant expediency of the worldwide internet, those eager to inflict an information war and falsehoods on a particular group of people have never had it so good. Using entertainment, sensationalism and outrageous falsities on AM radio, cable TV, cell phone texts, satellite channels and social media, a weak and fragile brain can be turned into mush quite easily. Imagine what happens to unhealed or ignorant people who are listening to highly opinionated and cleverly packaged talk radio every day on their commute to and from work? It's how people get indoctrinated and often radicalized to the point of no return. Sensational lies get all the attention and go viral across a broad spectrum of demographics. Yet a boring truth goes unnoticed and gets buried in platforms like Twitter or YouTube. It is also a fact that repeated claims of untruths over time become half-truths or full-blown new realities. So when I hold up a banana and tell you it's an apple — and when I repeat this lie enough times — you see the banana as an apple. Your newly adjusted reality is especially compromised when you're sitting in a dark hole of ignorance, desperation and internal rage. Mind control combined with the human emotion of outrage produces an intoxicating condition in the brain that turns dangerously seductive and addictive—and is counterintuitive to our emotional stability.

As an American immigrant and a colored person, it is disconcerting to me to personally witness the veracity of Mr Trump's four year white-lashing of immigrants in America. It's actually oxymoronic and very un-American, if our definition of American is still based on compassion and diversity. I thought I'd escaped the wrath of an African racist dictator as a child — only to revisit his white counterpart's ideologies four decades later. How insane is that. Although the damage done is deep and long lasting, it is my hope that its venom will be more medicinal than it is poisonous. The rebuilding of a nation is not achieved with the same tools used to destroy it. As a nation built by the blood, sweat and tears of immigrants and African slaves (and stolen from the Native Indians), the idea of pitting one race against the other and discriminating on the basis of skin color is a white-colonial mindset that only diminishes America's diversity and greatness. By succumbing to this divisive and racist philosophy, we're all as much to blame as the wounded perpetrators that concoct it. The blame game is in America's DNA and its history is proof of it. Just look at 9/11, the Great Recession and Covid-19, as the most recent examples. It is not a habit that goes away anytime soon. But what is attainable is the notion that both sides of the aisle have a lot more to lose by pointing the finger at each other than at themselves. In alignment with our highest self, it is only by having the wisdom to act like God that we cease to perpetrate ungodly actions against each other.

Chapter Takeaway:

What did this chapter do for you? Inspirations, lessons, comments? Look upon your own choices and actions toward people. Are you quick to blame others? Do you believe everything you see or hear? Could you make conversation with strangers who don't look like you? Take some time here to reflect and jot down anything you would do differently now — and then meditate for a few minutes before moving on.

10
Breaking Out of Our Boxes

"A journey of a thousand miles

begins with a single step"

— Lao Tsu

In order to understand 'ungodly' behavior, we must first understand the various man-made trappings that confine us to some of our human-based predispositions, choices and actions. Using The Healium Way lens, these trappings can be visualized as boxes. But what role do these various types of boxes play in our personal lives and how do we get inside them in the first place? I see these boxes in a rather binary way: one is physical and the other is non-physical or invisible. The physical is the shell we're born in and the planet we live on. We're stuck in both of those for a while so we won't try to change them. Within the realm of the physical box, we sit in smaller boxes, such as our country, town, community and home. Other interior boxes include our vehicles, places of work and so on. Changing some of these physical boxes is necessary for our overall health and is easier to fix than the invisible ones — i.e., relocating, changing jobs, or moving into a different community. But the invisible boxes are the culprit of our many imbalances and woes. Therefore, the invisible boxes are the ones worth investigating, observing and understanding, as they can help us get into a healthier balance of the body, mind and soul. Some of these boxes will be harder to get ourselves out of than others. It's just the harsh reality of life and why we're reminded that we are flawed beings.

THE CREATION AND EVOLUTION OF THE BOX(ES)

How we get inside of these boxes is quite complex but explainable. Some of these are inherited, some are imposed upon us and others we willfully step inside. The moment we exit our mother's womb we are gifted with some pre-set boxes (compliments of our Creator) called DNA and our genetic codes that determine our sex, skin color, intelligence quotient, physique and so forth. Some genes are healthier than others and many are handed down to us through our lineage and ancestors. Although we have little control over them (at least in the year 2021), they do control our behaviors, choices and actions with other non-physical boxes that we get ourselves into. Once we've exited our mother's warm and comfortable box, we enter into another box, the biospheric blue and green box, called planet Earth. During this welcoming period, we unknowingly but surely get thrown into more man-made boxes such as our culture, our family, our traditions, our religious beliefs, our living environment and our economic status. All these boxes have their dogmas, protocols, conditions, methodology and value systems. So before we even have a chance to think for ourselves, we've been placed inside the various physical boxes, all of which see, hear, process and get programmed into our newly formed soft-tissue brain. This spongy organ absorbs everything — good and not so good. It is the king of boxes and more akin to a black box flight recorder on an aircraft — as it is so complex and is mysterious to the user. As we grow, we're thrown into even more boxes: our learning institutions, our interpersonal and communal interactions, social norms, government rules and regulations, our environment and so on. Our boxes are not just inherited from our parents, but they're either imposed upon us by society or self-induced. The societal-imposed boxes are difficult to get out of as they're conditioned with harsh punishment (i.e., going to jail for not paying taxes, getting a speeding ticket, etc). The self-induced boxes are easier to break free from as we get into them willfully without anyone putting a gun to our head. Some we'll walk into as a form of escape from our reality, and some will be to enhance our reality. Examples include social clubs, college fraternities/sororities, country clubs, membership-only groups, neighborhood associations, gender race-specific clubs, social media platforms and online chat rooms. Interestingly, we fool ourselves into thinking that we're improving ourselves by joining these clubs. In truth, most of us choose these boxes as an extension of our pre-programmed beliefs: to confirm our predispositions and justify beingin our preset larger boxes (aka, confirmation bias). Instead of entertaining diverse points of views to grow and expand our mind, we simply dig deeper into our shrunken pigeonholed brain. It's quite fascinating why we do this, but we're all guilty of it.

For instance, If you're an avid gun collector, you're more likely to join hunting clubs and participate in gun shows, rather than be a member of animal anti-cruelty clubs or vegan groups. Over time, our brain is overloaded with so many invisible little boxes that it is incapable of knowing that it is operating from a set of commands predetermined by everyone else, but you.

In many ways, the brain is robotic rather than organic because it is being told what to do, how to do it and when to do it. Therefore, for the most part these boxes by design lend themselves in more ways than not to shape us to be even more imprisoned in our limited thinking. These restrictive boxes are the ones that we need to break out from as much as we can. They can suffocate our growth and reduce our personal power while throwing us off a healthy balance.

Since our goal is to transform ourselves from ordinary to extraordinary, we must therefore look inside and open the Pandora's

Box of all our boxes: our brain. There are a plethora of invisible boxes that sit inside the brain at any given time. We're just not aware of many of them. But what do these boxes look like? For one, they're the nesting kind, a box within a box, within a box... And we sit comfortably in all of these types of boxes throughout our lives. They're instrumental in identifying us, shaping us and guiding us on our life's journey. As a controlling microprocessor, we can surmise that our brain is our ultimate restrictive box that has the power to get us out of our other unhealthy boxes. As a common example, this box houses another rather controversial and restrictive-minded box called religion that's handed over from prior generations. In its development stage, our brain is trained not to question this box in any way, or it faces punishment from the ultimate box maker in charge: God.

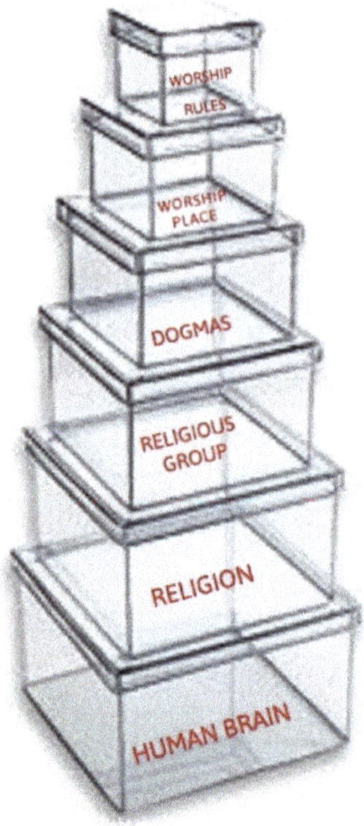

An example of our nesting boxes

THE MOTHER OF ALL BOXES

As I've mentioned before, The Healium Way of manifesting our transformation is by our intention to change. With this intention comes awareness, which is a prerequisite to taking the appropriate set of actions. And taking action is our ticket to self-autonomy and liberation.

By having a broader lens of the particular boxes that we're looking at, we become better observers of our imbalances and myopia. For instance, we start thinking about how stuck we are in our thought patterns in relation to someone else, what kind of filters we build into our boxes to diffuse our higher self and what defense mechanisms we use to justify sitting in them. The one box that effectively breeds all these conditions without fail is religion. In my assessment, organized religion is the mother of boxes. It is passed on to us at birth by heritage and therefore easily absorbs into our unsophisticated brain; it has mass universal appeal; it attaches itself to all races; it has celebratory holidays; it has little or no barriers to entry; it bypasses many government rules and regulations; and it offers to fix and save us all from harm. Holy sh*t … that's an amazing gift box for mankind, isn't it? Well, not really.

So let's remove the gift-wrapping and take a peek inside this box. For one, it's a box constructed not by God — as we're made to believe — but my man. Since man had no clue as to how and why he got here, he had to concoct some explanation. My view is that we were bored stiff and needed something exciting to do. And there was no better way to get stoked than to pick a fight with people who didn't look like us. So we used our free will to judge each others' different skin tones and facial features to define beauty. Our color differences gave us the perfect excuse to form a separation mindset that we called *tribes.* We became proficient at pitting one group of people against the other. But we needed to justify these tribal wars with our maker. Hence, we learned to organize ourselves into larger groups and formed a coalition between mankind and this invisible maker, who we called our Almighty God. Interestingly, this God never showed itself or approved or disapproved of our divisional scheme. But we persisted anyway. As middlemen to this creator, we elected some enlightened Souls to be in charge and sacrifice themselves for the good of our respective tribes. We also figured that people were pretty naive and would pay the tribe a tithe to please this God. And so was born a members-only group (aka, organized religion) or what I call "warriors of separation" across our civilization. Soon we realized that the more rules and restrictions we put on people, the better they behaved and obeyed. Eventually, we got everyone to conform and get indoctrinated to all the rules, by staying inside the restricted fence of the tribal boundaries. We learned to use the coping tools that our God gave us, with our daily imprisoned conformities: *fear, ego, judgment and pretense.* These four hooded horsemen that act as our filters justified our greed and our self- righteousness. We didn't use the weapon of guilt yet, because we wanted the non-members and rebels to carry that burden. Guilt was then complemented with shame, as God's punishment was to torch people in his fiery dungeon if they didn't obey and pay up their fair share of dues. In my view, this is how man cleverly created the organized religion box.

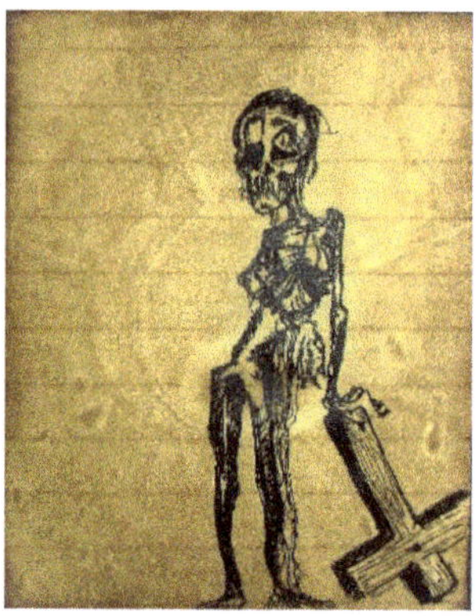

"Crutch"

(Pen on paper) Artist: Haseena Peera

For some people this box provides a security blanket and a sense of community and structure. For others, it is a crutch and a divisive mechanism that suffocates the autonomous self. Whatever your view is, undisputed fact is, man has weaponized religion and killed more people and enriched himself in the name of God, with his preference of beliefs, than any other phenomenon. As we look deeper into this controversial man-made box, we find proof of its nesting character; in that the dogmas, traditions, places of worship, etc. are all smaller subsets of this big box. The third observation of this box is that it is time sensitive. The longer we stay in our boxes, the worse it consumes us in restricting our minds. As a result, the older we get, the more difficult it is for us to break free of our respective trappings. Even worse is the replication of tunnel-visioned behaviors in other areas of our life. Often it has a detrimental effect on people close to us and their offspring. Organized religion by design is a closed-loop bubble of separation. The worship of a specific book, theology or messiah is oxymoronic to the ideals of higher consciousness and unity. On one end, the faith-based teachings promise to bring us peace — and on the other, these teachings succumb to the dark side by destroying the boxes that it doesn't like and justifying wars.

The man-made ideology of division, fear and punishment is counterintuitive to leading a life of authenticity and balance. It breeds all the low-vibrational conditions in our flawed human toolbox. Most of us end up swapping one imbalanced lifestyle with another less destructive one when we join any conventional religious organization. But sometimes it's so subtle that we just don't know it. In the process we give up our self-identity and personal power. We then justify it by congregating in groups and slowly get indoctrinated in our respective tribes. Soon we're ostracizing others who don't think or act like us, and in time we isolate ourselves into our own little box, one that believes it's prettier, smarter, better and more special than the other boxes or anything around it. I've had my share of experiences with this toxic philosophy.

At The Center I recently confronted a yard maintenance person who refused to cut our grass because we housed a church as a tenant. Upon further investigation, I learned that the young man was a deeply indoctrinated Jehovah's Witness who openly despised anything associated with Jesus Christ. Despite my attempts to shine the light on his divisive and hypocritical views and to separate our business from his personal religious beliefs — he double-downed on justifying not servicing my property. When he said that, it reminded me of people who practiced similar ideologies in my own family.

While he was middle-aged, one of my uncles willfully stepped inside of his religious box after experiencing our family's uprooting crisis in Africa. The authorities put him behind bars for a short time to make an example of him, and when he got out, he was demoralized. He double-downed on attending the mosque to find salvation and reclaim his inner peace for himself. But his indoctrination was a trade-off for his loss of individualism and intolerance of other belief systems. I recall a time when he banned us from eating at a restaurant owned by a Sunni Muslim family — a division of Islam that we were programmed to view as inferior to ours and treat with enmity. Once upon a time, my uncle was a progressive, carefree, creative and adventurous man. And then it all faded, as he surrendered his power, his personal freedom and his life to a costly and caustic middleman called organized religion. I'm not sure how happy or at peace he was with himself shifting into that myopic mode, but his blind faith seemed to have sucked the joy and fun out of his life. Sadly, my uncle sacrificed much of his life, family and money defending that proposition. He got increasingly dogmatic and closed-minded until he died in his mid-80s. I saw that as a huge red alert signal in my own family, and decided to take corrective action before I too lost my mojo and walked around with a self-righteous stick lodged in my derriere.

I, like my uncle, was born and raised a Muslim, of a minority Shia sect with esoteric and non-radical views. I had absolutely no choice being in this box as my ancestors were Muslims as far as we can date back. The Islamic religion, like Christianity, is split into many smaller boxes. For one, Allah (Muslim name for God) is separated into two disparate boxes: Sunni and Shia. These hate one another and have destroyed each other's lands and people throughout history. An example of a modern-day Sunni state is Saudi Arabia and a Shia nation is Iran. Like India, with the Hindu religious tribe and Pakistan, these two countries are always hostile with each other because of religion. Within these two types of religious boxes, you have many other boxes separating Muslims even further, to the extent that the walls of the boxes are too opaque to differentiate between the man-made labels. As a Western Muslim, you can get away practicing a watered-down version of the faith by drinking alcohol, smoking and even eating pork. In the Middle East, you will often find the other extreme: radical Muslims praying five times a day, with adherents mutilating themselves with chains on their back. Within this lies another box, a patriarchal method of control and power, and the separation of men and women in prayer and social congregations. Each nested box further dilutes our autonomy as free-thinking individuals. The smaller boxes are able to fit inside the other boxes, and the more opaque the bigger boxes get, the less clarity you have. Hence, the term "blind faith."

THE SPECIAL ONES

Growing up, I followed the more moderate version of Islamic protocols, traditions and teachings. But it didn't matter, the boxes still kept multiplying, physically and invisibly. At school, we were told that our faith and sect was better than any other, as our spiritual leader or Imam, His Highness The Aga Khan, is a direct descendant of the Prophet Muhammad. As a result, we were smarter and more holy than our other Muslim counterparts and any other religions. We were beyond the realm of the "chosen ones" — we were told that we were the "special ones!"

I was too young to decipher or question the validity of this claim, but looking back this should have been a huge red flag. Taken at face value, this separatist and privileged claim is antithetical to the concept of Divine oneness and inclusion. But it's another box I was thrown inside and one of the three *ugly truths* of The Healium Way that we've discussed before. As I got older, I questioned the many preset ideologies and monetary-based memberships that separated people into secret hierarchical clubs. But I never got any satisfactory answers. Apparently, the more you paid, the closer you got to Allah by being indoctrinated into more special and secretive clubs. I am not sure what these member-only prayer clubs did behind closed doors, but the folks coming out of the rooms were tight-lipped and walked around with their noses up in the air. I don't think they realized how self-righteous and stuck up they looked. I just knew I wasn't going to be one of them. I never understood this blind faith ideology, but it seemed to give them a false sense of power and pretentious high status. These folks were making their own self-serving little boxes within this box of faith and seemed to thrive on it.

Each of the boxes further mutated withindifferent mosques, to where each location had its own egotistical clergy, ignoramuses and subjective rules. When I wanted to marry my Asian-looking wife, they imposed on us that she convert to Islam from Catholicism. But because she looked physically different than any conventional Muslim in the mosque, they judged her further, using their patriarchal power to delay her conversion. I saw the box within a box system as divisive — not representative of any Divinity or spirituality. So I voiced my opinions on many occasions. But the more vocal I got, the more I was ostracized for questioning the dogmatic servings, and told to never doubt the authorities or their protocols again. Soon I was tagged as a rebel and troublemaker for asking questions. The elders instructed me to follow the faith unconditionally and obediently, but I couldn't be silenced and doubled down on my queries. The more I pressed on finding answers to many sticking points, the more resistance I got from the clergymen and some members of my family who were also indoctrinated to the fullest. I discovered much ego, superficiality and self-righteousness with the many attendees. Each time I went to get some peace of mind and salvation from the local mosque, the less I felt connected to my God or experienced any spiritual enlightenment. At best, I felt some calm and meditative benefits listening to the various Sufi and Indian chants. But those blissful moments were overshadowed by God-fearing sheeple, who were going through the prayer and motions without even understanding what they were doing. To make things even more interesting, many of the prayers were in Arabic: a language most of the Western community in our sect doesn't even speak or understand.

Unlike most places of worship that allow respectful humans to walk in and visit, our "special" mosques are only for us "special" people and don't allow anyone of any other faith to walk in — let alone pray. Over time, my wife and my kids simply got tired of the ill will and hypocrisy of the sheeple trying to size you up competitively rather than honoring their maker and being God's children. Slowly but surely, we began a systematic withdrawal from organized religion's various restrictive boxes, including our local mosque in Atlanta. We just got sick to the stomach of the pretentious small minds stroking their big egos, judging us and instilling fear in our hearts. It felt great breaking free of the shackles of conventionality and bigotry.

Today, my wife and I pray to our maker in our own way, at our own sanctuary of peace in our home, at our Center or anywhere we are in the world. We do it on our own terms, and it feels great. We consider ourselves to be out-of-the-box spiritual beings, not belonging to any theological boxes or toxic middlemen. We've never felt more at peace with our Divinity, and it doesn't cost us a penny to be close to God. How novel and liberating!

In the Spirit of The Healium Way, let me be clear that I have no ill feelings with a particular religion, sect or mosque or its clergy.

That would violate The Healium Way teaching of practicing non judgment. If organized religion gives you peace and joy without collateral damage to your freedom, personal power and self-autonomy, feel free to stay in that entire box. It's your free will and I'm happy for you. For me, the cost of its trappings far outweighs any benefits. My experience with organized religions have been quite ungodly, and do not fit the beliefs or philosophy of my higher self and Divine consciousness. And it's OK for us to have a difference of opinion and agree to disagree. I also have respect for our religious leader; The Aga Khan, whose selfless dedication, philanthropy and contribution to society in poor and developing countries is worthy of a Nobel Peace Prize.

"God is not about our punishment

We've already done that job to ourselves"

- Jim Peera

THE AMERICAN DREAM BOX

The textbook definition of the American Dream is the belief that anyone, regardless of where they were born or what class they were born into, can attain their own version of success in a society where upward mobility is possible for everyone. This ethos is achieved through sacrifice, risk-taking and hard work, rather than by chance. So in effect that would make me a living example of the American Dream. Yes, it strokes my ego and boosts my self-esteem to say so, but I'm not taking it for granted, I am not self-consumed by it, and I'm spreading its benefit across a larger ecosystem to the best of my ability. Because for me, the American Dream represents much more than making a better living for myself and my family. Rather, it's that I espouse the allocentric way of measuring my blessings— by working to make the world a better place. The American Dream with a healthier balance, if you will, a sustainable condition that has positive cascading effects on others. For many however, this balance is rather challenging given our competitive nature. If appearances and material wealth are the only metrics Americans use to define the dream, then we've boxed ourselves into an unhealthy trap.

Actually, it's even more complex than that. I came to America for its opportunities and freedoms, but soon saw its flip side — a seducing capitalism-based materialistic mindf*ck that pits the *haves* versus the *have-nots* and breeds class warfare. I soon realized that no amount of material possessions and status will fill the void in the Soul to give us joy, contentment and inner peace. Even worse, this hyper-competitiveness takes a toll beyond our own health and wellness by destroying family relationships, friends and careers if we don't practice balance. It's a man-made and self-inflicted metaphorical bubble or box no different than many other such boxes we trap ourselves into.

To be in a box means to be confined in a certain polarized mindset and be willfully or unwilfully trapped, with walls that close in around us. These invisible walls are symbolic of the restrictive-minded and low-energy environment shaping our behaviors in other aspects of our life. In the case of the American Dream, we're fooled into believing that the chase, the grind and the sacrifices of going up the ladder are all worth the price to take us to a place of eternal bliss and fulfillment of our ambitions and better lifestyles. It has become the ultimate measure of our success. But it falsely induces us to act as if we are more special than others, demand privileged treatment and have the arrogance and license to shame and ostracize those who're *not* sitting in our status box. Our illusive reality falsely numbs us with materialism and pretenses that we tightly hold on to, at any cost. So in many ways, the American Dream is a classic example of a box we willfully walk into and justify to stay in, to further separate us from our higher self. Inside this box, there are smaller boxes of more trappings that give us a false sense of security, power and status. The danger of sitting in a box and within its respective boxes is that it not only robs us of our self- autonomy, but throws us off into a healthy imbalance with everything else, which is not in alignment with The Healium Way.

THE MONEY BOX

America is essentially a big box that houses the world's best-known capitalist society (another box, by the way) that contains within it the box of money, which houses within that container other restrictive and low-vibration containers of thought. For me, the concept of money is about financial freedom. It gives you more choices about what to do with your life. It's about having the freedom to do what we want,when we want to and how we want to. In one way, it gives us the power to be our own bosses, not be enslaved to those not in alignment with our values, and to exercise our higher virtues. It also allows us to become owners of assets instead of renters or borrowers. As an underdog, a short and brown-skinned man with a funny accent, having money has allowed me to be respected and be taken seriously. It has enabled me to send my kids to college without incurring debt; to travel to exotic places; to provide an above-average life for my family; to live life on my own terms; and to stay in a healthy balance and contribute positively to society by being altruistic — such as opening The Healium Center. Therefore, when used responsibly, money is a great tool to liberate us in positive ways. But when we're not responsible with it, it can boss us around and have an ugly stranglehold on our wellness. This stranglehold powered by greed, ego and busyness causes harm (on us and others), makes us corrupt and deviates us from our higher self. So the price we pay in accumulating it, managing it and dispensing it, makes for a particularly nasty box.

If we're financially more secure than the average person, there's a false sense of comfort and self-entitlement that stops us from journeying inward and freeing our Soul. Financial success cleverly camouflages our imbalanced reality and gives us a temporary sense of comfort and happiness. Soon, America's infatuation for this box gets filled with pitfalls and unhealthy imbalances. Combined, these boxes can take us into a tailspin of all sorts — risking family, health, friends, career, relationships and so forth. Some of us come to our senses and break out of some of these boxes, but many of us don't. Our country's global reputation has certainly suffered as a result of it. As one taxi driver in India recently told me; *"America's hyper-capitalist model has made it more spoiled, selfish and stupid over time."* And as a result it suffers, I added. How America's perception has changed. Just 30 years ago, I met a taxi driver in Egypt who dreamed of coming to America and envied its freedoms and its smart, generous and innovative citizens: *"I love America. It is my dream country,"* he exclaimed.

THE WORKAHOLIC BOX

So what has tarnished us over the years, and how do we polish it backup? For one, money is a universal man-made trap. Many of us worship it, hoard it, kill for it and succumb to it — falsely believing we'll somehow take it with us when we're six feet under. But what's killing us today is not just the lure of money, but how we're working for it. Specifically, our overworked habits or workaholism, which is another invisible, restrictive box. In some way, money and workaholism are codependent partners in crime.

I know many successful people who are self-admitted workaholics using work as an excuse to cover up relationship problems and not look in the mirror. These people use work as a crutch and a pacifier to hide their underlying problems and get stuck inthe grind. A Brazilian musician I met in Portugal put it succinctly: *"In my country, we work to live. In America, you live to work."*

I couldn't agree more. I became aware of work as an unhealthy self-induced box when I was in my 30s. As a highly ambitious entrepreneur, I pushed myself incessantly and in consequence was hospitalized with a minor heart attack. It was the wake-up call that reminded me of my dad's premature death at just 52 years of age. I began to reprioritize and rebalance my life by not taking it too seriously, working smarter and reducing stress by not competing with anyone but myself. This shift helped me look at life holistically rather than materially. I spent more time with my family, exercised regularly and devoted more time connecting with the arts. My personal goal was to be the best father to my children, the best husband to my wife and the best human being I could be. This was radically in contrast to many of my real estate buddies whose daily mantra was to make as much money and not factor the negative trade-offs for the incessant grind and chase. And many of them have paid a heavy price, such as divorce, ill-health, drug addictions, alcoholism and even suicide. I knew many individuals who went from yuppies to puppies — those who got obsessed with material values and overextended themselves and suffered losses during the Great Recession and the financial crisis of 2008. Their imbalance simply tipped them off a cliff. Luckily (and thankfully) for me, my even-keeled lifestyle and disciplined savings protected me from financial harm. Sadly, many folks never come to grips or get out of their self-induced containers. In many cases, they comfortably box themselves into a routine of their particular profession and don't know what to do with themselves besides their work. I've met such people at our Center who get a jolt out of seeing soulful, middle-aged people come alive and have unconditional fun. In a way, a place like The Healium Center is a reminder to them of manifesting a life outside of their boring and unhealthy grind.

SHINING THE LIGHT

If our path to change comes from awareness, then each of us must remove our blinders and be willing to see each of these boxes for what they are and how they negatively affect us. In order to step out of our trappings, we must first shine a light on them. There's a certain complexity to these various boxes as they are not all separated but codependent. The important fact is they successfully inhabit our brain since we're born and expand in size and volume during our growth into adulthood. On the path to our extraordinary-self, we must identify as many of these low-vibrational trappings, reduce their imposition on us and break out of as many of them as we can. At the very least, we must strip out their worst characteristics, which are in effect the little boxes within these bigger boxes. In order to accomplish this, we must have a strategy to get us the optimum results to identify the boxes and take corrective action to reduce their stranglehold on us.

Stepping out of the boxes

The Healium Way gives us an easy *six-step* method that can be applied to any box as follows:

1. **Have a curiosity about the subject.**
2. **Be aware with both eyes open.**
3. **Observe the box objectively.**
4. **Identify your emotions.**
5. **Visualize the trappings.**
6. **Act to remove the trappings.**

Let's put this method into practice for the above example of the *American Dream* box:

1. **Have a curiosity about the subject.** Set the intention to learn about the subject matter at hand. When you care enough about something, it will care for you. In this instance understand what the American Dream actually means to you. Is it about making a better life for you? Is it about competing with others? How will it change your life to live it or not live it?

2. **Be aware with both eyes open.** Give the subject all your undivided open-minded attention without a myopic lens. By opening both eyes,we get a truer perspective. Do you see it as a two-sided coin with positive and negative attributes? Is this box about status, wealth, power, lifestyle change, altruism or other benefits? Or is it an overrated term without much merit?

3. **Observe the box objectively.** See it for what it is, not what you think it is. By relating to others who are in the box, we can see ourselves in it better. Do you see people you know who sit in this box?

   How happy are they? What do you like or don't like about them? Doyou feel intimidated by them?

4. **Identify your emotions.** What emotions fill you when you imagine yourself sitting in this box. Is it your higher-self ones such as generosity, joy, kindness and empowerment, or lower consciousness ones like anxiety, fear and greed, etc? Or a combination of both types of emotions?

5. **Visualize the trappings.** Looking through your mind's eye, what happens when you remove all the low-energy attributes from this box. Feel the difference in your heartbeat, temperature and breathing, as you throw out the dead weights of these negative emotions. How much better do you feel without them? Do you feel less pressure to compete or measure up?

6. **Act to remove them.** Now that you know what the subject matter is, what it does for you and its pitfalls, you're ready to take action and visualize yourself *without* these trappings. These low-energy elements housed in the smaller nested boxes do not serve you. In this particular case, you can still be on your path to pursuing the American Dream(the bigger box, that is), but you have now identified all of its trappings better. Now you are in a better position to know how to

manifest a healed and balanced version of the American Dream and how to maintain it by not being self-consumed by it and even seeing being altruistic within it.

The above steps are how we get to a healthier balance for our overall wellness. This method can be used in identifying any boxes that you want to remove from the bigger boxes. Many of our earthly trappings can be undone in this way. We must also believe that we are a powerful creative being, capable of overcoming any problems and getting out of anything we trap ourselves into.

Obviously, these boxes don't just exist in America, they exist all around the world. As an example, one could easily argue how many boxes exist in Eastern cultures, with their various dogmas and restrictive/ separatist patriarchal rules for women and intolerance for looser Western values. As we look at our own Western model, we see how its more liberal values have given us empowering movements for women and black people and also abortion rights, legalization of alcohol, cannabis and gambling, the plight of runaway capitalism and so on. Not all of these man-made things or permissible conditions make for a better society. If we look objectively, we find how all these freedoms are relative and subjective depending what demographic you fit in. Indeed, what seems like a restrictive condition in one part of the world is not one in another. And vice versa. This difference in our opinions, tolerances and choices therefore makes it more difficult to decipher what boxes are more harmful for us. Some boxes that restrict us also protect us, and are beneficial to society, such as some government laws, regulations and various public institutions. Others, such as paying taxes, are impossible to escape. So we suck it up and accept that as a way of life.

The good news is we have common sense, logic and critical thinking available to us. They help us make better decisions to take corrective actions and help us get out of the boxes that we do have control over.

In other words, I won't tell you what boxes you need to get out of. You'll need to put your thinking cap on and figure that out yourself.

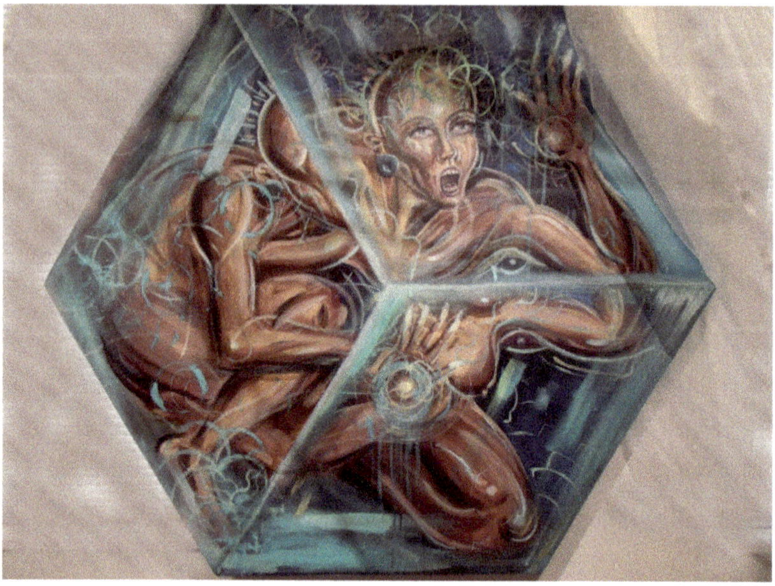

"Breakout"

(Acrylic on Canvas). Artist: Miguel Dominguez

Interactive Exercise:

Spend a few minutes interpreting the painting called 'Breakout' created for Healium by artist Miguel Dominguez.

What emotions do you feel when you look at it? Can you relate to it? Do you see the box as an attachment to a dead-end job, a bad relationship, loss of power, unhappy marriage, ill health, etc.? What part of yourself is in the box — the anxious and curious one in front or the hesitant one in the back? Put yourself in the box and looking from the inside out, what do you see outside of this glass box? Is there a better and more joyful version of you? Or do you see other people? Considering the bigger picture, how do you see yourself in relation to what's out there? What form of enlightenment is outside of this box? Are you feeling disconnected from that light at all? If so, why? On a personal level, do you see this box as a self-induced prison or a society-created confinement?

Do you want to break out of this box? Are you courageous and ready? Or are you afraid that breaking out would be too difficult and risky? A key component of this exercise is to ask: *Am I capable and as powerful as I can be to get out of any trapped environment?* Your answer may reveal a lot about yourself and lies in prodding deeper and being honest about your true intention.

Ask yourself these three questions:

1. **Have you given your power away by knowingly or unknowingly outsourcing it to others?**
2. **Do you feel disconnected from your true self?**
3. **Are you living a life that is in a healthy balance?**

Your first gut feeling will give you the most honest answer. But if you are struggling with any of these questions, you are not alone. Most people have not given much thought to these three hidden underlying factors of our modern-day ills. Interestingly, you know when you're operating from inside a certain box because you manifest many of its symptoms, such as loneliness, depression, anxiety, lack of self-esteem, obesity, greed, cruelty, etc. All of these symptoms are self-induced and therefore can be reversed by self-correcting.

THE AQUARIUMS

The Healium Way of perceiving these low-vibrational conditions is to understand that the boxes we've trapped ourselves inside are glass containers, akin to aquariums, not concrete tombs. This is a critical point. The former type gives us hope and possibility necessary for our transformation. We know many of our boxes are not permanent jail sentences, because in our subconscious unfiltered mind we can see the better, the extraordinary and the more enlightened versions of ourselves. We may be flawed beings, but we're not doomed. We're quite clear on that. Where we get opaque and f*cked up is by our own myopic lens and egotistic mindset. As we remove the blinders, the resistances and the veils of our self-defeating trappings, we know that there's a better version of us inside somewhere. Therefore, there's hope in raising our own bar and operating in a higher consciousness within ourselves. We also have clear evidence in our history of mortals who became enlightened and truly extraordinary: these *roots*-type humans include The Apostles, Buddha, Jesus Christ, Prophet Muhammad, The Dalai Lama and many other Divine examples. By their own volition, they were imperfect beings who had to work on getting to that level of extraordinary condition. But what does extraordinary really mean in the context of The Healium Way?

THE SHIFT TO *EXTRA*ORDINARY

Extraordinary is not the same as *extra*ordinary, especially in the context of The Healium Way. The word '*extra*' in extraordinary is the main differentiator and it helps refine its meaning. It is why the entire word can mean different things to different people depending on how we use it. As a Latin word that means "outside" or "beyond." It becomes easier to understand its relevance and importance in The Healium Way. But it can be misinterpreted. The truth is, the vast majority of us are not going to be the embodiment of truly enlightened and exceptional beings mentioned above: the truly extraordinary. So although we look up to these exceptional humans in high regard and adulation, most of us mortals do not have the discipline to have the light shine upon us and not be blinded by greed, power and other man-made low-vibrational attachments. Therefore, we must be careful to not emulate these rare humans and feed our egotistic beast, as it will falsely make us feel special and superior. There are a lot of people who don't get this memo and eventually self-destruct in their pursuit of wannabe prophets, messiahs and false Gods. Human history is full of evidence of this man-made trap. The more sustainable option is to not strive for that high level of exceptionalism or even look for those qualities in people. What is more realistic is to simply step outside the parameters of being ordinary, predictable and conventional. It is about focusing on doing and being the *extra* in the ordinary. In this way, the *extra*ordinary person goes the *extra* mile and the *extra* step beyond the ordinary in their dealings with people.

The *extra*ordinary person strives at all times to be *extra*-kind, *extra*-generous, *extra*-compassionate, *extra*-creative, *extra*-courageous, *extra*-loving, *extra*-peaceful, *extra*-logical and *extra*-everything that is good! This type of condition is consistent with a *roots*-type individual, who operates at a higher vibrational sphere of energy.

WHAT'S WRONG WITH ORDINARY?

Being ordinary is also not so much about being boring, irrelevant or financially strapped, because it's not a metric of temporary happiness or economic status. I translate ordinary to mean mediocre. In The Healium Way of seeing ourselves, we want our life to be much broader than settling for mediocrity. We want our life to be more in alignment with our higher consciousness and the vitality of the universe, which embodies beauty, expansion, adventure, radiance and energy — as opposed to being stagnant, monotonous and lifeless. When we're operating in a low-vibration mode, it seduces us into being comfortable with our malaise. This malaise leads to our attachment to the many unhealthy boxes that encapsulate our ordinary self. It doesn't take much to push this type of ordinary individual into unethical behaviors such as hurting, screwing, knocking, hating and destroying others — rich or poor, weak or strong. It's a lot easier stealing money than it is putting in the effort to make it honestly and with integrity. It's also a lot harder to make money the legal way than to monetize what you're selling illegally. When we are desperate or destitute as individuals, we'll easily sink into a dark hole without remorse or concern for others.

For example, a powerful person who uses his authority to incite mayhem on people for the sake of control or more power, is quite an *ordinary* individual. As is any person who hacks into another person's bank account to steal money for fun or revenge, or a billionaire who preys on the poor. These are all ordinary people in The Healium Way definition, even if they're masterful in attracting masses of people to follow them on social media, are wealthy or smart. We have to apply the same moral standard to all types of people, even those who are conventionally successful. In order to strive for our *extra*ordinary self, we must not be afraid to explore the possibilities that exist outside the conventional wisdom and ordinary conditions. This shift of operating from our higher selves doesn't happen in a vacuum or a push of a button — it happens incrementally and gradually with practice.

Not all ordinary people will be unhealed, but I know from experience that most *extra*ordinary people are more healed than not. The art of being *extra*ordinary is therefore not so much about reaching a particular destination, as it is about the intention, effort and action toward that worthy goal. It is the cornerstone of The Healium Way Principles and part of our daily transformational regimen. So understand it well if you want to operate your life from a higher vibrational Divine-inspired condition.

Knowing that this unknown but powerful force of creation is the embodiment of oneness and unity with the all-loving, all- encompassing, all-inclusionary, all-compassionate, all-powerful characteristics, one must ask why we're constantly doing stupid and self-defeating things to ourselves? Why do we choose to deviate from our maker's highest value system? Why don't we try to get closer to these virtues without infecting them with our man-made agenda- based toxins of greed, ego, envy, competition, dishonesty, divisions and so on?

Perhaps looking at some examples of our unhealed-selves in action, may awaken and inspire us to ditch our self-induced toxic boxes.

MR. ROGERS IS NOT HAPPY

As a society that is quick to pull triggers on symptoms but is slow to diagnose its underlying causes, we Americans are constantly in a state of repair. The more interesting revelation is to consider how most people in the wealthiest countries have self-sabotaged their lives and fallen prey to an unhealthy imbalance of the body, mind and soul, relinquishing their own power to others and being disconnected from their own truth. Tragically, many people don't even know it. Many of us are simply too busy making a living and providing for our families to take the necessary time to operate from a higher state of being. In other words, we're not even aware that we're sitting inside a trapped environment. Unless there's a medical emergency or loss of a loved one, most ordinary folks are on life's hamster wheel, grinding away without time to heal themselves until it's too late. Having lived in the West for most of my life, I've witnessed the casualties of its many trappings. Beside the previously discussed *American Dream* box, one of my biggest pet peeves is the *Keeping up with the Joneses* tendency; to compare oneself against the benchmark of neighbors in matters of social class. This trapping is a good example of the superficiality and fragility of the many boxes we put ourselves into. Today, though, we're not even talking to the Joneses, or the Steins or the Patels on our block. Our competitive model coupled with our busy lifestyles have shut us off from engaging with our neighbors altogether. Sadly, the days of neighborly interaction and starting new friendships that way are behind us. The only time we become "neighborly" is in moments of imminent crisis or inclement weather conditions and disasters. We've conveniently turned ourselves into a nation of transactional acquaintances. We don't have time to be nice, courteous, friendly or make small talk. It's all about getting to business, and even that is usually not face to face. It's a pity because we've boxed ourselves into our own egos and hotheads even more than the days of *keeping up with the Joneses*.

In the last two decades we've gone from Fred Rogers' "*Won't you be my neighbor*" America to "*Stay off my yard or I'll blow your head off!*" America. In those more innocent days of Mr. Rogers, a ring on our doorbell meant a visit from friendly guests, neighbors and at its worst; pushy Jehovah's Witness recruiters. Today, the doorbell-ringers are cops, crooks and your local code enforcement officer. My next-door neighbor actually called the code enforcement authority instead of talking to me about an ongoing puddle of water in my backyard.

What's up America, don't we even have the social etiquette or courage to knock on a neighbor's door to discuss any concerning issues anymore? Are we so socially inept or afraid to talk to strangers? All the guy had to do was come knock on my door and express his concerns. But he was either too fearful to approach me, too fragile in the mind, too withdrawn as a person, or he had some other issue. His behavior is not excusable and definitely not an anomaly. In a second example, a neighbor was outright hostile and ready to blow my head off. I bought a beautiful piece of land in the North Georgia mountains overlooking a river to build a vacation home and rental cabins. But unbeknownst to us, our family was not welcome in this highly racist redneck town. While I was playing with my little kids in the river, the neighbor across the river stood atop a rock and fired his rifle into the water a few times to scare and intimidate us. "*This ain't your side of the water. It's mine. You folks ain't welcome down here!*" he shouted. My little kids were traumatized and never wanted to visit the property or that town again.The excitement of building a quaint mountain retreat quickly faded and diminished the more I visited that area. The town and its people soon revealed their true colors and gave me nightmares akin to the famous dueling banjos scene in the movie "Deliverance". Perhaps that man did us a favor! I quickly put that property on the market andsold it a few months later.

In both these cases, fear and ignorance of new or unfamiliar people propelled their toxic behaviors. Whatever the reason, we're withdrawing and depersonalizing each other more than ever. We put up more fences, buy more guns, install security cameras and domesticate guard dogs to alienate us from people — particularly those we don't understand or look like us. We conveniently retreat into pricey condo towers and gated country club communities that further separates us in tribal fashion. How far have we drifted from the basics of common courtesy and common sense in just a few short decades? Mr. Rogers is probably turning in his grave right now!

MISSED OPPORTUNITY

Both the above unneighborly experiences are good examples of ordinary beings. Those guys were sitting comfortably in their respective boxes and were confined to their low-vibrational versions of themselves. They did *nothing* to change their pre-conditioned mindset. They could have done *something,* such as refraining from making judgments about my family, taking the time to talk to us, or simply not unleashing their respective vitriol. How things would have turned out different and better for both sides. All options would have required some *extra* work and effort on their part, however. As a result, it was a missed opportunity for their transformation into *extra*ordinary versions of themselves. And in hindsight, it fermented a 'coulda, shoulda, woulda ' situation from our perspective.

Although many of our boxes may not be as easy to get out of due to our own rigidity, cultural norms, ancestral programming, and other predispositions, The Healium Way allows us to look at possibilities outside our existing reality by incrementally reducing the trappings that restrict our personal growth and power — and by layering the Principles that will be outlined in the later chapters. First though, we must try to take incremental steps out of our smaller boxes. For instance, you can still seek salvation through one religion,but be open to educating yourself about forms of spirituality such as Buddhism, Shamanism, Rastafarianism, etc. By gaining knowledge on a broader spectrum of beliefs, you begin to open your mind in other areas of your life too; such as loosening your grip on patriarchal control in your own family, not hating people who don't worship like you, respecting nonbelievers and gays, and so on. Eventually, you'll step out of the many conformities that do not serve you, and make friends outside of your rigid sphere. These are some practical ways in which you can step out of your comfort zones or boxes. This is not about converting you or imposing on your faith, culture or beliefs, but rather showing you other possibilities outside of your shrunken world.

Our next goal is to uncover the convenient cover that we've been hiding under for a long while, so we can rediscover what we've been missing. This uncovering piggybacks on the box metaphor by going into the subject of "personal power" in more detail. One of the most challenging aspects of this new objective is to launch yourself on a difficult inward journey to see how you've slowly disempowered yourself, not just by being inside many boxes but by succumbing to our *trade-offs.* Most important, I will demonstrate how to empower yourself, first on an individual basis, and second on your relationships with others. In the following chapters we will explore our disempowering relationship with others and how the arts can actually help us recover to feel more in control and, ultimately, be self-autonomous.

11
THE UNCOVERING

Have you felt afraid of standing up for yourself? Is it difficult for you to make hard and important decisions? Do you look at other people to lift you up? Are you always living in the shadow of others? Do you feel your voice does not matter? Do you have a difficult time speaking your mind to others? If you answered "yes" to any of these questions, you are experiencing a common problem that is undermining your ability to be courageous, take risks and be at your highest potential. It is the self-induced cover-up of losing your own power to others. This is not power for the sake of control, greed, corruption or destruction, but rather the soft, personal, invisible and spiritual power that resides within each of us. It is an energetic force that guides, protects and strengthens us as Divine beings. It's important that we understand how to uncover our unhealthy patterns of behavior that are constantly disempowering us with our own self-defeating ways. Once again, it all relates to having a healthier balance of power rather than having one party call the shots in a relationship.

THE CONUNDRUM

No matter how well we think we're doing career-wise with the respective labels that define us, we're probably losing some sense of our personal power unknowingly to others. It's all to do with our trade-offs, which for many of us is a conundrum. Many of us are too afraid to uncover the layers and layers of habits and programming that has us held hostage to our own true identity and higher self. For some, it's a pattern of behavior from our childhood that grows like a cancer that we don't get until it begins destroying our self-esteem, self-worth, self-power, self-identity andultimately self-love. The reality is we're only as good as what risks we are willing to take to initiate this uncovering. The reward is an authentic, blame-free, well-grounded and powerful you. This is thepayoff. But in order to remove all the obstacles that weaken us, we need to shed the dead weights of our man-made ways that justify our resistance to change. Moreover, we need to understand how societal-bred conditions weaken us and inhibit our ability to empower ourselves. As innately powerful beings, we can either use our power for our own benefit or to our own detriment.

But we must be very careful not to give it away. Sadly as adults, most of us simply relinquish it without much thought. We go from empowered spiritual beings to a disempowered man-made version of something or somebody else. Indeed, we are all guilty of surrendering our power at some point in our life. I will give examples that show how we fall into self-defeating traps in culture, dogma, societal norms and addictive habits, similar to the examples discussed in the boxes metaphor. Now, though, these traps have us on the one hand voluntarily engaging in the act of building our personal power while simultaneously relinquishing it. This conundrum has us pay a price that is quite heavy and can paralyze us and run the risk of redefining relationships, families, communities and countries for generations. We've grown so comfortable outsourcing our power to others that many of us have become sheep and robots in return. Often, we do it without much thought in the workplace, at home and in social settings. Sometimes it's an evil necessity to get us the desired results. However, these trade-offs that we make on a daily basis have destructive boomeranging side effects.

Consider the typical example of how women use their beauty and often sex to weaponize their bodies as a means to combat gender inequality at work. It's a quite common occurrence in male chauvinistic corporate America. I've observed it from the perspective of women who express its toll and toxicity through art at The Center. They frequently reveal a disempowering exchange or trade-off. On one hand the woman believes she's empowering herself by her mutual exchange, but she is unknowingly creating a problem — disrespect and distrust of herself, which devalues her character and self-worth, that in turn decreases her personal power in other aspects of her life. Similarly, we're always outsourcing our power by our dependence on and allegiance to our government leaders. We feel empowered by voting for them but quickly disempower ourselves by absolving our civic responsibilities, attaching too much faith in their promises and blindly following their orders and rhetoric. It is only when the elected officials fail to do their jobs to our expectation, that we realize our unhealthy over-dependence on them.

In the latter example, this dichotomy clearly manifested during the Covid-19 pandemic as America failed due to lack of leadership in its race to combat the crisis. The ship's elected captain steered the U.S. ship so poorly and recklessly in the global crisis that people in local communities took control of their own tugboats before they too cracked and sank. It is as if the virus became a mirror and a lesson for people to wake up and become involved in their own destiny — not to have blind faith in any elected leader(s) or government institutions. Outsourcing our power has dire consequences for our overall well-being in many ways. For one, it is a form of imbalance that permeates into other areas of our lives like a domino effect. For instance, a person who worships a guru or is fanatical about a particular group or belief system will mimic that polarized servant/master behavior by being either subservient or authoritarian at work or at home. In both cases it's an unsustainable condition that ends up in broken relationships and loneliness, or both. This inability to honestly look at ourselves through a lens of truth takes us off the hook from our own duties and responsibilities in all areas of our life. How we consciously or unconsciously disempower ourselves in our daily lives has a direct effect on how we relinquish our power as a group or society as well.

Is it possible that our choice to lose our power is to win over others' approval and fit in? Or is it due to our cultural norms, ancestral programming and patriarchal conditioning? I believe it is a combination of all of those reasons, because the subject of losing our own power is quite complex from a social science perspective.

MASK OF THE DAY

Quite often this loss of personal power is situational and necessitated in exchange for giving up your identity and wearing a fake social, metaphorical mask. Take for instance how so many of us have to wear what I call our *mask of the day* on a daily basis to survive. In most cases it exists in a social setting, personal relationship, learning institution or at work. I saw it a lot in Alabama, where black people would dress, act and behave white to fit in with their segregated environment. I was guilty of doing that myself when I first arrived in America, trying to have an American accent, wear American clothes and have American mannerisms. It was a survival technique not to draw attention to myself and to blend in with my surroundings. During the many nine-to-five jobs she had in her 20s and 30s, my wife was also a great example of putting her social mask on in her various positions.

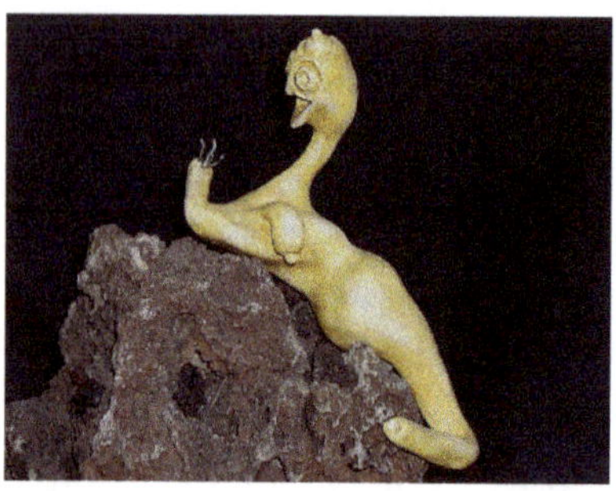

"Untitled"

For YOUR interpretation!

Hint: It's to do with loss of power

(Clay on Rock)

Artist: Jim Peera

I recall when she worked for a Jewish organization, she hid the truth that she was married to a Muslim man and had converted to Islam. I know from the tribal and closed-mindedness of her bosses, that had she revealed that tidbit of personal information on her job interview she would have not been hired. But since neither of us were that religious anyway, the uncovering was not necessary. It was too risky to test it out. As struggling newlyweds, we simply couldn't afford losing her job. Fortunately for us, although the mask was never removed, it didn't have any collateral damage or disempowering effect on our freshly new marriage. On the other hand, I had a different experience while studying to be a fashion designer in the early 1980s. In this example I wish I had a metaphorical mask to wear, but I couldn't for obvious reasons. Almost every male in that fashion institute including the teachers were gay. There were only two heterosexual males in my class, and I was one of them. The other guy and I bonded immediately as minorities in a class of mostly females and gays. The first few weeks were quite discomforting for both of us as we'd get ostracized by the gay students and get weird looks from the females; "*Are you guys really serious about being in fashion design?*" or "*Are you sure you're in the right class?*" were the prevailing reactions. We even got ridiculed or ignored when we presented our homework in front of the class. At one point, we both looked at each other and thought maybe we were pursuing a career in the wrong industry. But it was too late, we'd paid a lot of money to be there and we had to make the best of it. We had no covers or masks to hide behind and had to tough it out by proving ourselves and working harder than others. And we did. Over time we earned everyone's respect by producing critically acclaimed collections, and it didn't matter whether we were gay or straight. We all mattered equally and kept our self-autonomy without trading off our personal power. In the ensuing three years in the fashion industry, I had some of the happiest and most rewarding times of my life, designing, pattern making, sewing and dressing beautiful women from L.A. to London and Paris.

I created some pretty amazing haute couture and matching

accessory jewelry and belt collections that still turn heads today.

I called my fashion company Status Sphere:

Jim's designs modeled by wife, Donna. (Los Angeles, 1984)

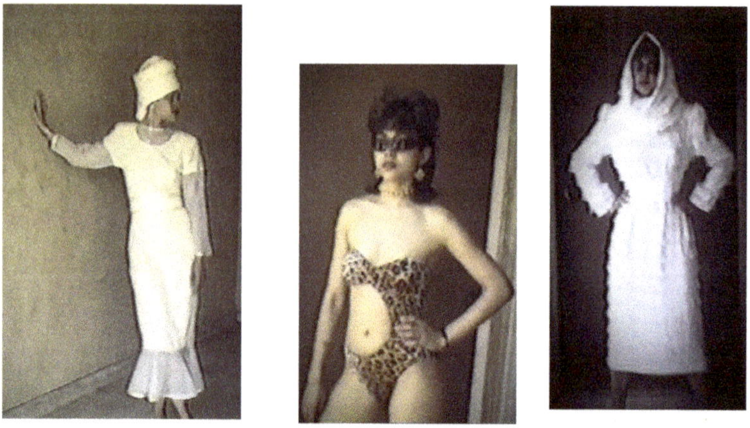

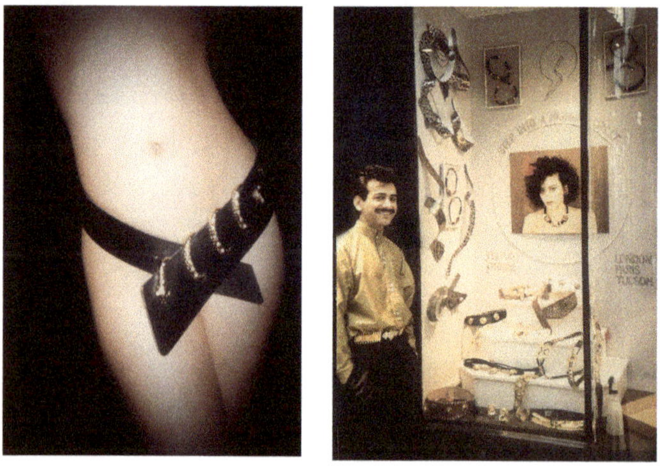

Jim with his jewelry and accessory collection. (London, 1985)

HONESTY IS SUCH A LONELY WORD

In both of these personal cases, there was no loss of individual power or lasting damage during the cover-up. But that's not always the case. Most typically destructive is when this phenomenon exists in intimate relationships and marriages. Indeed, a disempowering relationship can be allowed to grow like cancer for years without being fixed and can spread into other generations too. By convenience, culture, fear or a handful of other reasons — one or both spouses choose to live in a matrimonial container of hell by not being open and true to each other from the onset. *"Honesty is such a lonely word. Everyone is so untrue,"* the words of musician Billy Joel's song have never been so valid and haunting. Because covering up the truth has become our modus operandi in order to avoid conflicts and retain our positions of power. I've seen the condition of dishonesty and mistruths exist in many relationships. Even so-called long marriages are hollowed out on the inside but stay conveniently functional on the outside. In long marriages, the stiff and old covers are usually difficult to remove because both spouses have either lowered expectations for themselves to keep their sacred vows or function unhappily in a lie or fear of the other. More often it's a marriage of convenience or agenda. Without raising the bar too high, it's a mindset of fulfilling some basic minimum needs for each spouse. In a traditional marriage, that bar is reached quite easily. For a woman, that minimum is usually finding a man who can be a good provider. For a man, it's finding a woman to bear children and be a good homemaker. Having a spouse who's able to provide more than those basic requirements and not experience friction or infidelity is rare. In both cases, we're still conforming to the whims of a *man's world* society. I've seen marriages in my own family where a woman's role is diminished by losing her power to a man (from a military or strict patriarchal background) where she is held hostage in her pretentious, dysfunctional glass box. Often, she has anxiety attacks and faces emotional bullying due to her own self-captivity to an unhealed man, who uses his temper, manipulation, money, power and control as a convenient defense cover. If this imbalance is not readjusted, over time each spouse will enable the other and justify their covers to suit their agendas. In new marriages, the uncovering can get complicated if both partners are working and have little quality time to spend with each other. The truth bucket gets kicked even further down the road while mutual trust dims.

I've seen many of my friends who lead a double life, wearing a suitable mask at home to please their spouse but manifest their displeasure by overworking, drinking or cheating until the relationship erodes. In this situation, it's imperative before a child is brought into the mix as a distraction that this couple remove their respective masks, lay out their unhealed trauma and come clean. If not, you sow the seeds of an unhappy relationship that manifests in infidelity, loss of self-esteem,job loss, divorce, mental instability and so on. It's a nasty domino effect that sucks out the Soul that most people never recover from. In many cases, it repeats itself in the next generation of children. This weakened state and deviation from our own true self eventually destroys us from the inside out.

Whether you are a victim of domestic violence, bullying, sexual abuse, racism, workplace discrimination, arranged marriage, etc., you've made some trade-offs and tasted loss of power — and it's not a pleasant feeling. But you *have* the ultimate power to either fix it or break out of the self-induced box you put yourself in. It is never too late. You are an empowered being with your self-charging power generator box. So act like it and reclaim your personal power and self-identity. In my own marriage, I saw this train wreck coming at the onset when I began mimicking the ancestral and cultural patriarchal control on my 19-year-old virginal wife. I noticed my habit of wanting to control every aspect of her life and I quickly made a U-turn before it suffocated our relationship and disempowered both of us. By not being under my thumb or silenced by me for my own selfish reasons, she found her independent voice and blossomed to her full potential. And so did our marriage. Today, we have mutually empowered our relationship by respecting one another, listening and communicating more, giving each other freedom to express our opinions and not being afraid to disagree with each other. We're each other's best friend, lover, therapist, critic and soulmate. We've worked hard to get to this point and are truly blessed to have a healthy balance. Because being yanked into an unhealthy imbalance is dangerous. I've seen stories of male acquaintances who've allowed a woman to totally control all aspects of their marriage and become subservient to the point of being kicked out of their own home and sleeping in their car in a domestic dispute. And vice versa. It's a recipe for a disastrous relationship. For me, it's more about respect and responsibilities rather than power. As long as my wife respects my decisions and handles her responsibilities well, I am happy with that dynamic. I'm open and true with what I like — and so is she. It's a win-win condition when we take a mutually beneficial approach. Decisive acts such as this, not only stop the formation of an unhealthy behavior cycle in marriages but they diminish its spread onto the next generation. This is the power of facing our destructive habits with truth, courage and honesty.

Is it possible then to impart some hard truths to uncover the metaphoric lid we've put on ourselves? This lid that has us trapped in our own self-inflicted bubble actually weakens our ability to cope, connect and heal at the expense of a life of joy, purpose and balance. Now is the time to remove the veils of denial and to reassess the various roles you're playing on your life's stage. Is it all a momentary harmless act to please those around you? Is it a situation necessitated by keeping a boss or spouse happy? Or has your act become your reality — a real-life horror movie that is eroding your personal power?

In the next chapters, I will relate more loss-of-power stories from my personal experiences and elaborate on creative solutions that you can take advantage of to address your own situations of disempowerment.

Chapter Takeaway:

What did this chapter do for you? Inspirations, lessons, comments? Draw upon your own uncovering towards people. Are you comfortable being you, or do you automatically put a convenient cover on at work, in public, etc.? Take some time here to reflect and jot down what you would do differently now — and then meditate for a few minutes before moving on.

12
PUTTING ALL YOUR EGGS IN ONE BASKET

No matter how well you think you're steering yourself on this wild ride called life, one thing is for certain: We are at best a co-pilot.

On any given day, our aircraft captain is an invisible higher force who holds many surprises for us. Some show up as beautiful blessings, and others as ugly curses. On one particular day in the spring of 1970 when I was 9 years old, this Divine power planned a head-scratching event for our entire family. Although it was a man-made calamity, it was a moment in our family's history that we definitely saw as a curse and an unprecedented nightmare.

We were uprooted from our homeland of Tanzania and sent on a one-way ticket to any strange land that would accept us. Our once-beautiful country known for its world-famous wildlife safaris and Africa's highest peak, Mount Kilimanjaro was suddenly ripped from us. It became an ugly, dark place and now those idyllic days of the past are a distant memory. A black populist movement championed by a despot named Idi Amin formed an insidious plan that would make America's white supremacists celebrate in awe. This diabolical, unhealed madman who ruled Uganda, wanted the neighboring East African countries exclusively for black Africans, and expelled others, including the rich, educated and entrepreneurial brown-skins like us. We were seen as a formidable threat to their race and sovereignty — akin to how Hitler perceived the Jews.

But we were spared our lives in exchange for being stripped of all our assets and dignity. We should have read through the tea leaves when they coined us East Indians *The Jews of Africa.* With a swift heavy hand, the authoritarian governments of the three East African countries — Uganda, Kenya and Tanzania — selectively nationalized thousands of Indian families' properties without warning. Once a British-colonized country, formerly known as Tanganyika, this newly independent country turned a blind eye to five generations of East Indians who had been brought by the English from India as slaves to build Africa. My father was one person who took that Indian diaspora on the chin. And for good reason.

My dad was an ingenious entrepreneur and visionary who was born in a dirt-poor family in Zanzibar, a beautiful island off the mainland of Tanzania. He worked his butt off, sacrificed, stayed creative, took risks and built a formidable empire 20 years later. He went from selling empty Coca-Cola bottles to sailors on British ships to selling stamps, to becoming a millionaire filled with adulation and respect in his birthplace and homeland. But his success was short-lived. Fate would have it that our entire livelihood as we knew it was shattered without any advance warning. My father trusted the leaders and their governance so much that he had put *all his family's eggs in one basket* without a fallback position. When the authorities came out to seize all our assets, we were caught off-guard and lost everything we owned without recourse. I can't imagine my dad's state of mind and pain of being betrayed by the same leaders he befriended and given gifts of precious Tanzanite stones from my family's mine.

Legend has it that my family gave Julius Nyerere (Tanzania's president at the time) with a 400-carat Tanzanite gift in the late 1960s (worth about $1 million today). But none of that mattered. As the youngest child of five siblings, I remember the trauma of being rushed into a plane in Africa and only hours later landing on a tarmac in Paris, France. The only sentimental item I carried with me was a white Porsche toy car in a handbag, a gift my brother had picked up for me in England. Unknown to me, my uncles and parents took the extreme risk of hiding precious gemstones in our travel baggage and underwear. It was all quite scary and surreal for a short, slinky kid who'd left his friends, pet monkeys, tortoises, and African grey parrots behind forever. We had just gone from a country that no longer wanted us, to a strange land where we had to start all over again. Sadly, my father's health was never the same after losing everything he had built for his family.

COULDA, SHOULDA, WOULDA

In this segment I will attempt to show how a blind faith attachment to one country, leader or person is a common mistake many of us make that results in our own loss of power. In this case it is a lesson from my dad and my mom. The two years I spent with my dad in Paris were my best memories of him. Soon after, I was sent to a boarding school in England and I saw a lot less of him except on summer vacations. On one particular summer trip in 1974, as I entered our apartment in Paris, he told me how proud he was of my good grades in school. My mom had me sit on his lap for what seemed like an eternity. I sat shyly with my red report card in my hand and we chatted and bonded like never before on a red velour-cushioned black armchair. He never looked happier, as he hugged me tightly and told me how I made him so proud. Until then, my dad had never shown his affection openly or complimented me on any of my achievements. In fact, he was a perfectionist who was quite hard on all of his children. So for him to display that rare gesture of admiration was mind-blowing for me. That memorable moment is embedded in my brain forever, as it would be the first and last time I'd sit on my dad's lap.

As a surprise gift to themselves, my parents had planned a month -long trip to see my brothers in the U.S. About a week into their trip, my dad developed a sudden brain aneurysm a few minutes after he fell asleep. My mom recalls how on that night he was partying, dancing, cracking jokes, and had never seemed happier. Interestingly, he removed his watch and packed it into his suitcase right before he went to bed. He'd never done that, according to my mom. "*It was as if he knew his time was up,*" she would later say of that ill-fated night. Tragically, his case was fatal. Within 48 hours, the doctors pronounced him brain-dead and soon the decision was made to pull the plug. He was only 52 years young. The heartache and anxiety from the African calamity killed him. I was in Paris when I received the news of his death. I was shocked, distraught and traumatized as any 14-year-old son who loved his father would be. Somehow, I knew our family was never going to be the same. As the main provider and leader of our large close-knit family, the tragic loss of my father shook the community and devastated us all financially and emotionally. Being that he was the main pillar and foundation of the family unit, the entire household collapsed without his presence. Our dependence on this one man paralyzed us and left us powerless. When he died, it seemed like we all died. There were a lot of coulda, shoulda, woulda reflections from every member of the family. Looking down upon us from heaven, I bet my dad thought the same thing about himself. Could he have prepared his family better for a day like this? Was he too controlling and overprotective as the leader of the family? Why didn't he leave a will and a life insurance policy for his family? I know as a father today, those regrets would torment my Soul. One thing was clear: My mom was not mentally strong enough to deal with his passing. In fact, she fell apart at the seams, stayed medicated for months and could not provide much stability or direction for us. Although she tried her best, she fell victim to a patriarchal culture and quickly felt disempowered and disillusioned. There was a huge leadership vacuum in the family dynamic and no one knew how to overcome it. My oldest brother and my uncles did the best they could to fill my dad's void for me, but it was not possible for anyone to fill his big shoes. The man was larger than life, and now it was up to each and every one of us to pick up the pieces and walk our own path.

Each year after that passed with much difficulty as we missed my dad's guidance and support. Without him to keep peace and forge unity, the family unit began disintegrating. As the youngest sibling, I manned up pretty fast and eventually left the household to start my own family. My other siblings parted their own ways too, and it would take almost a decade after my dad's death before they were strong enough individually to recover and rebuild. My widowed mom paid the heaviest price. Although she took turns living with her five children in different parts of the world, she would not regain her life as a sexually active woman or wife.

Mom was a short but attractive and passionate woman with a strong and vibrant personality. She was also unconventional in her thinking, fearless, a natural salesperson and spoke her mind freely, similar to myself. So it didn't make sense to me why she wore an ankle bracelet of fear after my dad's death. As much as she longed to go out on dates to meet a man, she fell prey to our cultural dogma and my siblings' discouragement — they were afraid of letting her go and overprotected her. During the years that followed, I questioned why she wasn't seeing a man, much less getting remarried. In her blunt and matter-of-fact way, she complained how many in the family shamed and ostracized her for going on dates with any man. She often confided in me how she missed a sexual partner; *"You know your dad would say that sex is very important for our health, but they don't want me to have a man,"* she complained. *"That's absurd, Ma! You shouldn't care about what they say, and just go find a man,"* I'd yell at her in frustration when she visited my wife and me in Los Angeles. But my mother had lost her spunk and courage to exercise her free will. Year after year, the dependence on her children increased. Then, her situation worsened with the passing of my Uncle Jeff, her advocate in her plight to find a man. Jeff was one of the most generous Souls that kissed this earth. I loved him so much that I gave my son his middle name in his honor. The youngest of my dad's siblings, he was progressive and unconventional in his thinking and often longed that my mom would find a suitable male companion to regain joy in her life. But after he tragically died in an apartment fire, my mom lost a friend and confidant. She was now in her 70s and 20 years had passed since my dad's death. And still she was regrettably man-less.

On her 85th birthday, after she had climbed the thousand-foot granite rock of Stone Mountain in Georgia without any crutches, I remarked at her strength for her age. I asked her where she wanted to go for her birthday and she looked at me in frustration and unapologetically replied: "*I want to see naked men with large penises dance!*" My mom was dead serious, and I should have taken her up on it. But I knew my siblings wouldn't approve, and I regrettably didn't honor her wish. That was my own coulda, shoulda, woulda lost opportunity moment with her.

BLIND FATE

During the course of writing this book, I buried my mom at the age of 98, a victim of Covid-19. Although we were blessed to have her live so long, I can't help reflecting on her half-lived life with regrets. It's sad but a painful truth that is a lesson for us all. One of the culprits of any regret is losing our own sense of power and paying the price for it. Loss of personal power doesn't come in a wave or a vacuum — it builds up in layers over time. It starts off quite harmlessly when you innocently attach to someone larger than life or feel small about yourself. We do it all the time. We put so much trust and faith in our leaders, clergymen, gurus, teachers, therapists, financial advisers, doctors, life-coaches and spouses that we become distrustful of our own unfiltered and self-induced decisions and actions. This type of blind faith toward authority seduces us to a dangerous game of deception and illusion. It turns into *blind fate.* On one hand it gives us the false comfort of relying on others. This of course, makes good sense to do because these people are professionals in their fields and we trust them to have our best interest in mind. But on the other hand, it gives us the perfect alibi for scapegoating, blaming them and absolving our responsibility when things go wrong.

To demonstrate my point on a more personal level, I'll use the example of my father. Being a successful businessman and visionary, he earned the respect of an entire community in Tanzania. In a weird way, he was a martyr when he died. A humble man, he commanded a quiet authoritative power in the family. Having the head of the family treated as a demigod figure is not unusual in patriarchal Eastern cultures. What is significant is how this power-dynamic manifests itself within the family members. I'm certain my siblings, my mom and my dad all regretted relinquishing their personal power in their respective ways. In my siblings' case, while my father was alive, they gave up their power by their own volition to him. Dad was the one authority and the man of the house who made all the decisions for the family, even when they were grown adults. Right or wrong — he was the executive decision maker who no one dared to question. So when he died, the entire family collapsed and it was unable to progress for many years. For my mom, the loss of power manifested after she became widowed. She not only relinquished her freedom and decision-making to her children, but she was culturally pressured to grieve for an unknown time. In this period that lasted about a decade, two interesting things happened by her own choice. Being mentally unstable, my mom leaned on her children (except me, the youngest) and was dependent on them for shelter, food, financial and emotional support. From her children's perspective, they felt a sense of guilt caring for an emotionally fragile person and became overprotective in the process. This Eastern ancestral programming of the offspring fulfilling a duty to care and support the parent(s) was thrown on autopilot. Personally, I think this cultural responsibility is a noble cause if it's done without pressure or guilt. Unfortunately, pressure and guilt are the mainstays of our East Indian culture. They work to a certain degree to wield power and control over people, but there are limits and when they backfire — people get hurt. At the onset, there was a mutual comfort and grieving exchange that worked for all. But when Mom was ready toregain her womanhood, she encountered resistance from many of her kids. The more she persisted, the more they resisted in allowing her to go out on dates. It was not a forceful resistance, but rather a guilt and shame-based one. In patriarchal cultures, the woman submits to the will of males (in this case, her sons), especially if she's dependent on them. Instead of exercising her free will and having the courage to break out from the comfort of her self-imposed incarceration, my mother willfully gave up her power. She suffered by not having her freedom to live by her own terms. Ironically, my siblings suffered as well. Each xperienced a rash of problems in their marriages due to my mom living in their homes and infringing on their privacy and intimacy. By the time the siblings realized what had happened, my mom was too old to care and became a bitter and joyless woman (lack of sex will do this). In my mom's case, the universe would have it that she lived for a very long time and two of my siblings were her caretakers and babysitters. She was pampered and treated with dignity until her last breath.

COMFORTED LOYALTY

The lesson in this story is the danger of not just outsourcing our power to one entity, authority or person, but being held hostage to a cycle of disempowering comforts and a false blanket of security. It is a similar trap to my dad putting his eggs in one basket in Africa. He was comfortable on one hand and disempowered on the other. This amounts to what I call *comforted loyalty.* My dad made a mistake of trusting his entire fortune to a leader and a country, and he paid a heavy price for his comforted loyalty. My mom made the mistake of trusting her life to my siblings and similarly regretted her own comforted loyalty. Both of my parents put all their eggs in one basket in different ways and suffered because of it. This is what loss of personal power looks like when we put our blind faith in others.

Our entire life is upended and we lose our self-worth, freedom and joy. Again, the most disturbing aspect of this failing is the effect it has on future generations. I learned from my father's reliance on comforted loyalty and did not put all my financial eggs in one basket, by resisting to be the top dog ruler in my own family dynamic. I prefer to spread the risk and have my wife and children equally responsible for decision-making. I know that if I croak tomorrow, they won't be lost orparalyzed to make decisions. For one, they're a lot more independent- minded. Secondly, unlike my father, I am fully transparent about my assets with my family. But, alas, I'm an exceptionin the patriarchal and secretive Eastern culture. Unless my siblings and their children adopt an approach like mine, they too stand the chance of repeating the same mistakes of my parents. Such a disempowering cycle will continue to spread and mutate generationally.

How does this example help you recognize your own imbalances with your relationships, attachments and money? Are you selfish with people you love? Do you dangerously attach yourself to people, outcomes, things and places? Are you in a relationship where you're over reliant on one person? Are your baskets of eggs with finances, family and friends in need of a healthier fine-tuning and balance? Take this time to reflect honestly on your own situation and make the appropriate changes now.

MESSAGES FROM ABOVE

It was Sunday late afternoon on April 12, 2020, and I was about to put some finishing touches on a new piece of artwork from the previous night. It was the final piece of my five series Covid-19 collection. While all the other pieces had a dark message and made a statement about the economic enslavement of Americans during our isolation period, my fifth piece was going to be more transformational and uplifting in its theme. I visualized a person perched on a granite slab encapsulated in a glass tomb (a cylindrical flower vase turned upside down) with half its body inside reaching up to Divine light, (white crystal stone sitting atop the roof of the cylinder), while the lower part of the body was morphing into the roots of a tree, coming out of the tomb. The concept was inspired by a poem I wrote called "within" a tribute to our internal personal growth. With most of the clay body and face completed, I began to work on the final phase, adding one arm with its hands open and reaching to the top of the tomb. Halfway into it however, I changed course and began adding a second arm and turned both hands toward each other in a joined open-handed position. I don't know why I did that, because as a surrealist artist, I almost never sculpt with symmetry. Rather than create an image of the person reaching to the sky, I changed it to a person praying in gratitude to the Divine light. After looking at it closely, I immediately felt a sense of joy and peace permeate my Soul. Without any hesitation, I felt satisfied with it and decided not to alter any part of it. It was a breakthrough piece for me as I had just done something I had never done in all my 20 years of sculpting: create a gratitude/praying position character.

As I was removing my apron and ready to get up from my chair, my wife yelled at me from the living room below my loft studio: *"Something terrible has happened to your mom at your brother's house, we need to go right now!"*

My mom had just collapsed on the kitchen floor and died.

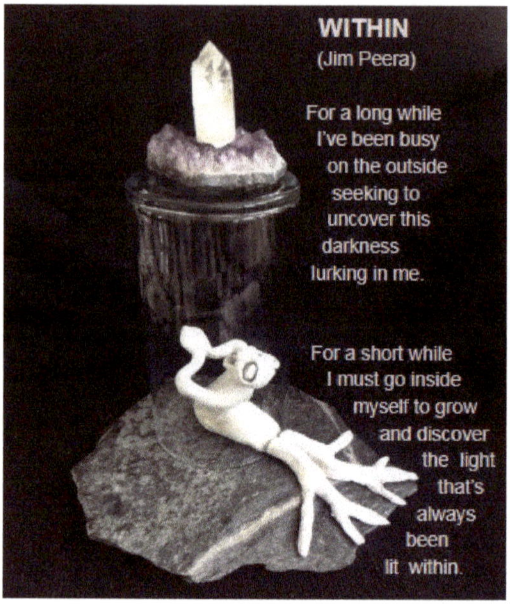

"Within"

(Clay, Amethyst, Crystal, Rock). Artist: Jim Peera

There was no doubt in my mind at that very moment that Mom's Spirit had something to do with the way I switched the arms of my character. The timing had to be Divinely inspired. But that wasn't the last time I'd feel her Spirit. As we had finished packing the last shovel of dirt on my mom's grave, I prayed for her Soul's freedom with Allah and the angels. I was happy that she was finally liberated to do what she had robbed herself for 47 years, to be with a man. Standing by the grave that was sprinkled with her favorite candy, Kit Kat, and was surroundedby her favorite flowers, carnations and roses, I noticed a bright ray of sunlight beaming like a spotlight on her buried body. I looked up to theoak trees nearby and it was odd how a laser-focused beam of light made its way through all the foliage and leaves and shone on her grave with such precision.

I snapped a photo of a precious image with my cell phone and breathed a sigh of relief for her rested Soul. For me, this sign marked her powerful and a serendipitous ascension to her maker.

She was exactly where she needed to be — reunited with her first and last love, my dad. "*Have lots of fun up there, Mom!*" I whispered to myself as I looked to the blue sunlit sky. I felt her Spirit look down and muster a smile with a sense of relief, freedom and peace. Now, it all made perfect sense!

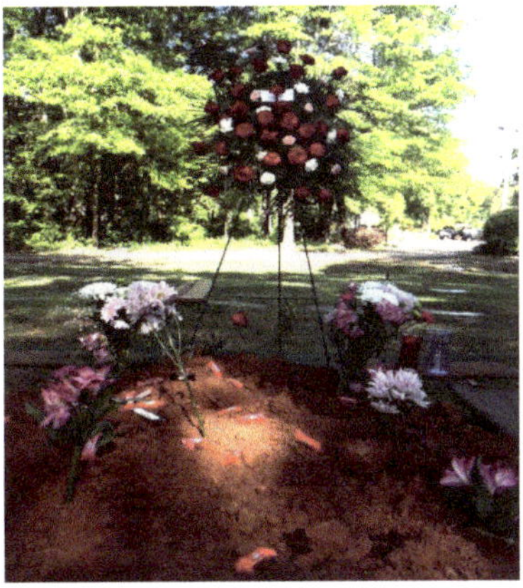

R.I.P Sherubanu Peera (Jim's Mom)

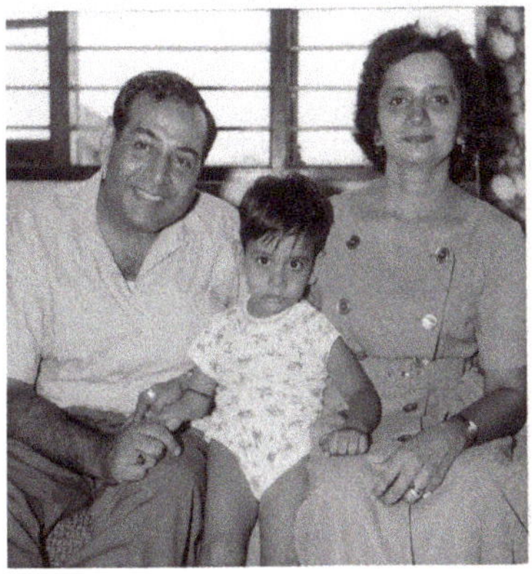

Jim w/ Dad and Mom (1963)

Chapter Takeaway:

What did this chapter do for you? Inspirations, lessons, comments? Find an example of loss of power in your own family. Take some time here to reflect and jot down anything you would do differently with the situation now — and then meditate for a few minutes before moving on.

13
THE ART OF REGAINING YOUR POWER

"Never underestimate your power to change yourself.

Never overestimate your power to change others."

- H. Jackson Brown.

In the last chapter, I recounted some family stories from my perspective that did not have a happy ending. Perhaps because the disempowered individuals did not use the healing medicine of the arts to regain their personal power. I know that was true for my mom and my siblings. None of them opened their inner creative portals to communicate their true feelings. In fact to this day, all of my siblings harbor deep unhealed scars from their childhood, the African diaspora and my dad's untimely death. Sadly, I am the only one out of my five siblings who has self-prescribed the arts as a healing medicine and licked those disempowering wounds. In this chapter, I will contrast two loss-of-power stories that had a better outcome for their victims.

The stories will demonstrate how art helped to heal and build a bridge in these young adults' violent relationships.

THOSE LYIN' EYES

Domestic violence is a huge problem in our society. My wife experienced it in her family with her dad, but I never thought I'd experience it through the painful stories of my own children, who were physically abused in their personal relationships. In each case, they were first cuts that bled for a while. They both also demonstrate the dangers of relinquishing power by being bullied, manipulated and allowing to be pushed-over in the excuse of love.

I recall the night when my lesbian daughter had just turned 18, packed her bags and ran off with a girl I'd only seen once. "*You guys have been great parents, but I have to go on my own now and live with this girl ofmy dreams!*" exclaimed my daughter as she rushed out the door slightly after midnight and into her girlfriend's car. This older girl had apparently blinded her with what my daughter said were *beautiful mesmerizing eyes.'* But these were lyin' eyes. A couple months later, I got a call from her that the two of them had been kicked out of the girlfriend's mom's house and needed a place to live. As a landlord of a house in the area, I offered them a top level of a duplex for a reduced rent. This way I could keep an eye on my daughter.

Several months passed, and I could see that they no longer seemed as smitten with each other. The more the rent was delayed, the fewer smiles I saw. Then one day, I saw a trail of trash from the steps down to the driveway. I confronted my daughter about the trash, and she bowed her head and said she wasn't feeling well but would take care of it. This was the first clue of domestic abuse: shame. I should have noticed bruises on her arms, but I didn't pay close enough attention at the time. Apparently, her girlfriend was highly temperamental and would physically punish her for not taking the garbage on time. There were countless other episodes that left not just physical but deep psychological scars on my daughter. When I walked into the apartment after it was emptied out, I could feel the ghost of fear and smell the violence in the rooms. There was evidence of angst and pain throughout the house with dents, scratches and holes on the walls and bruised doors. When I questioned her if she retaliated against her abuser, she just shook her head and said that we'd taught her not to use physical force with people. Since I am not a therapist, I am not going to analyze the particularities of the abuse as much as remark how surrealism-styled art and composing music saved my daughter's life and mental sanity. Using some of the Principles discussed in The Healium Way, we can see how she was able to self-transform and better cope with her trauma without resorting to harmful drugs, addictions or suicides that many in her circle of friends fall prey to.

During and soon after this tumultuous period, my daughter created some of the most heart-wrenching songs and jaw-dropping drawings I've ever heard and seen. To this day, I still tear up when I hear those songs. The raw unfettered outpouring of emotion is quite remarkable and a testament of the power of art at its most authentic level. My daughter used this episode in her young life to propel her artistic talent in ways I couldn't have imagined. I've showcased her music and art pieces at our Center and have seen thousands of people over the years relate to it and find therapeutic benefits for themselves.

Check out Jim's daughter's heart-wrenching music:

SCAN ME

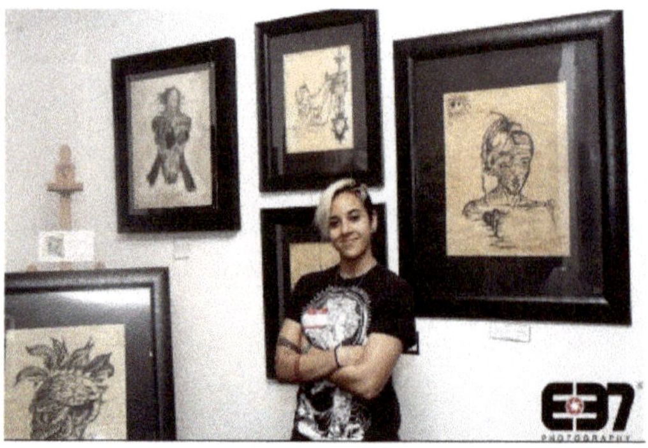

THE FIRST CUT IS THE DEEPEST

It was a pretty quiet Saturday night when we returned home from grocery shopping to hear the phone ringing off the hook. When I picked up the phone, I was shocked to hear the panicked, terrified voice of my son. He told me he had just been stabbed in the arm by a homeless person while he was walking home. His voice was shaking, but he assured me that he wasn't in grave danger. He asked if I could send him some money to go to the hospital and have it checked. He was six hours away so he suggested I just use Western Union for the money transfer. I sent him the money, but I was worried for him throughout the night. My wife and I followed up with him the next day and she got a slightly different version of the story. In the following days we found out that he had a violent domestic dispute with his girlfriend with whom he was living near the Georgia coastline. He had been having a long-distance relationship with a girl for some time and decided to move in with her while she was going to art school. We were against the spontaneous move, but he was adamant and anxious to get out of Atlanta. When the truth slowly surfaced, we learned he had been stabbed by his girlfriend and was too embarrassed to tell us. As we prodded deeper, we found out that he had been frequently abused (and often quite violently) by the same girl. My daughter, who had already experienced her share of domestic violence, tried to knock some sense into him to ditch the girl and come back to Atlanta, but he resisted. We tried repeatedly to end the chaotic attachment, but it continued its slow and persistent downward trajectory for three years. The abuser was an unhealed Soul from a prior rape incident unleashing her pent-up rage on my son. He, on the other hand, was a rather naive and confused young man experiencing the trials and tribulations of his first love. The lyrics from a Sheryl Crow song fits his situation well; *"The first cut is the deepest."* Indeed, it was a relationship made in hell and both were too ashamed to admit their self-destructive behaviors. During the stabbing attack and other prior similar episodes, the girl used her white skin privilege to advance her vitriol and demoralize him with a mindf*ck such as, *"No one's going to believe you. I am a pretty white girl and you're a brown piece of sh*t!"* On one occasion, the cops were called and my son had to show his wounds to be believed as the victim and not be taken to jail.

By being madly attracted to fairer-skinned individuals, both my son and daughter fell into that subservient racial rabbit hole and experienced their own diminished sense of power in the process. They also quickly discovered that in trying to be a fountain for others, they drained themselves. In my son's case, we learned that he too had been physically abused (often slashed) for a protracted period before he cut the cord and got help. As a man, it was difficult for me to comprehend why he allowed himself to suffer as he did. If it was me in that situation, I would have packed my bags and left the very first time the girl cut me up. Because the longer one stays in a disempowering and abusive relationship, the harder it gets — and the longer it takes to recover from it. Sadly, I've encountered many tales of men in the West who forget to take back their power with unhealed, manipulative and aggressive females, only to face dire consequences. When my son finally did have the sense to get out of the relationship, it would take him another few years to fully heal the emotional scars.

It is not uncommon to see unhealed people resort to dark entities and even sorcery to get what they want in relationships. But we all have free will and in the end these experiences teach us as much about ourselves as about the people we chose to love. I know for my kids, having supportive parents and self-prescribed art therapy helped each cope with their respective emotional and physical pain management. Since the emotional wounds were so deep, they each sought the professional advice of psychotherapists. Luckily, we had the financial means to provide our kids with the therapy they needed to aid in their eventual recovery, a luxury that is not available to a majority of Americans. Many teenagers and adolescents are left dealing with domestic violence without much societal and parental support, paving the way for a multitude of collateral damage from suicide, depression, alcoholism, drug addiction and mental illness.

Throughout the ordeal and during his healing period, my son used music as his therapy. I remember him coming to me with a unique sound where he'd combined screaming vocals with rap, hip hop and electronic dubstep. I've never cried listening to a rap song before. You can hear the raw emotion bleed out his heart.

Check out Jim's son's powerful music!

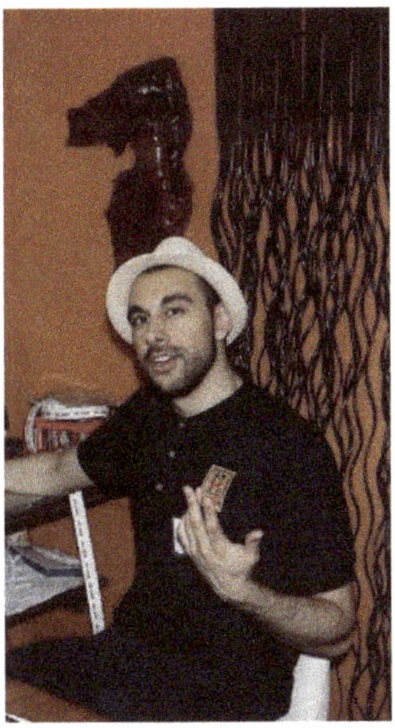

SCAN ME

Chapter Takeaway:

What did this chapter do for you? Inspirations, lessons, comments? Do you have your own story of regaining your power with art or music? Take some time here to reflect on your past relationships and jot down anything you would do differently now. If you're currently in an abusive relationship, does this chapter help you take action sooner and prescribe creative self-expression for your healing? Meditate for a few minutes before moving on.

14
The Art of the Heal Project

"The only way to fix narcissistic people is to show them with art what they really look like."

- Jim Peera

The Bee Gees wrote three number one hits: "Shadow Dancing," "Tragedy" and "Too Much Heaven" all in one afternoon. That's a surreal milestone by any metric. Most successful artists will tell you that some of their best works were created in a quick burst of time rather than a protracted period. Often the inspiration is triggered by our connection to a particular environment or an emotional state of mind. And when we're aligned with inspiration's magnetic force field, it manifests in beautiful ways. I had such an experience, conceiving one of my best ideas for Healium Center. It was about 6 a.m. on November 9, 2016, and I hadn't slept all night awaiting the American presidential election results. As I wept like a child following the victory announcement for Donald Trump, I was exhausted and could barely see through my tears. I walked into my office looking to find a book by the Dalai Lama to calm my nerves, but instead knocked over a book by Donald Trump called "The Art of The Deal." For a split-second, my watery eyes read it as "The Art of The Heal." I didn't think much of it then, but in the following days after witnessing how devastated and disempowered the Healium community was feeling after the election, I had a lightbulb moment. What if we could get people to freely paint out their pent-up emotions on Trump and send those paintings to the White House? I discussed the idea with my family and they loved it. Within a couple weeks we created a promotional video and a website and launched *TheArt ofTheHeal.org*; *The People's Gift to Trump (aka: AOTH.)* I even mimicked the gold font of Trump's book. It was an immediate hit and our Healium community embraced the project with open arms.

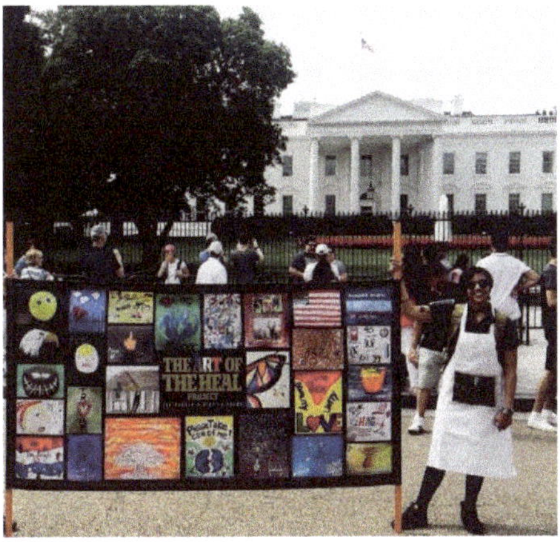

The Art of The Heal goes to the White House.

My goal was to mail out 100,000 canvases but oddly we got a lot of push-back from many schools and institutions citing it was too political. In 2017, we traveled to Washington, DC, and showcased some of the art in front of the White House lawn. It was not a demonstration but rather a soft protest that got total strangers into open dialogue in an empowering way. Tourists from all over the world reacted in a very positive manner to see Americans being innovative, creative and unapologetically displaying uninhibited self-expression. One French reporter even commented to me how the project gave back power to its disenfranchised people. I told him it was simply a First Amendment right shining its bright light on America's darkest modern period. But since Americans are a pretty fickle bunch, over time we experienced Trump-fatigue and interest in the project waned. In the end, we sent 1,000 paintings to 1600 Pennsylvania Ave., and found it quite remarkable to see the level of public enthusiasm generated from "The Art of the Heal".

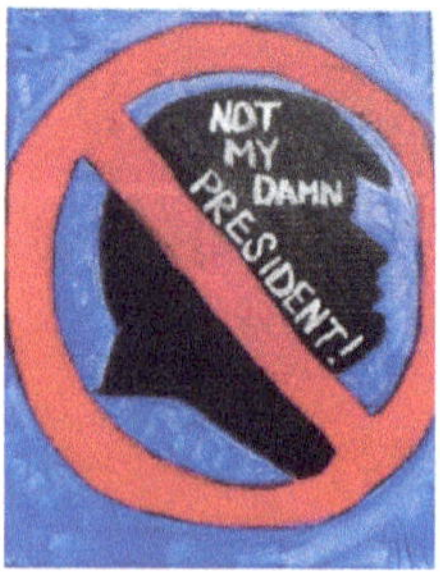

Giving ordinary people a freehand to unleash whatever they had on their mind and release their emotions to the most powerful man in the world was empowering and liberating. The exercise helped people heal in ways we'd never seen. Each time someone completed the painting, we asked them to write a personal message to Trump on the back and sign it with their name and other personal information. We then snapped a picture and put it on social media for people's comments before we packaged it for mailing. In many cases, we witnessed people cry and connect with other artists in cathartic ways. This was truly the power of art at its best: to open dialogue, empower, be a healthy therapeutic release and even unite people. I specifically remember one story of a young family who came with two small children. The wife told me how Trump had divided them to the point they couldn't sit at the dinner table together. She'd heard about this project and wanted the kids to paint.

The husband was on the opposite side of the political fence. They looked sad and frustrated, but the wife wanted to change the dynamic. This intention was important for the AOTH to succeed as intended. Once I heard their story, I knew it was going to be a transformative evening. I asked them to separate while they did the exercise.

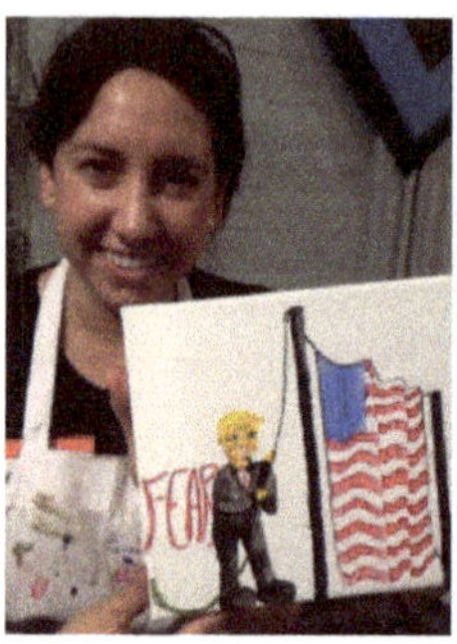

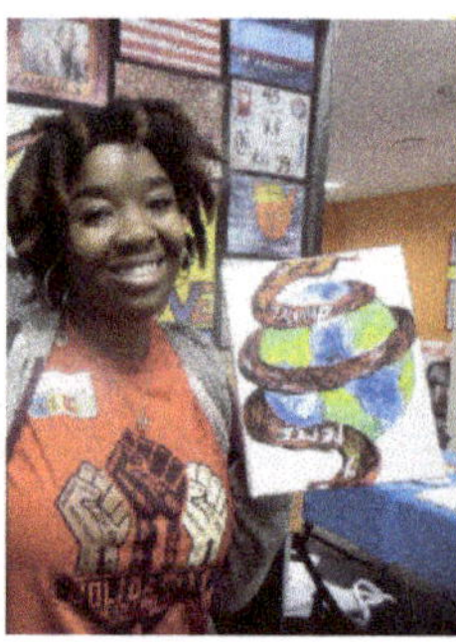

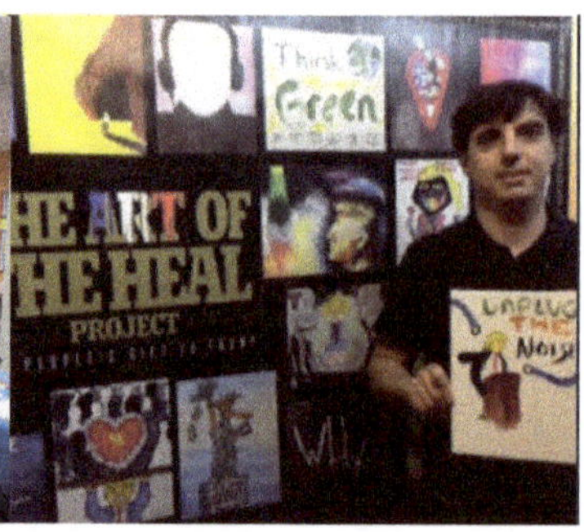

Then I convinced the parents to mix in with the other adult participants and not bother the kids. When they saw how other people were letting loose, they too were inspired to participate and paint. Within 90 minutes or so, I noticed how the kids were smiling and the parents were laughing. They were talking about each other's pieces and exposing their Souls without any inhibition. The father may not have liked the theme of his kids' paintings, but he was not upset. The evening changed this family, who were now hugging and kissing each other. They showed me their respective pieces and the kids' paintings were raw and shocking, especially for their age. The wife expressed how helpful the exercise was in bringing the family together and thanked me for creating the powerful project. I teared up. When one of the kids asked me if Trump would even open the package, I told him it didn't matter as the art exercise was more for him than for the new president. I hung the art on our gallery wall at The Center for people to enjoy for a couple of weeks and then shipped them out with many others. We were stunned that some of the boxes were actually opened by White House staff, who sent us 'Thank You' postcards in the mail. From a legal viewpoint, we were also told that since the packages were sent as gifts that by law they had to be warehoused and archived. So to that extent each participant made a bit of American history by participating in The Art of The Heal project!

I wonder what Donald Trump thought of that 13-year-old white kid who wrote, *"Trump you're a dick,"* in his painting to him? I know the artist himself felt quite empowered and liberated getting that message off his chest!

A painting by the 13- year- old kid:

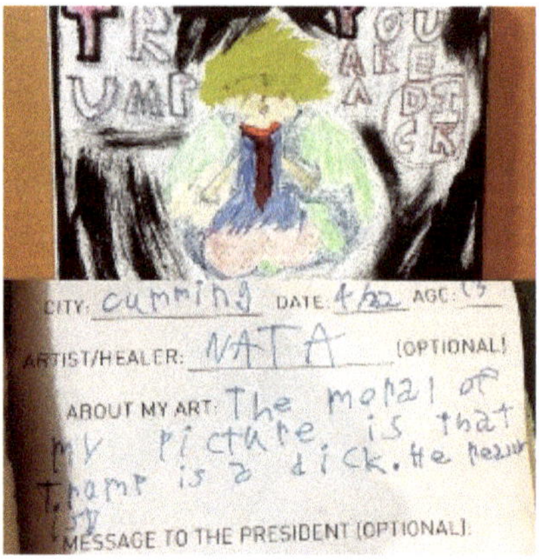

A sampling of paintings sent to the White House for the project:

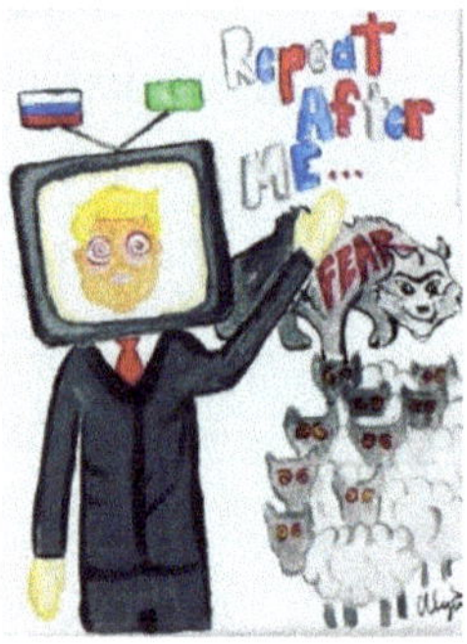

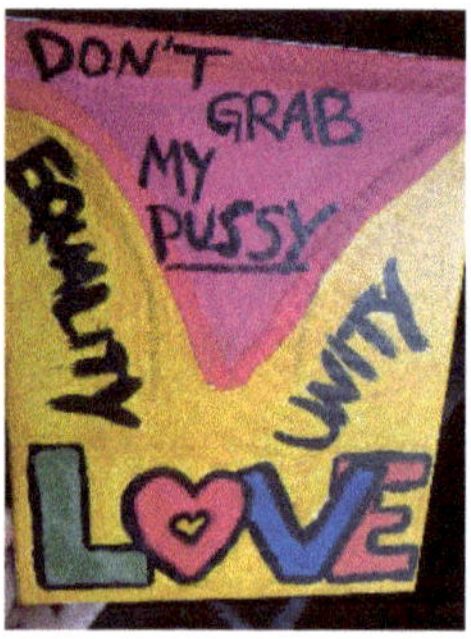

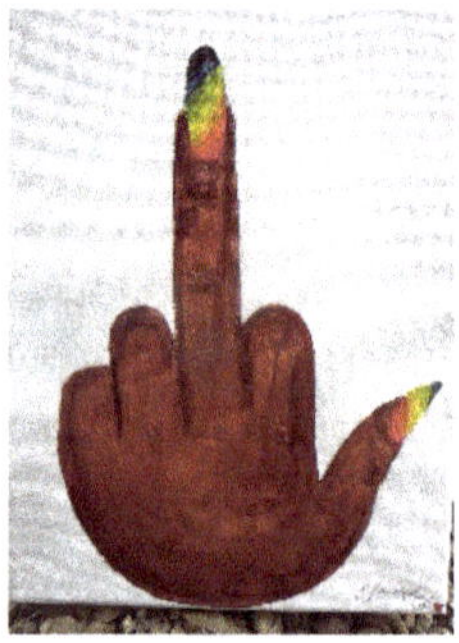

Chapter Takeaway:

What did this chapter do for you? Inspirations, lessons, comments? Identify someone in your life today who warrants a gift of self- expression to ease YOUR stress or anxiety. Perhaps you can send this person an honest, creative piece of art straight from your heart! Meditate on the power of this idea for a few minutes before moving on to the next chapter.

15
"THE MAN" DOES NOT HAVE YOUR BACK

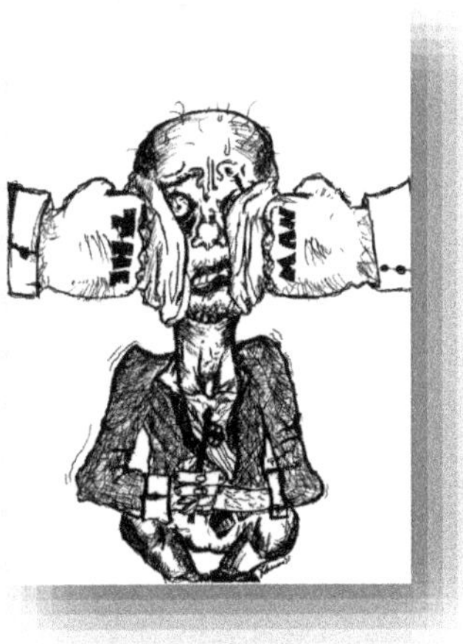

Imagine you're having a pretty peaceful day driving on the way to go see your friend. You come to a stop at a red light, and as you're enjoying zoning out on some New Age music, you are jolted out of your seat and rear-ended at 50 mph. Your car is totaled, and as you manage to step out of the car, you feel shocked and dizzied. The driver at fault admits guilt to her insurance company.

End of story, right? Wrong. Over a period of a year, you rack up thousands of dollars in medical bills for your injuries — only to find out that this corporate giant insurance company doesn't believe your condition to be serious, denies paying the bills and sends you a final check for a depreciated value of your totaled car. You're contemplating this offer when it happens again: A guy on a phone rear-ends your car at 60 mph while you're legally waiting for another red light. You're in total disbelief and your life just went from sh*t to f*cked up sh*t. Your back is so badly messed up that you're on a wheelchair for months, at the mercy of chiropractors and physical therapists. You lose your job and become unemployed, but are denied employment benefits.

It's now been over three years since your suffering began, with two back-to-back faultless accidents. You're still in pain, desperately trying to find a fix and don't have your normal life back. In both instances the insurance companies failed to have your back, the lawyers left you straddled in debt and the doctors want to cut you up. As you try to sign up for health insurance,the Affordable Care Act (ACA), you realize there's nothing affordable about it. The insurance premiums and high deductibles would soak up almost half of your poverty-level wages. So you're left with two solutions; suffer and file bankruptcy or call your parents for a lifeline. Lucky for you, you can choose the latter alternative and have parents who have the financial means to ease your hardship. This is my daughter's disheartening story. A few years ago, she took out her pent-up frustrations on corporate bullying and greed in America by creating art. She drew two corporate fists squishing a person's face — a symbol of how we're getting screwed and enslaved by "The Man," aka, corporate America. Sadly, it all came true for her.

THANKS TO THE GIPPER

My daughter's story is not unique. I've met many Americans whose lives have been derailed by powerful corporations in all sectors of the economy such as insurance companies, retailers, airlines, service companies, manufacturers and so forth. This license to screw the American people (aka, runaway corporate capitalism) sowed its toxic seeds during the reign of the nation's 40th president, Ronald Reagan (aka; the Gipper), a Hollywood actor turned conservative superstar for the wealthy. His two-term presidency, from 1981 to 1989, set the stage for the erosion and the decline of the middle class with *Reaganomics* paving the way to empower and enrich big corporations. Once deregulations and lowered corporate tax laws took effect, *the man* got stronger, greedier and devoured any small competitor that got in the way. Today, with our weak consumer protections coupled with unlimited litigious power of corporations, the American people are powerless and often at their mercy. Just 30 years ago when I had my first car accident similar to my daughter's, the insurance company not only paid up without any hassle, but the agent sent me a get-well card — a year after the incident. That's a utopian America compared to now. In those pre-Reagan days, some people got greedy by scamming insurance companies and boasting bumper stickers that read; *"Hit me, I need the money."* Then auto injury lawyers multiplied like mice and insurance companies responded with vengeance. They doubled down on becoming powerful cartels, with authorities and litigators in their back pocket. Their arrogance is not only dished out in unwarranted premium hikes, but it permeates through the entire chain cycle in the name of customer disservice and bullying. And it's downhill from here unless we begin to rebalance this reality by our awareness and willingness to stand up against the corporate powers. I noticed the signs of corporate power's influence during the 1996 Summer Olympics, which were held in my hometown of Atlanta. Back then I was pretty naive of the dangers of free-market capitalism and America's profit-over-people values. I even wrote a comic book championing it. But beneath the obvious superficiality of showcasing America's shiny image to the world and Muhammad Ali's iconic torch- lighting moment, we were corroding our own core values and dimming our light. The record investment that was generated to host the Games catapulted the city economically, but the benefit was unequal. Money flowed freely into the airport, real estate projects, infrastructure and downtown commercial developments. Most of that benefited crony capitalists, crooked politicians and powerful elites, while the average Atlantan saw no real increase in their wages, or in their pocketbook. The corporate sponsors such as Coca-Cola, Delta and Chick-fil-A spent millions of dollars strengthening their brands, but fell short in sprinkling some of that money for downtrodden neighborhoods. Even worse, they scalped you in sports arenas with high ticket prices and concessions and built bigger and badder sports domes to further feed their ego and enrich themselves. The ball players, managers and owners made egregious amounts of money while the average Atlantans struggled to pay their rent, worked two jobs below the minimum wage and buried themselves in more debt. Today, billionaires see this profit-over-people culture as normal, as it slowly engulfs our moral fabric and widens our economic gap. Sadly, though, that sort of greed and individualism mindset is not exclusive to corporations.

THE VICIOUS CYCLE

There's an unspoken but nasty philosophy that I call the *capitalistic vicious cycle*. It affects a lot of us on an individual level. Most of us are caught up in this cycle of dishonesty and greed by passing the buck without much thought. It's an automatic default loop that we normalize as our survival tool. If you're a small business or an entrepreneur, you know this conundrum well. In a typical example, it shows up in situations where you're overcharged on a product or a service such as during an emergency car repair or a plumbing service call. Because you don't bargain (a Western faux pas), or you may not have a choice, you're stuck with an uncomfortably high bill. In order to ease your emotional and economic pain, you turn around and (consciously or unconsciously), make up for it by overcharging your customer, who repeats the same pattern on others. This silent but obvious act to make up your shortfall and stick it onto others is justified without shame or guilt. In fact, it becomes a necessary tactic for many of us in a dog-eat-dog-survival-of-the-fittest capitalistic model. It works great when the scheme keeps circling, but it doesn't when you're unable to do it anymore. It's only when you're caught or rejected by the receiving party that you give thought to the vicious cycle trap. Often, it's via customer complaints, bad online reviews or competition that you curb your dishonesty and greed. The American free market economic model ferments this vicious cycle well and has contributed to our inequality gap and high debt levels. It is also a contributor to our rising prices and real inflation that's not accurately measured by conventional methods.

So be aware of this low-vibrational condition and avoid participating in it; if you want repeat business, respect and keep overall consumer prices in check. By arresting it on your end, you may have a contagious effect on others to follow suit and keep everyone honest in your cycle. It may sound idealistic, but it's very doable!

THE CYA SOCIETY

*"You know what capitalism is? Getting f**ked!"* is another famous line from the movie "Scarface" that the Western world, specifically America, understands well. Personally, I don't think capitalism is our downfall as much as it is our mishandling of it. Americans are good at taking a good thing and f*cking it up with our overzealous extremist habits. We take the free-market concept and turn it into a "greed market" that infects our moral compass and slowly suffocates us from the inside out. Greed breeds economic power. And economic power rests in the greased hands of the corporate elites and the mega-rich. Today's corporate America wields so much power against us that it has the arrogance and the audacity to stick their middle finger in our face without flinching. Its dishonesty and flagrancy is displayed openly, and shows up in our daily lives at all levels. Often there's very little we can do about it, due to their sneaky practices and legal jargon that's buried in their cumbersome policies, also known as the CYA, or Cover Your Ass, clause.

A good example of this occurred when our Center experienced an insurance scam similar to my daughter's car accident story shortly after we began operations. We were paying top dollar for insuring our historical property and never had a claim. One winter our roof collapsed following four days of heavy rains, and the insurance company refused to pay for the damage, citing it as a non-eligible coverage in the policy. Sound familiar? The eye-straining lines of legal jargon buried within the 50-page policy had CYA clauses that excluded standing water on the roof as a reason for denying the claim.

I had a fit! I wrote a complaint to the Georgia Insurance Commissioner, but it was a waste of time. They said there was nothing they could do unless I took them to court. The desk clerk confided in me that the insurance industry was too powerful for most consumers to win against their grievances. Perhaps, I thought, I needed to invent my own CMA (Cover My Ass) policy to counteract their CYA! I spent more than $40,000 out of my own pocket and was closed for three months. To put salt on my wound, the insurance company raised my premium. So I fired them. But they input my (unpaid) claim in the central data system, so the other insurance companies red-lined us and would not insure our building. We operated without insurance for two years until we were in the clear. This is the heavy-handed power of "The Man". I have many stories that confer corporate thievery such as this, but I'll recount my most recent one that will blow your mind as it can happen to any of you. It is about an uninvited guest bird that resides in our home; a daily reminder of living in today's America.

THE GUEST BIRD

About a year ago my wife wanted me to replace our problematic seven-year-old refrigerator. She specifically insisted that we purchase a good quality brand from a big box retailer to ensure our satisfaction. One morning we made a trip to our local national-brand hardware store and were excited to pick out our new appliance. After about thirty minutes of comparing and testing the various models, we settled on a $1,300 unit. It was the most money I'd ever dished out for a fridge. As we were paying, the saleswoman kept insisting we purchase the extended warranty, which was a quarter of the sales price. I refused.

So she had me sign off a fine print waiver to relinquish their responsibilities. I never buy extended warranties as they're a rip-off. She had me check off a box absolving any worthwhile warranty on my receipt. What I didn't know, because it was buried in fine print and the saleswoman neglected to tell me, was that the home improvement giant was not responsible for the unit three days after delivery. Of course, our problems began within a couple of days after the installation. I heard an annoying chirping noise emanating from the freezer area. It sounded like a bird singing. My first thought was there was a bird's nest stuck behind the wall, but I couldn't find any birds and it kept up with its occasional chirping. By the fourth day, I suspected the noise was inside the unit so I recorded a video of it on my cell and took it to the store clerk to file a complaint. She looked at my receipt and told me I was out of luck: "*You didn't listen to me and now there's nothing I can do about it*" she exclaimed. I was confused and furious and took the matter to the store manager. He told me the same story and said my issue now lay with the manufacturer of the refrigerator. He got them on the phone for me, and I knew in the first five minutes that I was getting the old runaround. The company denied that there was any irregularity with the sound — contending it was a normal noise. They sent out three technicians over a period of a month: all of whom said the problem was a manufacturing defect in the refrigerant line and could not be fixed at my home and that the unit needed to be replaced. Yet the manufacturer insisted it was normal and refused to replace it. I spent the next three months doing everything I could from sending videos of the problem to higher supervisors to no avail. I went back to complain to the retailer, which said I should have bought the extended warranty. As I researched the internet, I found over fifty people scattered on different sites mirroring my problem and how corporate headquarters gave them all the middle finger. I decided to stop wasting my time and not pursue a lost cause. Some battles are not losing hair or a good night's sleep over. For me, the importance of fighting is not so much in the expectation of "winning" as it is in the act of *trying* — and having the satisfaction to "right the wrongs" and raise awareness. Today, my wife and I live with that occasional annoying chirping noise every day. We've trained our ears to think of it as a guest bird in our home. The sound it makes reminds me of a sickly baby bird crying for food — an eerie metaphor symbolizing the moral decay of America at the mercy of powerful corporations.

THE SQUEEZE IS ON

The above stories are real and I'm sure you too have your own nightmare versions. If you don't, don't worry, it's coming — the squeeze is on the American consumer! From egregious bank overdraft fees to costly warranties; every profit hungry company is ready and eager to scalp your pocketbook. Indeed, how America has changed. If I bought anything at any big box retailer 30 years ago, I would never be asked to buy a separate warranty and would have no trouble returning a defective product. There would be no qualms about it. In fact, some companies back in those days would even offer apologies by reducing the price or issuing you a discount coupon — just to keep you as a customer. Sadly, those days are behind us. The elite-class and corporations, rule with their one-way ticket agendas of squeezing the most profit for their shareholders by being dishonest, greedy and above the law. Once one company gets away with their dirty game, others join in to play with rigged rules and eventually join hands to reset the laws in their favor. They've monopolized and sabotaged our economy from Silicon Valley to Washington, D.C.; they've penetrated our government as lobbyists, lawmakers and bribing agents. They're the puppet masters of our news dissemination by controlling what we see, hear and process on the airwaves. Many don't pay their fair share of taxes; they overcompensate their bosses; and they throw crumbs at their dispensable workers. Over time these big fish eat the little ones to become "too big to fail" conglomerates —screwing America in every aspect from enslaved foreign labor to genetic food engineering. And we're gobbling it all up like fat, unhealthy turkeys on Thanksgiving Day — thanks to our stupidity. Their profit squeeze shows up on our end as clever packaging, reduced volume, low quality parts, fillers in food, planned obsolescence, useless warranties, automated complaint departments and a litigious modus operandi.

In essence we've gone from a culture of *customer service* to *customer no-service* to *customer dis-service.*

RAISING YOUR HAND

Often our dissatisfaction with something is resolved by raising our hand, figuratively speaking — in order to complain. It's common at restaurants. We've all had situations of being dissatisfied with a service or a product and having two outcomes — voicing our grievance on the spot or letting it go and bitching about it later to others or on social media. The Healium Way is about taking the former path first, to get a satisfactory resolution. It's your right as a paying consumer. This route often involves face-to-face contact that's becoming rare in our socially deficient and fear-based society. Yet, the service or product provider cannot read your mind, and there's no need to feel bashful. If you don't bring the problem to their attention, how do they know it didn't meet your expectations to fix it? You're actually doing them a service by being upfront and speaking your mind. I always take the complaint straight to the top, but I do it tactfully. You'll be surprised to discover how you'll get the desired results, often even get something better out of it. Americans are known around the world for bitching and complaining when they don't get it their way – so why lower your bar in your own country? More important, you'll help American businesses stay honest and go from ordinary to *extra*ordinary!

PUTTING ON THE GLOVES

But what happens if we cannot talk to a human or have bigger unresolved issues? What can we do? America's greed is not going away anytime soon, and The Healium Way is not to get railroaded by anyone — human or computer. Therefore, you'll need to put on your boxing gloves and learn to be your own private investigator, litigator and defender. It is no different than learning to be your own doctor and therapist for physical and mental health. You've also got to protect yourself against private entities and public monopolies, like your local utility provider. I'm sure you've got your horror stories of being overcharged by your city or county for water, sewer, gas, electric or property tax bills. The culprit of unmerited hikes can be departmental red tape, employee incompetence or outright thievery due to budget shortfalls. I've experienced it all in my long real estate career. I've also gone through the dog and pony shows known as appeals boards. They're not fun to attend because they're often rigged, are intimidating and you seldom get your way. These low vibrational situations can be stressful and frustrating, but the alternative is that you don't bother fighting — and they win, and repeat their wrongdoing against others. I've talked to many people who are held hostage by the monopolies and end up paying the ransom for fear of losing service. It's pure extortion. So why not make these folks work for it and be a necessary thorn in their side. What have you got to lose? Go down fighting like Tony Montana at the end of Scarface. In any dispute, it's vital that you have to get in front of it when you're feeling the squeeze. The earlier you act, the better. Be persistent in your complaints and do not be afraid to stick your neck out. The more stink you make, the better your chances are of being taken seriously. Definitely ditch the "robots" whose job is to pass the buck to other order-taking robot supervisors. Take your complaint straight to the higher ups and do not be intimidated. Write to the department bosses and document all conversations and people you talk to and keep good records. Regrettably, the tools available to individuals to combat injustice and malice are limited. You can find consumer advocacy groups in your area that may help give you fighting tips; or you can use the internet to identify, expose and shame the dishonest players. Social media works too, to raise awareness and find allies. Local news teams can help break the squeeze, especially if your story shows a pattern of abuse or has "wow" newsworthy appeal. Calling your county representative or politician sometimes helps, particularly during an election cycle. A more costly recourse is to join in a class action lawsuit if evidence of corruption or ill will is established. This choice only works for a non-governmental agency — since government monopolies are often protected by sovereign immunity clauses that give them unlimited power to screw us. The least effective and slowest recourse is to report a wrongdoer to a government protection agency. Albeit for me, this route has been mostly a waste of time. In cases of private corporate malice, the most effective weapon is through the use of strikes and boycotts. The French are masters of this technique. It's more difficult to implement these tactics in America, as many workers don't belong to unions and consumers are too spoiled to turn off their shopping switch. The idea is to hit the companies where it hurts them the most — in their pocketbook. We can do it as groups or individually by closing our most powerful weapon: our wallet.

The moral of this chapter is what happens when we take our freedoms and free market philosophies too far. It's the price we pay for feeding large corporations with special tax breaks, and not holding them accountable for unfairly squashing mom and pop stores. That's the ugly side of *Walmartization* of America. When large corporate entities are left uncontrolled, they morph into monopolies that then mutate into monster companies which become too big to control and punish — or even fail their own employees. Our consumer protection agencies are weak or understaffed and our elected leaders get bought off via lobbyists and special interest groups. In this process, we get thrown into an imbalance with our core values of trust and honesty, and forget to keep a check and balance on runaway capitalism.

Before we know it "The Man," whose primary interest is about shareholder profits has turned into an uglier beast. He's now emboldened by not caring a rat's ass about you. He not only fails to look out for your back — with his substandard products and services — but is happy to twist it, step on it, break it; and now more than ever, try to get away with it!

This folks, is the ugly face of the 21st century America we're living in. It is partly brought to you compliments of the Gipper, who opened the floodgates of laissez faire, free market capitalism and unleashed the worst greed and dishonesty in us.

Chapter Takeaway:

What did this chapter do for you? Inspirations, lessons, comments? Have you been screwed by anyone, company or entity and had no recourse to fight back? Take some time here to examine your past inactions and see if you would do things differently now — and then meditate for a few minutes before moving on to the next chapter.

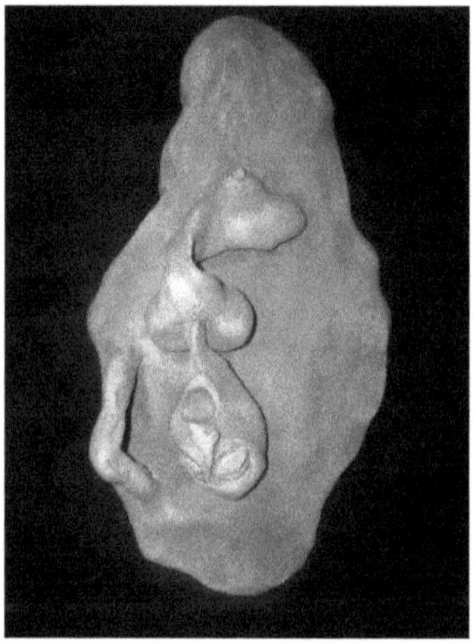

"Pain"
(Clay). Artist: Jim Peera

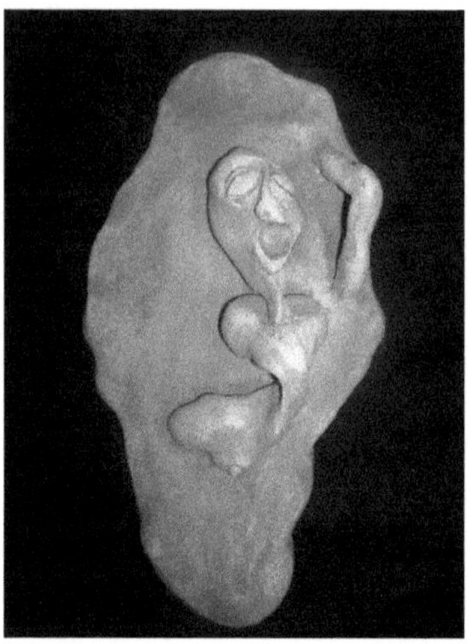

16
MAYBE IT'S YOU

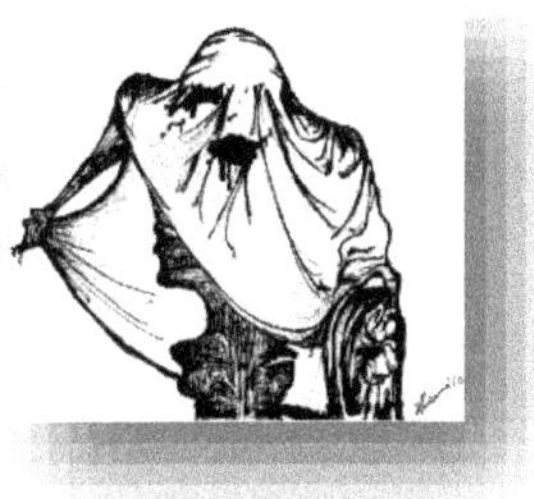

In Chapter 3, you did an art exercise that asked you to interpret a drawing from your own perspective. Get the notes out now and let's look at this piece again. If you haven't done so yet, please take a few minutes and write down what you see and feel. Besides the specifics of your emotions, the most important thing is if you see the person as a*) trying to remove the cover* or b) *trying to cover itself.* There is no right or wrong answer, we are just determining your current state of being. The artist only seeks to expose the fears and resistance within you. If you see the image as a cover being removed, it means you're comfortable being vulnerable and are ready to expose some hard truths, pain and darkness within. If you see it the opposite way, then you're perhaps hiding something unpleasant and are not ready to reveal your mistakes or transgressions just yet. This second response is quite normal. Most of us hide some secrets we're not comfortable exposing in fear of the consequences of telling the truth. Perhaps the secrets are too old and harmless to jeopardize a healthy relationship. Quite often you're not ready to open a can of worms anticipating a blowback from your partner. For others, it's not about admission of secrets but about neglect and regrets. Maybe you're a parent who's regretting not spending enough time with your children. Or a person who's tormented over the guilt of neglecting a deceased spouse. The important thing is to unearth the problems that are weighing on your conscience. I am not suggesting that you confess every bit of your past wrongdoings but that you realize how the truth can set you free — especially if you've done some horrific things in your past and that by carrying that beast of burden it is engulfing you from the inside out. The idea is to come clean, free yourself and restore your Soul. Living a lie is counterproductive to discovering your higher and authentic self as it affects everything you do. Even worse, you're doing a disservice to others close to you who are suffering along with you.

REVALUING OUR VALUES

One of the most common deterrents to our path to self-transformation is our own resistance. I'll elaborate on this subject when we discuss the Principles in Part 2 of The Healium Way. We're all quite good at making excuses and putting up defenses to justify our actions or inactions. Sometimes this obdurate behavior is programmed from our upbringing and quite often it's a result of adulthood conditioning and our societal labels. The most typical excuse people use for inaction is money. Specifically, the idea of having it, not having it or not having enough of it. It's always a fascinating debate for all of us. Interestingly, we can all agree that it's our own man-made problem — and therefore our own to fix. In this realm of our societal conditioning, money is the culprit of many of our resistances and an impediment to our personal growth. The dichotomy is real. On one side of the coin, it's our addictive drug and friend to celebrate when we attain it. And on the other side, it's the evil monster when we lose it. Money's two-faced reputation is embedded in the fabric of our daily lives that is unraveling us due to our handling and imbalance with it. In the context of The Healium Way, we know from our own experience at The Center that having the intention and allocating the time toward self-improvement supersedes being able to afford the low entry fee to many of our activities and events. Yet many people choose to do the opposite. They'll forgo life-changing Healium events and instead, buy material things they don't really need as a way to temporarily fill their Souls. In the process they go broke and go into an anxious tailspin. It's a convoluted way of thinking that begs reprioritizing our values, managing money better and undoing material-based societal norms. Buying a 10th pair of Nike shoes instead of taking a healing session at The Center is a false *feel-good* trade off. And that's where The Healium Way Principles come in: to help you re-balance your time and money where it matters the most. A trip to a nail salon or a shopping mall is less of a necessity (a need) than a material satisfaction (a want). There's nothing wrong with splurging and treating ourselves on special occasions — until the treats become superficial pacifiers that overtake common sense and throw us in debt.

Eventually, we attach to them habitually and justify their hold on us without good reason. It is not rocket science to see that spending our time and money by seeing a play, creating art or going dancing is more beneficial to our mental wellbeing than excessive shopping. My millennial kids are teaching me the value of practicing a 'needs-based' (aka; resourced-based) economy; as opposed to a 'wants-based' one that my baby boomer generation flaunts.

HUMAN CAPITALIST

Our future is looking bleak if we don't start correcting our unhealthy imbalances now. We'll end up not valuing people based on their human capital, but rather for their for-profit material productivity. If "The Man" is hung up on providing shareholder value at any cost; it will be the people's responsibility to reverse this trend. This means you and me! Using The Healium Way lens, we can start doing something and take some baby-steps towards this rebalancing. Let's begin by equalizing the playing field of human labor and the overweighted service-based economy in America.

We'll need to get creative and make some changes in our definition. Why not combine the positive aspects of capitalism (such as innovation, freedom, opportunity and entrepreneurship) with the holistic core values of humanity (generosity, kindness, reciprocity, and trust) and call it *human capitalism*? Look at it as a form of social enterprise to uplift the *underdogs* and the *under-appreciated* in the American economy. Since we've arbitrarily lifted some professions and left others to bite the dust such as teachers, artists, social and health workers, janitors, first responders, delivery people, etc., it's time to revisit this imbalance. For one, these professions are all essential to our livelihood, but are under-compensated and undervalued in relation to investment bankers, insurance brokers, computer programmers, stock traders, lawyers and so forth: the conventional corporate-defined for-profit generators. In part, this dichotomy is due to our rapid technological revolution and scientific advancement, which has made some professions more valuable than others. That's all fantastic for improving our civilization in one way. But such a bias leads to an imbalance, creating unhealthy economic disparities across our entire social and economic ecosystem. Often it leads to inefficiencies of human resources within communities, that can snowball into bigger problems. For instance, when a math tutoring outfit in a small town can't find qualified teachers to service its students, it struggles and eventually shuts down. But if the town leaders incentivized and paid its teachers more money, it would attract and retain more of them for the town's benefit. By increasing the value of such professions, other low-paying workers who service the higher-paying professionals would also be better compensated; the janitors who clean their restrooms; the factory workers who make their suits; the baristas who pour their lattes; and so on. By reprioritizing and adjusting the way we value and compensate human capital in this way, we start transforming the entire cycle of productivity — a positive chain reaction. In the business of the arts, this 'human-capitalist' model can be a game changer for our society's wellness. Let's take the arts as an example.

By increasing our economic value of artists, we start paying more for art, workshops and art events. When those interconnected components generate more revenue, art centers in turn show profitability and don't just survive, but thrive— enriching a community. Now instead of looking at art centers as charities and artists as starving talent, we view them as financially viable and investable entities that help improve people's mental health and fill the Soul. This in turn produces a healthier and more productive workforce, which will attract the interest of capitalists seeking a good return on their *wellness investment*. This more balanced and efficient system of capitalism using a social enterprise and human capital model is a win-win proposition for everyone. Therefore, when we have a spiritual arts sanctuary such as Healium Center that pays for itself, it becomes sustainable and even expands into other territories. We can have a multiplicity of similar types of Centers spread across the country — no different than coffee shops, nail salons or bars. This scalability translates into a higher volume of attendees who are spread across various communities and cities, resulting in a more connected, uplifted and empowered population. We start seeing an immediate positive effect in our society such as less depression, reduced anxiety, lower obesity, less violence, higher self-esteem, more joy, increased productivity and healthier balance etc. It's a beautiful chain of events that makes a trip to a neighborhood wellness-with-the-arts center as easy, accessible and ubiquitous as walking into a coffee shop, a brewery or a sports bar anywhere in the country — only it's a lot healthier for the body, mind and soul. Not to mention more fun! This reprioritizing and rebalancing is the ticket to our wellbeing. Now instead of seeing ourselves as capitalists, socialists, progressives or whatever labels we assign ourselves, we will find that being a *human capitalist* makes a lot more sense. It brings us into a healthier balance not just individually, but communally and collectively. But before we can arrive at that level, we'll have to understand the way our present reality thinks and functions.

WE ALL 'HAVES' IT

In many ways our material mindset has us programmed to believe certain mistruths, not just about our needs and wants but about the *haves* and *have-nots* of our society. Although the conventional definitions may be technically valid, the status-based *haves* fall short of demonstrating that they are a lot happier than the *have-nots* in America. That's because we must redefine success by re-examining what we mean by the *haves.* If our metric of the *haves* is overweight by a myopic financial standard, then our measure of success is purely monetary-based, and flawed. If you have money and material wealth, well then, you're in the *'haves'* box. But if we expand the definition of success to include our human capital such as health, family, education, personal freedom, community impact, altruism, wisdom, leadership, spiritual upliftment, creativity, etc., — excelling in either all or some of the attributes we change the way we look at the *haves* vs. *have-nots* dynamic. Now a Buddhist monk, a teacher, a musician, a firefighter, a social worker, a father and so on, are all successful people in their own right and belong in the *have*s column. In effect, when we remove the singular lens of what success and the *haves* really means, it changes our view of the *have-nots* as well. Let me elaborate.

THE DOC AND THE HOUSEKEEPER

Dr. Alan was a wealthy male doctor in his 50s who I met during my 10-year carpet-cleaning career. He lived in a luxurious country club mansion and was attached to a high-status lifestyle — owning multiple luxurious homes, wearing designer attire and driving expensive cars. To those who didn't know him well, he appeared to have it all: money, career, family. But beneath his high-status image, was a man living a lie and carrying baggage of his unhealed past. He manifested his scars and discontentment by cheating on his wife, overworking and ignoring his two teenage children. I knew that backstory because I saw how unhappy his family was. In our exterior package-oriented world, this doctor's smokescreen gives him a pass as a successful *haves* person. But what if we change the metrics? How successful is this doctor in relation to his *have-nots* housekeeper who was struggling financially, yet had a healthy loving marriage, was trustful and was blessed with more inner peace and contentment? Sadly, half of today's America will probably look the other way on the doc's immoral transgressions and keep looking down on the housekeeper. It's our male chauvinistic societal programming coupled with status-based values at play. In The Healium Way of seeing things, Dr. Alan is just ordinary, because non material human capital aligned with good character and morality is our higher value system. With this renewed lens, the housekeeper is actually the successful *haves*. This is quite a radical and antithetical way of thinking to most of us. But it's the direction we need to be heading toward in order to bridge our divide and build a more balanced and healthier society. We must start reinvesting in not just our country's roads, bridges and decaying infrastructures, but in fixing our own moral rot — or we're going to sink into a deeper dark hole. In the South it's called "putting lipstick on a pig." —a pretty ugly outcome. Using a humanistic metric of worthiness and success, we're therefore ALL already wired to be the *haves* in some manner and must think and act in this way as already "having" valuable human capital rather than always "lacking" material capital. It is this financial-scarcity mindset that traps us into being more insecure, competitive, judgmental, dishonest and entrapped to being the low-vibrational human. As a world traveler, I've witnessed this dichotomy operate in better balance best in the poorest of countries. The *have-nots* who are typically deficient economically are rich in the core values of generosity, kindness, respect, trust, hard work, compassion, humor, creativity, common sense, service and spirituality (The Healium Way definition of human capital). These qualities override the monetary advantage of the typical rich and make them prosperous beings whose wealth is measured by not just money but by doing good deeds and liberally exercising and sharing their human capital attributes.

DON'T BE A DICK

In the last three decades, we've also seen a meteoric rise in entrepreneurship, franchising, real estate investing, financial consulting, cannabis businesses, the green economy, multilevel marketing and so forth. I participated in this wave myself and made a good living for my family in many successful enterprises. It is what America does best: innovate, be bold, take risks and be a trendsetter for the rest of the world. Everything is positive with that model as long as we don't set the trend of stepping over others to climb our respective mountains. But when we include a system of corporate hiring that lifts only the best boats — paying six figure salaries to highly degreed IT employees but squeezing the liberal arts graduate to minimum wage levels — we leave a lot of people behind and create an unhealthy tipping point, an imbalance that shows up in a society with deep economic inequality, soaring debt levels and two-thirds of Americans living paycheck to paycheck. Social ills that emerge include racism, mental illness, crime, depression, suicides, drug addictions, violence, domestic terrorism and so forth. I am not an advocate of strangling or destroying free market capitalism, as many of my Republican friends are quick to blame a more middle of the road thinker like myself, but about its reprioritizing and rebalancing. First, let's bring to the forefront that the reason we are shrinking the middle class and increasing the economic gap has to do with our myopic and shallow view of success that's deprioritized the value of human capital. It's an unhealthy decoupling from our higher Divine self. But since it's all man-made, it's also reversible. There shouldn't be any argument or disagreement that we are broken as a society due to our blind spot on human capital. It's just a matter of our willingness to open our eyes, see the forest from the trees and point to ourselves as the ground zero solution.

Indeed, it's hard to get philosophical when you've got to work three jobs just to put food on the table. As of this writing some 50 million Americans (adults and children) are food insecure — not knowing where their next meal will come from. This third world statistic breeds desperation, which in turn creates dishonesty among people. And desperation is often an excuse for people to slip into a dishonest way of making a living, or succumbing to our lower vibrational self. But we must be careful not to get sucked into that vortex of immorality. Because those bad habits will follow us even when we're out of our black holes and financially secure. As an example, if you're a scammer when you're poor, you'll be a more sophisticated version of it when you're rich. It's programmed behavior in a capitalist *winner takes all* model — one that fuels the fire to burn our moral bridges without shame or guilt. In the earlier example of the successful but immoral doctor, I don't believe he was a saint before he gained his stature and wealth. Based on our experience at The Center, there is much evidence that a personality like him was probably burdened with unresolved past issues and manifested his disloyalty and infidelity growing up. His status and power position as an adult simply gave him a safe cover from his unhealed self. It camouflaged it on one hand, and accelerated it on the other. So once we understand that this doctor needs an honest housekeeper as much as his wife needs a mentally fit and trustworthy husband (not just his money), to have joy and contentment and no amount of monetary-based power or materialism will fix that imbalance — we can begin the rebalancing of basic human values together. We all benefit when we operate from empathy and see ourselves as part and parcel of others, not separate. It's the opposite to the shortsighted winner taking all seduction that has dangerously divided us. So yes, we can have upward mobility and all the success we desire… without being dicks at the same time!

WHY ZUCK SUCKS

From an economic viewpoint, we know the law of diminishing returns furthers the fact that too much of a good thing (in this case, money) is not necessarily that great. Studies from Gallup World Poll find that in the Western economies people's happiness level tapers off around the $75,000 to $100,000 annual income mark, and actually diminishes in the wealthier brackets. In other words, Jeff Bezos, Bill Gates, Elon Musk and Mark Zuckerberg (aka, Zuck) may not be much happier than the manager of your nearest fast-food joint. We just assume they are happier than us — based on societal programming that says increased wealth is correlated with increased happiness. So although there are many reasons to hate the founder of Facebook and Instagram for sucking the Souls out of our lives and making us unsocial beings, Zuck's life may suck more than yours in many other ways. We're led to believe that rap artists with gold teeth and real estate moguls with mega-mansions are the epitome of success and happiness. In reality, this ugly lie fermented by capitalist propaganda and clever marketing feeds a shallow brain and deepens the bog within. It's all simply an illusion fed to the American public that gets absorbed in the minds of the fragile and fickle consumer.

THE UNLABELING

I can't help re-emphasizing Wayne Dyer's masterful quote; '*When we change the way we look at things, the things we look at will change*' to underscore my point. The 1 percent to 10 percent of Americans that we've labelled as *haves* must start having an honest dialogue with the bottom 90 percent to reassess what *haves* or *have-nots* really means in a broader context. And visa versa. Instead of pigeonholing ourselves,we can all agree that the solution to bridge our divide is less about labeling ourselves as groups and factions and more about simply *un-labeling* ourselves and fighting for the same cause of having respect, trust, empathy and compassion for each other. We can also agree that although money is our man-made system of exchange and value (and necessary to conduct and operate our lives in this world), it is not and never will be an equal exchange to our higher-self ideals of upholding our core humanistic values. If you are still having difficulty understanding this truth, you need to hold up a mirror to yourself and take a good look at your face. If it's stressed, tired, frowned, puffy and always anxious, it's revealing the problem is not in what I am saying — but in you and an imbalance with your relationship with money, power and the labels you attach to yourself.

ART, THE MIRROR

In an equivalent manner to a Rorschach Test, the name of the drawing you interpreted at the beginning of this chapter is called *Maybe it's you.* It is the artist's clever and creative way to hold up a mirror using art, to open your mind and to get to better know thyself. Your interpretation is not so much a statement, as it is a question for you to answer. The way you interpreted the drawing is now your guidance to your intention and willingness — or resistance to discover a better and an *extra*ordinary you. Are you ready?

YOUR ADVENTURE BEGINS!

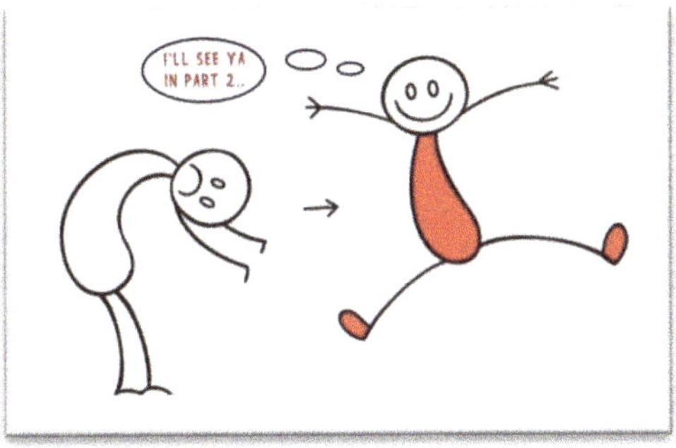

It is from this point, that you can begin your journey of untapped possibilities.

As you look forward to adventure into the self-help and application phase and the Principles of The Healium Way **Part 2,** you will be treated with ***21 life-changing ideas***. They're designed to help us create a more healed life for ourselves. They have helped change my life around, and I believe they can do the same for you. These Principles have been tested and proven to take you from ordinary to *extra*ordinary, and make sure you don't live a life without regrets. In addition, the second book is packed with more amazing stories, a peace plan for America, mind-bending art, practical solutions, poetry and fun online content that is sure to satisfy your literary and creative appetite!

CPSIA information can be obtained
at www.ICGtesting.com
Printed in the USA
LVHW072124121021
700249LV00019B/529

9 781737 595007